The Infinite Machine

The Infinite Machine

How an Army of Crypto-Hackers
Is Building the Next Internet
with Ethereum

| Camila Russo |

HARPER
BUSINESS

An Imprint of HarperCollins*Publishers*

HarperCollins books may be purchased for educational, business, or sales promotional use. For information, please email the Special Markets Department at SPsales@harpercollins.com.

FIRST EDITION

Designed by Elina Cohen

Interior art © Shutterstock by phochi

Library of Congress Cataloging-in-Publication Data has been applied for.

ISBN 978-0-06-288614-9

20 21 22 23 24   LSC   10 9 8 7 6 5 4 3 2 1

"Before anything else, you are a writer," my mother likes to say.
THIS IS FOR HER.

Any sufficiently advanced technology
is indistinguishable from magic.

—*Arthur C. Clarke*

Contents

Contents

A Note to My Readers

I don't consider myself a computer geek. I don't spend hours on end hacking away on my laptop. I'm also not into financial speculation. Watching it from a distance and writing about it, I love. Putting my money—and my stomach—through nauseating ups and downs, not so much.

So why spend years devoted to cryptocurrencies? The answer is at least slightly different for everyone I've asked this question to. For me, it's about freedom. If you push me a little, I might even say it's about revolution.

The first time I learned about Bitcoin was in 2013. I was living in Buenos Aires, reporting on the Argentine market for Bloomberg News. But I was more than reporting about it; I was also living it. As I wrote about double-digit inflation, the pesos I earned for those stories quickly depreciated. I started exchanging my salary to dollars as soon as I got it, until one day the president woke up and said, Nope! You can't do that anymore.

Could it be possible that the government was able to ban the purchase of the US currency, something I'd been able to do with a click on my bank's website? I went to check, and sure enough, the option to exchange pesos from my local currency account into dollars to deposit in my foreign currency account was nowhere to be found. One day it was there, the next day it was gone. The government was depreciating its currency with populist policies, and now it wasn't even going to let me protect my own savings against its economic mismanagement. This was perfectly legal. It was the government doing it.

Who could I turn to? Around that time, a colleague in another office told me about some weird digital currency called Bitcoin, which Argentines were using to get around this problem. I decided to write about it. The people I talked with for my article had been living with some form of inflation and/or currency controls all their lives and so had their parents. They understood right away how significant it was to be able to buy a currency that's not controlled by anyone and, therefore, can't be stopped or seized. Its issuance rate was dictated by algorithms and computer code, not by the whims of politicians and central bankers.

I thought this innovation was incredibly powerful and continued to watch Bitcoin and the growing cryptocurrency market until, in 2017, I got a chance to write about it again. By this time I was based in New York, still reporting on markets with Bloomberg News, and noticed that crypto was heating up. I started covering this strange market, at first sporadically, but as prices kept climbing, and more tokens kept getting issued, and crypto startups were raising millions in seconds, and everyone from celebrities to fund managers to CEOs was talking about it, it was soon consuming most of my time. By the end of the year it was clear we were witnessing a full-blown bubble. One of the most fantastic speculative manias the world had ever seen, and I had been privileged to cover it at one of the most respected financial media organizations.

At the end of 2017, when I took stock of what I had just witnessed in crypto, I thought, This needs to be permanently documented. From an early age, my dream had been to write about the real world with the drama and excitement found in fiction. I set out to find the best story to tell in crypto. I found that, while some great books of the kind I wanted to write had been written about Bitcoin, there was no history of Ethereum, the second-biggest chain, which had fueled much of the craziness of the past year. More important, Ethereum was unique in that it tried to take blockchain technology, underlying Bitcoin, even further than what the original cryptocurrency had. Bitcoin wanted to be peer-to-peer money. Ethereum wanted to be peer-to-peer everything. It wanted to be the "world computer," behind a more decentralized, freer world. Even if it failed in its ambition, the innovation in itself and the frenzy it caused were bookworthy.

That's how I set out to write the first book on the history of Ethereum.

To write it, I started with interviews with the small founding group of this network, the original cofounders—although you will now read there's some contention around that term—including the creator of the platform himself, Vitalik Buterin. From initial conversations, I established the basic chronology of how Ethereum developed, the major milestones and themes. Then I sought out the protagonists of each major stage of the project, those who saw its history unfold firsthand. They led me to contact others closely involved, who led me to talk with yet others. Then I went back and talked with many of them again. That's how after two years of work, with roughly six months focused on research full time, I compiled more than one hundred interviews, and many more hours of recorded conversations.

I also tried my best to follow them wherever they met. The Ethereum community lives all over the globe by design, so conferences and hacking contests are especially important as they're the few times during the year where many see colleagues and fellow Ethereans in person. At the dozen or so events I attended in the United States, South America, Europe, and Asia, I got a chance to meet even more people and get a better sense of what the broader community looks like, from what they talk about to how they dress and party. In other words I got color—and they're a colorful bunch.

Some of my sources were also generous enough to share their emails from the time, pictures, chat logs, and recorded conversations. In addition, I relied on other primary material, such as archived websites, blog posts, and videos.

A Note to My Readers

My goal with this research was to reconstruct Ethereum's history as accurately, and as close to reality, as possible. Everything I narrate is based on interviews with people who were there and materials from the time. I haven't reconstructed or condensed scenes for dramatism. The closest elements to fiction are dialogues, which I crafted from how those involved in these conversations or events remember they happened. All of the characters in the book are real people, and the names used are their real names. I didn't create composite or fictional characters. In only one occasion, I accepted a request to use a pseudonym, as it was a minor character and excluding his name didn't impact the documentation of Ethereum history. It is disclosed in the book.

One of the biggest challenges when writing this story was to decide on a single version of events when those involved remembered it in different ways. This was especially difficult when there wasn't supporting material, other than interviews. On those occasions, I went with the account that was shared by most participants, and the one that, based on my research, made the most sense. Readers will have to trust my judgment on those few cases. I did my best to make those decisions responsibly.

Of course, enthusiasts will hopefully enjoy learning even more about the network they support and work on, and get a peek at how it developed from its very early days. But if you're a non-techie person like me, and even if you had never heard of the word "Ethereum" until maybe just now, this book is for you. My intention is that anyone, anywhere, will be able to pick this up, without prior knowledge of blockchain technology, and be captivated by a fascinating story: an idealistic hero, his band of misfits, and the challenges they face to make their incredibly ambitious dream a reality.

By the final pages, I hope you will have learned more about this dream, about how this army of hackers is building an alternative to the way the world works right now, that is, concentrated in the hands of a few powerful entities. They're seeking to put that power into the hands of individuals, so that people can have greater control over the things they own, from assets to data, and more freedom to use those things in the ways they choose—that's what I meant when I said cryptocurrencies are about revolution. I hope you will also have learned about this technology, which I believe is here to stay and will be increasingly prevalent in the future.

PART I

Groundwork

1

Mooning

THE WEEK OF MAY 11, 2018. NEW YORK CITY.

At a booze-and-EDM-fueled yacht party with views of the Statue of Liberty, two randomly selected guests were gifted Aston Martins at the end of the night. One car had a Bitcoin "B" stamped across its door; the other had an Ethereum logo. At another event in a Brooklyn warehouse, the sushi served was advertised as being "on the blockchain," while wellness guru Deepak Chopra led meditation sessions, and a digital cat, alive only thanks to lines of code and pixels, was sold at an art auction for $140,000. At one crypto company–sponsored venue, Snoop Dogg smoked a blunt onstage and shared it with the audience. Wall Street bankers-turned-crypto-investors courted Silicon Valley dropouts-turned-crypto-entrepreneurs at a penthouse in New York's SoHo neighborhood. At another after party, Bitcoin bros raised champagne glasses to bethonged dancers in a fabled downtown strip club as a rapper sang cryptocurrency-themed songs flanked by oily poles.

Three Lamborghinis parked in front of the Hilton near Times Square greeted some 8,500 attendees who had paid $2,000 a ticket for a chance to get in on the cryptocurrency gold rush. Dozens of twentysomethings, who had raised millions of dollars overnight selling their own digital coins, manned colorfully festooned booths at the event.

All of that happened in the span of seven days, in only one city. It was New York's "Blockchain Week," where the crypto community had gathered to attend the parties and conferences parlaying promises into fortunes.

Indeed, in those seven days, sixteen startups raised almost $300 million in a crowdfunding mechanism known as an initial coin offering, or ICO, where anyone, anywhere in the world, could issue cryptocurrencies and sell them to investors equally spread out across the globe.

Still, the market had fallen hard after an eye-popping rally, and the question everyone was asking was whether the recent slump was a temporary pullback or the beginning of the end. Exuberance was tinged with a whiff of desperation, which made the over-the-top spectacles seem even more urgent. Most of the startups raising money and presenting at conferences weren't much more than promises in a website. The Lamborghinis had been rented.

The high point had been just a few months earlier, in December 2017, when the price of bitcoin, the largest and first cryptocurrency, spiked to almost $20,000 from around $1,000 at the start of the year. Veterans took the pullback in stride, reminding themselves that, since the digital currency launched in 2009, its price had gone through exponential rallies and crashes three times before. During those past spikes, bitcoin had represented most of the entire cryptocurrency market. But this time it was different.

Ethereum, with its digital coin called ether, had launched in 2015 and two years later, its price was shooting up even faster than bitcoin's. It had peaked in January 2018 at over $1,400, soaring from just around $10 twelve months earlier. That meant that anyone who had bought roughly $10,000 of ether at the start of 2017 and sold at the top had become a millionaire. At one point in the rally, some investors speculated it would overtake bitcoin in market capitalization as it grew even faster than the first cryptocurrency.

And there was good reason, some argued, for ether to rocket to the moon. Ethereum isn't only a network for its digital currency, ether. It's meant to be the base layer for developers to build whatever application they can dream of, including issuing their own coin. All they had to do was push out a few lines of code and they could mint cryptocurrency and trade it for bitcoin or ether, which could then be exchanged for dollars—the so-called ICO funding mechanism that demolished the barriers between those seeking to raise money and those willing to give it away for the chance of getting rich. Thanks to this novel way of raising money, thousands of new coins were popping up and adding to the crypto feeding frenzy.

Investors—really anyone with an internet connection—were throwing money at these cryptos and at the young developers building them. ICOs were over in minutes, sometimes in seconds—that's how fast these blockchain startups reached their multimillion-dollar targets. There wasn't much you could do with these coins, which exist only on the internet and are traded on lightly regulated online platforms. They aren't accepted by most merchants, and the decentralized applications, or "dapps," for which they were intended to be used are still experimental and glitchy. But using them was actually not the point. The point was to buy them before the price jumped and then flip them later at the next new peak. At least, that was the theory.

In 2017 the amount of money raised in ICOs surpassed traditional venture capital funding for blockchain startups for the first time. By the end of 2018, almost $10 billion had poured into this crowdfunding mechanism that year. For perspective, that's about what companies raised in the equity markets of Canada, Mexico, and Brazil in that time, combined. A new form of raising capital for early stage ventures, and a new avenue to invest in tech startups that just wasn't available to regular people before, had just been born.

As money clogged the works, some smaller cryptocurrencies soared even faster than bitcoin and ether. If you visited websites tracking their prices, all you would see were numbers colored in green and arrows pointing skyward. All the lines on the graphs were parabolic. It didn't seem to matter which coin you picked—any one of them would multiply its value several times over.

Everyone wanted to be a crypto millionaire. Google searches for Bitcoin surpassed searches for Donald Trump. Celebrities, some of whom were compensated by crypto companies anticipating a big payday, started supporting ICOs in their social media. Paris Hilton tweeted, "Looking forward to participating in the new @Lydian CoinLtd Token! #ThisIsNotAnAd #CryptoCurrency #BitCoin #ETH #BlockChain," and Floyd Mayweather posted on Instagram, "I'm gonna make a $hit t$n of money on August 2nd on the Stox.com ICO."

It wasn't just celebrities paying attention. Suddenly, big bankers and blue-chip CEOs started voicing opinions on cryptocurrencies and blockchain, the underlying technology. "I'm a believer," said Abigail Johnson of Fidelity Investments. "It's a fraud," said JPMorgan's Jamie Dimon. Lloyd Blankfein, Goldman Sachs's CEO, said he's "not willing to pooh-pooh it," while Warren Buffett, not one to mince his words, said Bitcoin is "probably rat poison squared."

Meanwhile, with millions of dollars sloshing around, regulators scrambled to make sense of how to deal with these newfangled instruments, if at all. Were they securities? Software? New currencies? Or commodities? Stories abounded of erstwhile crypto founders running off with their company's stash, hackers stealing bitcoin from ICOs' digital wallets and exchanges, and robots trolling social media trying to trick people into sending over their cryptos—it was the perfect environment for scammers, pirates, and crazy rumors.

And then there were those who genuinely wanted to create world-changing applications using blockchain technology. They wanted to build a world that would sidestep traditional institutions and allow users to transfer value directly with each other, without having to go through banks and other intermediaries. They wanted to put data and money back under users' control, instead of in the coffers and computer servers of centralized entities. For them, blockchain technology (and Bitcoin and Ethereum) would wrest power from the big corporations that control tech and finance and put it into the hands of the people.

Of course, nobody was actually preparing to overthrow governments, protest in front of banks, or clash with police on the streets. Rather, it was a revolution based on technology and cryptography, which would unfold in a parallel universe where traditional financial laws didn't apply, and everything was being built from scratch. At first, nobody would notice or care about these outcast hackers, so their logic went, until it would be too late. The revolution had started with Bitcoin, and now Ethereum opened up a whole new arsenal in this underground fight toward a decentralized future.

At least that was the dream many of these developers had when they dropped everything and joined the growing Ethereum army.

To write this book, I infiltrated this army.

I had first written about Bitcoin for Bloomberg News in 2013, when I was living in Argentina and saw how average people were using the digital currency to protect their savings against inflation and to skirt currency controls. By the time I moved to Bloomberg's New York office in 2017, "blockchain" was on the tip of everyone's tongue to the point where it became an empty buzzword. At the time, I was one of a few reporters at Bloomberg, and in the mainstream financial media in general, covering crypto and blockchain day to day. At the end of the year, I came up for air after covering one of the craziest bubbles the world had ever seen. I decided this explosion should be documented more permanently and that Ethereum was the most important story to tell.

I conducted more than one hundred interviews, of several hours each, with all the original founders and developers working on the protocol in the very early days to the ones building it today. I spoke with the investors, lawyers, regulators, communicators, designers, and researchers who have also shaped Ethereum. Those who talked to me were generous enough to help me unearth dozens of old emails, chat logs, documents, and pictures. I also dug deep into online forums, blog posts, and archived websites. I followed this colorful, idealist, brilliant crew to their conferences and hackathons in Prague, Buenos Aires, Toronto, Berlin, Denver, Paris, New York, San Francisco, and Osaka.

I felt like Alice following the White Rabbit into a world of impossible dreams: banking without banks, breeding digital cats, self-organizing companies with no CEOs, and talk of flying to the moon. Shaggy, unkempt young developers, whether they had dropped out of computer science programs or had fled companies from the other side of the looking glass—these were the magicians trying to make these dreams a reality amid a swirl of internet memes, rainbows, unicorns, and lines of computer code.

At the center of this circle of tech geeks, financiers, misfits, and renegades stood Vitalik Buterin, a nineteen-year-old genius hacker who came up with the idea that would become Ethereum. His dream prompted a cohort of believers from different corners of the planet and disparate backgrounds to join him in making it a reality. They're working on technology meant to change, at its very core, the way the world works, and this grand vision has drawn even more people in so that several thousands are now building it. Even more are trying to profit, legitimately or illegitimately, from it. Five years into the endeavor he's well on his way toward changing the world with the multibillion-dollar network he helped create, but it's been a turbulent ride, with malicious attacks from envious hackers, mind-boggling technical challenges, infighting within the early team, and the lure of near-obscene wealth, which all threatened to derail Vitalik in his idealistic quest.

High up on the list of distractions was the eye-watering growth of the cryptocurrency market. At the market peak on the first days of 2018, the value of digital assets had ballooned to over $800 billion from around $15 billion a year earlier. Thousands of new cryptocurrencies had sprung up in that time. But Vitalik wasn't happy.

"So total cryptocoin market cap just hit $0.5T today. But have we *earned* it?" Vitalik tweeted on December 12, 2017.

"How many unbanked people have we banked?" he wrote, and continued to ask, how many applications have a significant number of users or are moving large amounts of volume? How many people have been protected from hyperinflation? In a series of tweets, he questioned whether cryptocurrencies' impact so far was enough to justify the size of the market.

"The answer to all of these questions is definitely not zero, and in some cases it's quite significant," he wrote. "But not enough to say it's $0.5T levels of significant. Not enough."

As this book goes to press, the value of ether is hovering below $200, down ten times from its record in early 2018. Many of the speculators have cashed out, but true believers like Vitalik and his ilk continue to press forward with their vision. As with previous generations of internet-based revolutions, it's hard to keep that vision pure and pristine. All too often, it gets murky, muddled, and messed up in the face of reality. Visionaries like Vitalik dream of traveling to the moon and beyond, frequently underestimating the gravitational pull that mundane forces like human ambition, greed, and fear can exert. It turns out that revolutionizing financial systems may be easier than overcoming human frailty. There is no app (or dapp) for that yet, though undoubtedly some tech genius somewhere is working on that right now, too.

2

Cypherpunks' Fever Dream

In 2008, five years before the idea of Ethereum materialized in a white paper, Bitcoin was created. But even Bitcoin didn't appear in a vacuum. Cryptographers had been trying to come up with a private, peer-to-peer digital currency since at least the 1980s. Computer scientist David Chaum saw how the advent of electronic payments could threaten privacy and focused his research on ways to prevent that. He devised the "blind signatures" system, which enabled digital payments without having to disclose personal information, and used that technology to create eCash in 1983, an anonymous digital currency.

eCash wasn't a fully decentralized system. It relied on banks to sign the digital currency, so it could still be susceptible to censorship and corruption. Still, Chaum's innovation spearheaded what would become a movement. Its humble beginnings can be traced back to an office in the San Francisco Bay area, where a small group of computer scientists and engineers met to talk about how cryptography could help ensure that users' privacy wasn't violated in the dawn of the internet and personal computers.

Hacker Jude Milhon, better known by her pseudonym St. Jude, combined the words "cypher" (a way to encrypt information) and "cyberpunk" (a science fiction subgenre that depicts high-tech worlds where society has broken down) to christen the emerging group as the "cypherpunks." For cypherpunks, cryptography would be a tool to effect wider social and political change. Some of them even advocated for crypto-anarchy, a belief that cryptography would enable a world free from corporate or state control. The technology would be the "clippers which dismantle the barbed wire around intellectual property," cryptographer Timothy May wrote in the manifesto. Private, peer-to-peer digital cash would be at the core of this break from banks and governments.

Soon after the initial meetings, a mailing list formed so discussion could be broadened out from just San Francisco, and it quickly grew to hundreds of subscribers.

As cypherpunks made headway, the open source software movement, which would also influence the development of blockchain technology, was growing. Supposedly it all started thanks to a jammed printer at the Massachusetts Institute of Technology in the late 1970s. Richard M. Stallman, a staff programmer at the university, had written code for the lab's printer, which was on another floor, to save time by having the machine send a message to the lab's central computer when the printer got jammed. Eventually the printer was replaced and when Stallman tried to implement the same hack, he found he couldn't modify the code because it was proprietary information.

In 1983, Stallman responded by creating an operating system called GNU, which would be free and accessible to anyone. Next Stallman founded the Free Software Foundation and the GNU General Public License, which said anyone was free to use, copy, distribute, and modify software created under that license. The only requirement was that changes to the code had to be shared. Linux, an operating system that runs on the GNU license, started taking off in the mid-1990s.

In 1997, Eric S. Raymond published the essay "The Cathedral and the Bazaar," comparing two software development models: the cathedral, where code development is restricted to an exclusive group of developers, and the bazaar, where code is public and developed over the internet. The essay was credited to be the final push for Netscape to release the source code for its web browser Mozilla in 1998. In the decades after, open source continued to grow and spawned the world's most popular mobile operating system with Android, as well as multibillion-dollar companies with Red Hat and GitHub, while Linux is now used by most computer servers. "Software was meant to be free" is still a rallying cry for programmers everywhere.

At around this time, in 1999, Napster launched. The now-defunct website allowed users to share digital files among a web of participants, instantly making hundreds of thousands of MP3 songs available for free to anyone in the world. Then in 2001, BitTorrent was released, doing to movies and larger files what Napster had done with music. They arguably brought peer-to-peer (P2P) applications into the mainstream. Peer-to-peer networks interconnect equally privileged nodes with each other, allowing users to share and transfer data without the need of a centralized administrative entity. Systems using this architecture are resilient against censorship, attacks, and manipulation. Just like the mythological Hydra, there's no one head that you can cut off to kill it, and it gets stronger after each attack.

The original vision for the World Wide Web, as imagined by its creator, Tim Berners-Lee, was meant to be closer to a P2P network than how it works today, that is, behind a series of firewalls and fed to us through Google, Facebook, and maybe a handful of other mega corporations. Berners-Lee has publicly lamented the current state of the web. The original vision is what inspired and drove cypherpunks. They wanted a P2P network for money.

In the 1980s and 1990s there were key problems cypherpunks were trying to solve before they could get there. One is that digital coins, unlike cash, are just computer code that can easily be replicated and falsified. The problem, known as "double spend," can be solved using a centralized entity that keeps a record on the coins and authenticates them, but the challenge was to transfer value without having to trust a third party. Another issue to address in peer-to-peer, pseudonymous systems was Sybil attacks. Just as coins can be replicated in a digital world, so can identities. This is a problem in a network of equal peers because an attacker could create a large number of pseudonymous identities to gain a disproportionately large influence.

Researchers Cynthia Dwork and Moni Naor made the first break toward solving these problems when they invented the "proof-of-work" concept in 1993. Proof-of-work is aimed at deterring attacks or spam in a network by requiring the users of the service to do some work, so that it would be economically inviable to create useless or malicious data. Their paper focused on preventing junk mail by requiring the sender to spend some computing power to solve a function or puzzle. Cryptographer Adam Back proposed a version of proof-of-work called Hashcash five years later, which used cryptographic hash functions to prove work had been done.

In 1998, computer scientists Wei Dai came up with B-money and Nick Szabo invented Bit Gold. They both proposed schemes that allowed a network of users to transact with digital money without the need of intermediaries, but these were never implemented as they didn't fully solve the double-spend and Sybil attack problems.

For those living in developed, democratic nations, with relatively stable currencies and trustworthy institutions, cypherpunks' obsession for money that doesn't need banks and is free from government controls may seem puzzling. Surely this is just a scheme for drug dealers and tax cheats, right? But in much of the world, financial stability and security still aren't the norm.

Consider the case of Alvaro Yermak, a bank teller in a far-flung city in Argentina.

The seed that would lead Alvaro to seek money that's immune to government controls or profligacy was planted in December 2001. As he had been doing for the past eight years working as a cashier at a bank in Tucumán, a mountainous region in northern Argentina, he got in a little before 8 a.m. and took his place behind the counter. He sipped his yerba maté but it turned in his stomach when he glanced at the doors. People had already started to line up outside and would flood the bank as soon as it opened in a few minutes. He and the dozens of other cashiers sitting beside him knew it would be a difficult day.

It was Monday, December 3, and the Argentine government had published a decree over the weekend prohibiting savers from withdrawing more than $250 or 250 pesos per week, and banning most international money transfers. Essentially, it meant people's savings were trapped in the national banking system. It would also suck liquidity from the economy, paralyzing commerce and leaving those in the informal sector, or about half of the working population, with no earnings.

It was the government's attempt to stop a plunge in deposits as Argentines who feared a looming economic crisis took out their pesos, bought dollars, and those who could sent those dollars to bank accounts abroad.

The country was feeling hungover after previous governments had sold a huge pile of dollar-denominated bonds and gone on a spending frenzy. The growing debt payments and widening deficit were now unsustainable and the market started to fear a debt default was coming. The Argentine peso was pegged to the dollar (one peso equaled one dollar), which worked in curbing inflation, but it also made the nation's exports uncompetitive and slowed economic growth. Fernando de la Rua's government had promised the International Monetary Fund severe spending cuts in exchange for a loan to help tide the economy over. Those measures caused an already slumping economy to contract further.

By the end of 2001, Argentines, who had been through spectacular boom and bust cycles before, were preparing for the worst. That weekend at the start of December, the decree restricting withdrawals was the confirmation they were waiting for: the crisis had started.

Hordes rushed to the bank, and Alvaro looked on with dread as the line of agitated customers stretched for three blocks. Every single person who came in wanted to take all of their savings out, but Alvaro could only follow the new rules and reply, "I can only give you 250." He absorbed the barrage of insults and cries for help as best he could. He understood the people on the other side of the glass partition; he was one of them, too.

Alvaro had never finished his economics or information technology university degrees and got an entry-level job at the bank to help support his new wife and child. He was like so many other Argentine men in their early thirties, but suddenly he had become a face for the country's crumbling economy. Those who had decided the best way to deal with the crisis was to dictate what people could do with their own money were hiding somewhere inside the baroque government palaces in Buenos Aires, like cowardly war generals, while he was placed on the front lines.

The country descended into chaos as everyone, from the wealthy in gated communities to the poor in the *villas*, marched down the main avenues, banging pots and pans to create a metallic roar. Angry mobs started fires and destroyed anything in their path, particularly foreign corporations and banks.

Alvaro dreaded showing up for work. He would fix his eyes on his shoes as he walked by the angry crowds, trying to ignore the insults when someone realized he worked at the bank. The bank started to keep the steel blinds protecting its façade halfway closed during the day, letting in only ten people at a time. Some days, it simply didn't open.

De la Rua implemented a state of emergency giving armed forces more power but all he got was an even louder uproar. The police turned to violence, beating protesters to the ground and eventually opening fire. On December 20 the president resigned and soon after, a loud rumble drowned out the thousands gathered near the Plaza de Mayo square in front of the presidential palace. They looked up and saw a helicopter flying over them. A jolt of adrenaline pulsed through the crowd when it descended over the Casa Rosada. They realized it had come for De la Rua. It hovered very near the roof of the presidential palace and like that, without the blades ever stopping, De la Rua jumped on. There was a wave of incredulity, mixed with relief, mixed with anger, and all they could do was boo and whistle as it flew off.

The immediate replacement for De la Rua lasted only a week and Eduardo Duhalde, who followed, stopped the practice of pegging the peso to the dollar and established a new official exchange rate at 1.4 pesos per dollar, devaluing the currency by 40 percent. All dollar deposits were converted to pesos at the official exchange rate, effectively slashing savings. People still couldn't withdraw their own money. A fourth of the country was unemployed and half was below the poverty line.

In that moment, there weren't many options for people like Alvaro, but a solution was coming.

Cypherpunks had continued incrementally improving past work until the major breakthrough came in October 2008, when an anonymous person or persons going by the name Satoshi Nakamoto emailed the group. "I've been working on a new electronic cash system that's fully peer-to-peer, with no trusted third party," the email began, and linked to a nine-page PDF that underlined how the system worked. He said he proposed solving the double-spend problem by using a "peer-to-peer network which timestamps transactions by linking them into an ongoing chain of hash-based proof-of-work."

In the paper titled "Bitcoin: A Peer-to-Peer Electronic Cash System," Satoshi Nakamoto proposed a network of computers, where each computer holds the copy of the entire transaction history for the network, a ledger with what everyone owns. Anyone is free to download the ledger onto their computer and join the network. The full transaction history is open for anyone to see, but the users behind transactions are pseudonymous, only identified by their public keys, which are a jumble of letters and numbers. Only users control the private keys needed to access funds tied to their Bitcoin addresses, which are under their exclusive control. For the first time, people could genuinely be their own bank.

When a transaction is executed, it is broadcast to all the computers in the network for them to update their ledgers. Transactions are bunched together to form a block of data, and once that block runs out of space (1 megabyte right now), computers race to solve a complex mathematical puzzle to verify the transactions, seal the block, and record it on their ledgers.

This is done using a cryptographic hash function, which works like a magic scrambling machine where an input of any length spits out a group of letters and numbers of a fixed length. The computers, or nodes, use all the most recent, unconfirmed transactions as inputs in the hash function and try to combine them with arbitrary data in such a way that the result starts with a certain, specific number of zeros. This is very intense computing work and takes a lot of energy to do, but once one of the computers gets the answer, it's easy for the rest to check. They just need to feed it into the hash function and verify that it spits out the answer with the required number of zeros. Once the nodes agree that the seal is valid, the block is recorded and linked to the previous block using the accepted hash, forming a chain of blocks, thus the name "blockchain."

The computer that solved the problem gets coins and a fee as a reward. Transaction fees have rarely surpassed $1—though they've jumped to almost $40 at their peak. This process, called "mining," takes about ten minutes per block in the Bitcoin blockchain.

"The steady addition of a constant amount of new coins is analogous to gold miners expending resources to add gold to circulation. In our case, it is CPU time and electricity that is expended," Satoshi Nakamoto wrote in the paper.

To modify the ledger, all miners would have to agree and make the same change; that's why it's very difficult to hack into the network.

The innovation of blockchain technology was to create a network of distributed participants that anyone can join using a system to verify transactions, known as a consensus algorithm (proof-of-work in the case of Bitcoin), that doesn't require third parties. A block of confirmed data will contain a cryptographic hash of the previous block, which will link them together and make it almost impossible to modify the chain.

Bitcoin was its first application, but the same principles can be used to create different types of networks. In the case of Bitcoin, "Bitcoin" is the name of both the blockchain and of the cryptocurrency itself (uppercase "B" is used for the network, lowercase "b" is used for the cryptocurrency), while ether is the coin that runs on the Ethereum blockchain. There will be some blockchains that don't even have their own corresponding cryptocurrency, and there is no one, single blockchain. Each chain will have its own unique characteristics, which is why the term "on the blockchain" that's used ad nauseam should immediately be met with the follow-up question, "Which one?"

In keeping with the open source ethos, Bitcoin is an open protocol that anyone can join, modify, or even copy to create their own, separate version. Modifying the protocol is relatively difficult, though, and requires the protocol developers to add the change to the software implementation and for the majority of nodes and miners to run that new version of the software.

The first block of the Bitcoin blockchain was mined in 2009 and the chain has continued to grow ever since, confirming a new block every ten minutes and issuing a decreasing number of bitcoins as mining difficulty increases. The total number of bitcoins ever created will be 21 million. Hal Finney, who contributed to proof-of-work research and was in the cypherpunks' mailing list, received the first Bitcoin transaction from Satoshi Nakamoto. Programmer Laszlo Hanyecz made the first known purchase using the digital currency when he bought two pizzas for 10,000 bitcoins in 2010. (Those pizzas are worth $85 million at the time of writing.)

It was not a coincidence that Bitcoin was born in 2008, the year a global financial crisis exploded. Confidence and trust in the financial system soured after the US economy plunged into its biggest downturn since the Great Depression. Banks had sold mortgages to people who couldn't afford them, repackaged those loans in complicated derivatives they could bet against, all under the eyes of corrupt ratings agencies and toothless regulators, and then most got bailed out by the government when it all came crashing down.

Satoshi Nakamoto left a message in the first Bitcoin block ever mined, which read:

The Times 3 January 2009 Chancellor on brink of second bailout for banks.

The text was referring to the headline on the cover of the *Times* of London that day. It was proof that the first block was mined on or after that date, but it also provided a clue as to what inspired this peer-to-peer digital cash in the first place. It was an act of rebellion against what cypherpunks viewed as a deeply flawed system.

For the first time in history, people were able to transfer value in minutes and across continents without the need of an intermediary and free from censorship. There was no central bank issuing the coins and dictating monetary policy, no bank account required, no processor taking big fees in the middle of the exchange. No currency controls. All that was needed was an internet connection. The price of the coins was determined by the free and open market.

All the while, traditional banks can take as long as a week and charge as much as $50 for an international money transfer; they can refuse service to businesses they disagree with or simply defraud clients, and governments can devalue local currencies with reckless printing of new money to finance spending, or they can ban foreign currency purchases and limit withdrawals.

In 2013, Cristina Fernandez de Kirchner was running Argentina. Things weren't nearly as dire as during the *corralito*, or little corral, as they called the 2001 crisis when the government banned withdrawals, but the Argentine government was again restricting what people could do with their own money. Fernandez had banned people from buying foreign currency to stop the outflow of dollars caused by the country's recurring problems of soaring inflation and a devaluing peso.

That's when Alvaro saw Bitcoin pop up in the news, as it had recently spiked above $1,000 for the first time. He immediately got the value of uncensorable money and googled "how to buy Bitcoin in Argentina." He didn't have much in savings, but he figured he'd be better off putting them in bitcoin than keeping them in Argentine pesos. Bitcoin was trading around $600 when he bought in, and the Argentine peso was at 6 per dollar. The peso has since slumped 90 percent to around 60 per dollar at the time of this writing, while bitcoin has multiplied its value more eight times from its 2013 peak and was last trading at about $8,500, granted, with many wild swings in between.

It was around that time, between 2011 and 2013, that developers around the world were trying to use blockchain technology to do other things besides "just" transfer value from point A to point B. They were building applications on top of Bitcoin, using its code to create separate blockchains, and even starting their own networks from scratch. They were exploring uses like decentralized securities trading, property rights, and identity. Excitement around those projects and some merchant adoption pushed Bitcoin above $100 and then $1,000 for the first time in 2013. But practical uses were still unheard-of, and soon Bitcoin plunged back to around $500, leaving most of these experiments frozen in the first crypto winter. True believers kept tinkering, and the Bitcoin community kept growing, populated mostly by young men with some background in tech or economics, who leaned libertarian. They coalesced in the BitcoinTalk online forum and on Reddit. It didn't matter that most had never met each other or that they didn't know each other's real names. For them, Bitcoin was more than digital money. It represented a belief system, and those forums were often the only place Bitcoiners felt understood.

In March 2011, the community gained a new member. Vitalik

Buterin was seventeen years old, and his first post on the BitcoinTalk forum said:

> On the subject of economics, I could write about the concept like the social taboos around money and the practical inconvenience of paying anything less than about $5 with conventional tools like credit cards or PayPal (. . .) and how Bitcoin offers a way to fix this.

He would go on to make the biggest impact in the blockchain space since Satoshi Nakamoto, but at the time he was just looking to write for the Bitcoin Weekly blog in exchange for some bitcoin. He didn't have any and wanted to earn it.

3

The Magazine

Sitting on a bus rambling down the streets of Cristian, a tiny town in Romania's Transylvania region, Mihai Alisie looked at the faces of the commuters. The woman balancing a purse and grocery bags on her knees, the man with the creased face and blank stare holding on to a greasy pole, the teenager finding temporary escape in his earphones. He felt a surge of happiness. He had gamed the system. He had dodged this daily grind without ever holding a regular job.

Mihai—tall, thin, pale—was the kind of kid who took stereos apart to find the magnet inside the speaker. That curiosity evolved into an interest in computers as a teenager and eventually resulted in his enrollment at the Bucharest University of Economic Studies for a degree called "economic cybernetics."

He was spending his free time learning about poker, reading up on techniques and theories in the university library, playing with friends, and gambling online. The first time his girlfriend Roxana went to see him at the university they stopped at the photocopy machine to pick up six different poker books.

Determined to get better, he started handing over part of his win rate to a coach until the summer of 2011, when he became a coach himself and celebrated his poker coming-of-age and birthday at a casino in Spain. He borrowed 50 euros from his brother-in-law and won 500. The average Romanian made about $200 per month at the time, and Mihai was making between $350 and $500 in a good session.

But playing poker for a living was risky, so Mihai started to think about related business opportunities and the idea of some sort of poker players' social network formed in his head. He contacted the owner of one of the sites he used for downloading poker books to get a better sense of this worldwide community, and that's when he heard about Bitcoin for the first time.

The website's owner mentioned that many of his clients were paying for goods with a peer-to-peer digital currency that didn't have to go through banks. It was pseudonymous so, in theory, people behind the transactions were hard to track down. The idea went over Mihai's head in that Skype call but a few weeks later, lying in bed one afternoon, he remembered that part of the conversation.

He started going through all the links Google provided when he searched for more information on this digital cash, and those pages led to more pages, and the search for Bitcoin led to more obscure cryptography terms, and soon he had spent hours reading everything he could.

Like so many other Bitcoin enthusiasts, Mihai understood that the great innovation of blockchain technology is that it can cut out the middlemen and pass those savings directly on to the masses. It can hold the powerful accountable with immutable public ledgers. It can help the unbanked transfer value peer-to-peer and across borders. In essence, it could put wealth and control back in the hands of the everyday man. This was a powerful concept for someone who had seen the corruption in his country blasted on TV and splashed across newspaper headlines all his life.

Poker looked so meaningless in comparison, that he decided to give it up and focus on Bitcoin. Instead of creating some sort of platform for the poker community, he would do it for crypto.

As Mihai continued his search, digging deep into forum pages, little-known blogs, and YouTube videos, he kept coming across the name Vitalik Buterin. It appeared as a frequent byline of the now-abandoned news site Bitcoin Weekly, on the Bitcoin page on Reddit and in the BitcoinTalk forum. This Vitalik guy was able to turn complicated concepts into readable and accurate columns. In August 2011, after getting a no from the guy who ran Bitcoin Weekly, he emailed Vitalik asking if he'd be interested in building a magazine about the Bitcoin space.

Earlier that year Vitalik had been roaming the BitcoinTalk forum offering to write articles in exchange for Bitcoin, and he soon became a frequent Bitcoin Weekly contributor. In May 2011, he was writing about the recent surge in Bitcoin prices. The beginning of the article could have very well been dated 2013 or 2017: "Many are wondering why the prices of Bitcoin have shot up by over 1000% over the past month, and whether the increase is sustainable or merely a speculative bubble, liable to suddenly crash at any time."

Vitalik was enjoying himself, investigating a topic he was increasingly interested in, getting paid for it, and becoming a respected voice in this zealous tribe of cryptocurrency believers. When Mihai Alisie's offer to start a Bitcoin magazine came in his inbox, he immediately took it.

Vitalik and Mihai had never seen each other face-to-face, they hadn't even had a video call, and between the two of them, the only journalism experience they had was Vitalik's posts. But after a few chats over Skype about what the magazine would look like, they were fully committed to working together. They'd call their publication *Bitcoin Magazine*. It would feature articles about the Bitcoin community, business, and markets, and would be a reputable source for mainstream media journalists. Through the BitcoinTalk forum they invited a few other like-minded Bitcoin enthusiasts to join, and soon they had a team, albeit with no publishing business experience or even plain business experience for most, running what would become the first ever print Bitcoin magazine.

The first step was to incorporate the venture and, following the advice of one of their new recruits, they decided the fastest and cheapest place to do it would be in the United Kingdom. Mihai would deal with the administrative hassle while the rest of the crew got to writing and designing the first issue. The only problem was, he had spent all his scant poker earnings and didn't have enough money to get there from Romania.

Mihai's mother, who had been listening to her son ramble on about this currency of the future, wasn't going to let a few hundred dollars stand between him and his dreams. She opened her jewelry box and gave Mihai a gold necklace, one of her most valuable pieces, for him to pawn. Roxana's parents loaned him some cash, and with that, he had enough money for a plane ticket and a stay in the United Kingdom.

The original plan, at least in Mihai's mind, was to create a PDF version of the magazine. If people downloaded it, they could make a donation in Bitcoin or "fiat," as Bitcoiners liked to refer to government-backed money (like the US dollar), to support the publication. Once the magazine gained a following, the aspiring publisher would approach advertisers and then, maybe, they'd be able to print the magazine.

One of the new team members, a controversial character whom the crypto community loved to hate for his rambling YouTube videos and who went by the online name of Matthew N. Wright, thought they should move faster, and when the magazine was almost ready, he started pushing for the first issue to be in print.

"Let's dream big," he would type into the *Bitcoin Magazine* Skype chat from his home in South Korea as he was trying to rally the team behind publishing a physical magazine. He got some lukewarm support, but Mihai, who was getting ready to return to Romania after registering the business as Bittalk Media Ltd. in the United Kingdom, argued they didn't have enough money or experience to do something like that. Thinking that was the end of it, he boarded his flight back to Bucharest and by the time he got to a computer, hundreds of messages on the Skype group had popped up. As he scrolled down, trying to understand what was going on, he clicked on a link, and there it was, a press release stating in bold letters, "The First

Issue of Bitcoin Magazine Goes to Print." The statement declared that the publication would be "an industry standard 64-page glossy magazine, with an initial 5,000 issue run."

Mihai continued reading the press release with dread:

"U.S. subscribers should receive their first copy of Bitcoin Magazine by the 16th of May 2012," which was less than two weeks from that press release. "Delivery time may vary for international subscribers. . . . Naturally, Bitcoin is one of the available payment options."

Roxana and Mihai felt a huge sense of responsibility to deliver what was just promised to the community and decided they would somehow make it happen. The writing was done, mostly by Vitalik, and so was the design. Now it was a matter of printing and shipping the copies, which rested fully on their shoulders. The magazines were printed in the United States, they traveled in a container ship to the United Kingdom, and from there they arrived in trucks in Romania. Mihai went to pick them up at the customs office and when the police opened the boxes, the magazine's cover—the Anonymous mask, that glossy, white, smirking symbol used by hackers and protesters around the world—peered back at him. Mihai threw Roxana a nervous look, but the officer only inquired whether the magazine was about Occupy Wall Street. "Kind of," they replied. The officer asked for a copy. Relieved, Roxana gave him two.

As subscriptions started flowing in, Roxana entered them into a spreadsheet, wrote down names and addresses by hand on labels, stuck them on the envelopes, and slid the magazines in, all from their room at Mihai's parents' house in Cristian. Boxes of magazines started filling up the living room, which they then carried to the village's post office, to find that it didn't have enough stamps. It was the best business that little office would get all year, so the clerks there said they'd figure it out.

Subscribers got their magazines weeks late and angrily complained on BitcoinTalk, accusing the whole operation of being a scam, but the publication charged forward. Vitalik and a few other die-hards kept writing their articles, the whole process became slightly more automated (Mihai and Roxana bought a label printer), and soon the team had succeeded in their goal of creating the most reputable source for Bitcoin news out there.

In part it was thanks to Matthew's arguably overly aggressive ambition to see the magazine in print that got them there, but he didn't remain in the magazine for long. Matthew, who was editor in chief at the time, resigned in September 2012, just four months after the first issue shipped. His departure was a consequence of his decision to throw his support behind a crypto project called "Pirate" that was rumored to be a scam.

On BitcoinTalk, he challenged those saying the project was a Ponzi scheme or fraud to comment on his post saying how much they were willing to bet him the project was legitimate. If he won, he would pay them back double the amounts committed. Not surprisingly, with a name like Pirate, the project closed with allegations of lost investments discussed in online forums. He didn't pay back all the money he owed from his bets, his reputation was tarnished, and his apology letter to the community was endlessly questioned and ridiculed. He resigned his position from director of Bittalk Media Ltd. and editor in chief of *Bitcoin Magazine*. Vitalik and Mihai kept the magazine going.

4

The Rabbit Hole

Vitalik always sat in the same spot in Professor Alfred Menezes's lectures at the University of Waterloo in Canada: in the front row and to the left. Computer science had been an easy choice for him, and he started class in December 2012. What struck the professor the most about Vitalik wasn't the tests he aced nor his occasional brilliant remark in class, but the times he stayed behind to talk about Bitcoin. Menezes, who had coauthored several books on applied cryptography, was impressed by the clarity with which Vitalik spoke about the topic. Vitalik would chat for a minute or two and then have to run off to keep up with his busy schedule. Besides his five advanced university courses, he worked as an assistant to prominent cryptographer Ian Goldberg, who coauthored the Off-the-Record protocol, which is now widely used to encrypt instant messages. Vitalik was still writing *Bitcoin Magazine* articles and had also taken on some programming gigs on the side.

All that work didn't leave much room for friends, so it was a lonely time. Far from the heavy partying and drinking that's common for many college students, Vitalik would be on his computer working hour after hour at the university and at home, weekdays and weekends. He used bathroom and food breaks as a chance to change rooms, just so he wouldn't be sitting in the same spot for days on end.

He enjoyed the work, but he craved some human connection. Vitalik, whose calm, blue eyes retreat into some faraway place when the present fails to interest him and who sometimes mutters or laughs to himself as if he's locked in his own thoughts, was thankful for the Bitcoin meetups and conferences that were increasingly popping up, recently even in Toronto.

Not far from Vitalik in Waterloo, Toronto native Anthony Di Iorio had also been searching for a real-life version of the crypto community he had found online. He had recently become obsessed with Bitcoin and wanted to connect with like-minded enthusiasts in the area, but couldn't find anything, so he created a Meetup.com group himself. The first gathering was in November 2012, at Pauper's Pub. Just about a dozen people showed up. Among them was an awkward eighteen-year-old kid, fresh out of high school. Vitalik Buterin. Vitalik sat on one of the stools with his back curved and lanky arms forward. According to Anthony, Vitalik didn't speak much and when he was spoken to, he seemed a little bit startled before replying.

Up until that moment Anthony had pretty much coasted through a carefree but aimless life. His father, Lino, ran a construction company, a patio door business, and had invented and patented curling equipment that's now used by most Olympic medal winners. Income from those ventures had put the Di Iorio family in a sprawling, eight-bedroom, English-manor-style house in Toronto. The children went through some of the best private schools in the area, but Anthony hated being told what to do and was only an okay student. He would always rather be playing soccer or hockey, or sitting in front of his computer. His first machine, the boxlike IBM PC junior, appeared in the family den in 1986, when he was eleven years old. From then on he was hooked. He spent his summers in computer camp, where he would kayak, canoe, and learn to use massive mainframes with punch cards and no monitors.

Lino wanted their children to know the value of money, so even though they were wealthy, Anthony still had a series of jobs growing up, from working at a golf club, to bartending, to helping out at an engraving shop at the mall. But he kept gravitating to computer-related work. When he was eleven, he got a job with his father's cousin Reno, who had a business setting up modems. Around the time of his first year at Ryerson University, where he got a business management degree, he started developing websites with his brother Elio, a business that didn't take off.

Still, computers were just a fun hobby to Anthony. He got a marketing job at a catalytic converter company right out of college, which he soon quit to travel in Europe. When he got back to Canada, his father helped him buy a house near York University, which he moved into but also subdivided to rent out to college students. In 2008, his dad sold the patio door business and asked Anthony if there was an opportunity he could help him out with. That's how Anthony ended up owning a million-dollar drill. He thought clean energy was interesting, and one of his father's friends had a geothermal drilling company, which helps cool or heat up buildings without using combustion, but through pipes that run through the ground. The business was booming and needed more drills, so the friend would provide the projects and Anthony's company would do the drilling.

But something else was stealing Anthony's attention. It all started thanks to his brother Elio, who had urged him to "learn what money is." Elio had seemed to be heading toward a promising political career. He was elected international secretary of Canada's Green Party in 2004, but he quit less than two years later, accusing the party's leader of mismanaging finances. His brief path through elected office left him so jaded that he would drive without a license plate to assert his independence. He became convinced banks were behind a legalized scam, and fought in court to pay a loan for more than $170,000 with TD Bank with nothing more than a piece of paper with the words "consumer purchase" written on them—something like an IOU.

Anthony, who has long and narrow dark brown eyes, thin lips, wispy black hair, and a short, trim figure, decided to listen to his brother and look into money. It was around that time that greedy Wall Street banks, corrupt credit rating agencies, both hopeful and reckless US home buyers, and both gullible and sophisticated investors, sank the world into a financial crisis that's still causing ripples more than a decade later. So if you were like Anthony, googling about money in 2008, YouTube was full of postmortems explaining what's wrong with it, or at least what's wrong with the way it's handled. That's where he found videos of Peter Schiff, a stockbroker who paraded into Occupy Wall Street protests carrying a sign that read, "I'm the 1%, let's talk." The videos showed Schiff in 2006 and 2007, across major news stations, warning about a looming financial crisis. His arguments that governments printing money, overtaxing business, and overspending on welfare were inflating asset prices and causing economic imbalances made sense to Anthony.

By 2012 Anthony had graduated from those YouTube videos and was learning about Austrian economics and reading Ayn Rand. From there, Bitcoin wasn't too many links away. He heard about it for the first time on libertarian radio show *Free Talk Live* and bought one coin right away. The price was around $10. A couple of days later he bought eight hundred more at roughly the same price.

So after halfheartedly jumping from job to job, Anthony was becoming a hard-core Bitcoiner, hosting Toronto's first meetup gathering at Pauper's Pub.

By early 2013, he wasn't alone. The San Jose conference in May 2013, simply called Bitcoin 2013, was a coming-out party for the cryptocurrency world. Past conferences had drawn crowds of a couple hundred, but this time a thousand people filled the room. In past conferences, only the Bitcoin-famous were on the speaker list. In San Jose, the Winklevoss twins gave a keynote speech and venture funds like Draper Associates and Benchmark Capital descended from Silicon Valley. Everyone was happy. Bitcoin had just crossed the $100 milestone from around $15 at the beginning of the year.

Most of the Bitcoin-famous were in attendance, too. Cofounder of crypto exchange BitInstant Charlie Shrem, who in December 2014 would be sentenced to two years in prison for aiding and abetting the operation of an unlicensed money-transmitting business related to the Silk Road, was one of the speakers. So was Roger Ver, known as Bitcoin Jesus for his enthusiasm in spreading the Bitcoin gospel, who would later become an advocate of a spin-off from the first cryptocurrency called Bitcoin Cash. Other luminaries, including BitPay cofounder and CEO Tony Gallippi and leading Bitcoin developer Gavin Andresen, roamed the halls.

Vitalik positioned himself behind the *Bitcoin Magazine* stand, from which he could chat with a constant stream of loyal readers who dropped by. He could geek out about cryptography and decentralization with them and make nerdy math jokes and they would get the punch line. For the first time, he was part of the popular crowd. But more than that, it felt like he had been reunited with his long-lost tribe. He had finally found his people.

He took up a program at the university that allowed him to study for eight months, work for four months, study for eight, work for four, and repeat that for five years until graduation. His goal was to gain some experience at a crypto startup. In February, he asked Jed McCaleb, who had developed digital payments protocol Ripple, if he could join the venture. McCaleb quickly said yes, but to get the job, Vitalik first had to get a US visa. At the time, Ripple was too young a company to sponsor a visa, and after a long process trying other avenues, they finally gave up around May.

By then it was Vitalik's term break from university. Mihai invited him over to Europe to work on *Bitcoin Magazine* and a new project called Egora. Bitcoin still wasn't great at the use it was originally made for, that is, to be digital cash. Sure, it had become the primary currency used in the dark web, where illegal goods are sold, and by 2013 it dominated the Silk Road website. But the goal for many Bitcoin advocates was for mainstream online commerce to adopt the digital currency so Bitcoin could really become the "peer-to-peer electronic cash system" hailed in Satoshi's white paper. With that in mind, Mihai started to build Egora, an online marketplace meant to be a decentralized eBay, where buyers and sellers wouldn't have to rely on the platform itself. Instead, funds would be sent into an escrow account stored in a decentralized ledger. The money would be released only when the buyer and seller unlocked the account.

After two years of working together for the magazine, Vitalik and Mihai finally met in person at an Airbnb in Barcelona. They weren't there for too long when Amir Taaki, a prominent Bitcoin developer, convinced them to come join him in Calafou, an anarchist community near Barcelona. They decided to go both because it was cheap and because they hoped to meet interesting people with aligned values of minimal government and corporate control.

A ninety-minute train ride takes you from Barcelona to the tiny and ancient village of Vallbona d'Anoia, the station closest to Calafou. The agricultural town nestled in the Catalonian countryside has a dozen or so paved, crisscrossing streets that give way to farms and a couple of factories. The roads that lead to the anarchist community are flanked by houses of red tiles, earthlike colors, and iron-clad balconies. A car seldom drives by and the sidewalks are mostly empty. Faded stencils of red stars, hammers, and sickles are still visible on some of the low walls in front of the houses, along with graffitied slogans calling for an independent Catalonia.

At the town's outskirts, a cluster of crumbling buildings with broken windows and a brick wall form a border around the compound. Inside, one of the buildings is in slightly better shape, with windowpanes still intact and white paint covering most walls. A colorful mural featuring a great tree trunk, branches bearing dancing fruit with smiley faces and other fantastical shapes reaching into a purple sky, lit up the otherwise fading facades.

Calafou had been started by Spanish anticapitalist Enric Duran. Duran was infamous for having masterminded a pyramid scheme in which he would borrow money from one bank to pay loans with another bank, which would raise its limit and let him borrow more money, which he would then use to pay credit with a third bank. So went the cycle until he had borrowed 492,000 euros from thirty-nine banks.

He refused to pay, and fled Spain. This was in 2008, when the world was steeped in an economic crisis and Spain had been hit particularly hard. Duran published a pamphlet announcing and explaining his "act of civil disobedience." He claimed that getting half a million euros with no guarantees and in some cases using falsified documents revealed how the banking system "promotes indebtedness from families," ignoring risks and common sense. The Bitcoin white paper, which proposed a system that didn't rely on trust to third parties, would be published one month later, but Duran's protest already carried the same sentiment: "This system works on the basis of trust, so if we can spread mistrust by carrying on similar actions, we will then be able to abolish it (destroy it?)!" he wrote.

He didn't run off with the free money he was able to withdraw from the bank accounts in his scheme. At least not all of it. He used part of it to fund anticapitalist and anarchist movements. He cofounded the Cooperativa Integral Catalana, or CIC, which was intended to create a self-sustained economy outside of the state. Activists of the organization negotiated to buy an enormous piece of land complete with a decrepit factory complex. The owner was about to sell it to someone who wanted to turn it into a waste disposal plant, but the activists' bigger vision finally won. They agreed on a rent-to-buy scheme and the thirty or so radicals moved in to what they would call a "postcapitalist eco-industrial colony." They set up metal welding and woodworking shops, planted some crops, and created Calafou's "hacklab." That's where Mihai and Vitalik settled in to work.

The hacklab consisted of a few tables bunched together in one corner, a computer and monitors, and a fast and reliable internet connection for developers to build open source software. But no amount of thrift store sofas, chairs, and tables the community members had brought could fill up the place. It was a building made for machines producing industrial quantities of stuff, not for a bunch of anarchists making furniture. Anything that would have made it seem remotely habitable had long been stripped away, and the rooms were now barren concrete boxes, unadorned columns placed every few yards breaking up the empty space. Light flooded through huge windows several yards from the ground, which was fortunate as not all areas had electricity. They had arranged with the town's supermarkets to retrieve perishables they were no longer able to sell.

For Vitalik, the worst part about Calafou was the bathroom. It was an outhouse with a hole in the ground, and which seldom had toilet paper and always had flies. He did his best to ignore the flies, but sometimes he would give up and go to the forest. After that, he would walk another hundred yards to a different place where he could wash his hands. The cold shower wasn't great, either. He slept on a mattress so thin he could actually feel the ground.

But he loved being in the middle of nature. He would take breaks from working on Egora or talking about the possibilities for cryptocurrencies and go on long walks. His narrow, almost fragile frame would get lost between the trees, leaves crunching under his sneakers, as he thought about what to do next.

It was the beginning of August and he had been living in Calafou for about two months when Vitalik emailed the university to say he wanted to take a break for one year to work on cryptocurrency projects, earnestly thinking he would go back.

5

The Swiss Knife

Vitalik's worldwide Bitcoin tour started in New Hampshire. The state's libertarian-leaning ways had a strong appeal for Vitalik, whose father had instilled in him from an early age the idea that society as a whole grows stronger when individual liberties are protected, while big governments end up corroding nations. They were lessons learned from living in communist Russia. Less than two years before his visit, Vitalik had written in the BitcoinTalk forum that "government is bad because it's a monopoly more than for any other reason. You can think of the world as a free market anarchy where all the land is legitimately owned by 193 landowners that allow you to live on the land under certain conditions."

To Vitalik, like any monopoly, oversized government's lack of competition caused harmful effects and left most people with no choice but to accept disagreements about tax levels, public services, personal freedom, and so on. As with large corporations, to him, governments become "inefficient once they cross a certain size threshold."

As Vitalik drove into the state that bears the "Live Free or Die" motto, one roadside sign in particular made an impression on him. It said wearing seat belts was mandatory for those under eighteen. "That is, unlike every other state, *only* for those under 18," he wrote for a *Bitcoin Magazine* article. He was there for Porcfest, a festival hosted annually by the libertarian movement Free State Project. It was a weeklong gathering with liberty-themed panel discussions and a marketplace where merchants accepted silver, gold, and Bitcoin as payment.

New Hampshire's politics made a stronger impression on Vitalik than the Bitcoin developments happening there, which were mainly focused on increasing merchant adoption. Vitalik saw that people viewed the local government favorably and that it would be a truly ideal place to live "if only the feds would get out of the way." The age restriction on alcohol and bars at twenty-one led eighteen-year-old Vitalik to get kicked out of a Bitcoin meetup there. "The meetup group was nice (and righteously angry) enough to relocate to a different location," he wrote.

Next he flew to Europe, making a stop at a conference focusing on Bitcoin businesses in Amsterdam. He thought the absence of the mainstream finance community, which he had seen in a conference in London earlier that year, was a welcome change. He listened raptly to representatives from the Dutch central bank and the Amsterdam police discuss regulatory issues and hoped that Bitcoin's features—like providing a public ledger for transactions and the ability for exchanges to have funds kept in verifiable off-line storage—would get them excited about cryptocurrencies' possibilities and not inspired to strike against them.

The most important announcement to come out of the Amsterdam conference, he thought, was that peer-to-peer digital payments network Ripple would become open source. At the time, the primary criticism of Ripple was that the network was ultimately controlled by a centralized company called Ripple Labs, which was able to change the code without asking anyone in the community. Ripple Labs also owned all 100 billion of Ripple's cryptocurrency called XRP.

"It only plans to distribute a part of them to the community—the rest will go to early investors and the company's founders. When questioned about this at the Bitcoin conference in San Jose, CEO Chris Larsen simply replied that the company chose this distribution model to better attract top-quality Silicon Valley talent and investment—hardly a satisfying argument to those who believe that the main problems with the current financial system are inequality and greed," Vitalik wrote in an article.

Vitalik thought that making the code public didn't change criticism regarding Ripple Labs controlling XRP, but it did allow anyone to review the inner workings of the code, and join the network, and if there were a disagreement at some point, people would be free to copy the code, modify it, and start a new Ripple.

At the conference he met Amir Chetrit, who was working in Israel on Colored Coins, a project aimed at representing and managing real-world assets as tokens on top of the Bitcoin network. Amir, tall and bald with a black beard framing an easy smile, had joined the Bitcoin crowd after realizing its ability to provide an alternative monetary system and improve existing economic, financial, and social structures. Because of his parents' work, Amir and his four younger siblings grew up going back and forth between Israel and the United States.

He dropped out of computer science at a university in Maryland and worked briefly for a local government in the state as a software engineer. Hours went by with nothing for him to do in his small cubicle, so he learned firsthand that the state can be highly inefficient, slow, and even corrupt. He quit and moved to New York, where he followed his mother's footsteps into real estate. This was 2005, when risky mortgage loans repackaged into financial derivatives were cycling around Wall Street and pumping up what would become a bubble and its inevitable burst.

It started to dawn on him that the world doesn't work according to fair and prescribed rules. The government, he came to believe, is fundamentally flawed, and the monetary and banking systems are made to tilt the scale in favor of an elite few. He contributed to Ron Paul's campaign because he felt a strong alignment with the libertarian values of individual freedom. In perusing libertarian blogs, he found Bitcoin, a system touted for not being beholden to any central authority.

He started working with the Colored Coins team in Israel, which was building a system that would allow different currencies and assets to trade on top of the Bitcoin network. His new interest took him to a Bitcoin conference in Amsterdam, in September 2013, where he met Vitalik. Vitalik told him he planned to visit Israel at some point in his Bitcoin tour and Amir offered to put him in touch with his friend Ofir, who was also working on a Bitcoin-related startup in Tel Aviv.

Soon enough, Vitalik was sleeping on Ofir's couch in Tel Aviv. It's his preferred way of traveling: living out of a backpack and couch surfing with friends and friends-of-friends.

Amir dropped by Ofir's apartment to hang out with Vitalik, and saw he had built a website for his friend's startup in the two short days since he had arrived, something Ofir thought would take weeks to do. Later, he challenged Vitalik with a statistical math problem, which Vitalik was able to solve by writing a computer program in just a few minutes. He sat back in his chair stunned as Vitalik continued typing away on his own laptop.

In the land of deserts, ancient religious sites, and cobblestone streets winding through the same noisy markets for the past three thousand years, Vitalik found a cluster of entrepreneurs and developers who were making the biggest strides in the blockchain world. Teams there were trying to push Bitcoin's limits and test whether it could be used for more than digital currency. The idea was that traits of blockchain technology—such as having no central point of failure, being uncensorable, cutting out intermediaries, and being immutable—could also benefit other applications besides money. Financial instruments like stocks and bonds, and commodities like gold, were the obvious targets, but people were also talking about putting other representations of value like property deeds and medical records on the blockchain, too. Those efforts—admirable considering Bitcoin hadn't, and still hasn't, been adopted widely as currency—were known as Bitcoin 2.0.

One person Vitalik was excited to meet was Ron Gross, who was leading the Mastercoin team. At a cafe in Tel Aviv, Ron explained how he and a group of developers scattered all over the world were building a platform on top of the Bitcoin network that would allow anyone to create their own cryptocurrency and fundraise through those coins.

Mastercoin founder J. R. Willett ambitiously called his proposal for the protocol, published in January 2012, "The Second Bitcoin Whitepaper." The project went live in July 2013, starting off with a month-long fundraiser where contributors sent Bitcoin to a digital wallet address and got Mastercoin tokens in exchange (1 BTC for 100 MSC).

Ron had quit his job at Google to join a startup and then quit that startup to get into Bitcoin. When he saw the white paper posted on BitcoinTalk back in 2012, he was one of the few that responded with suggestions. Then in July 2013, when J.R. posted the amended white paper and announced he was selling Mastercoins in exchange for bitcoins, Ron was the first to reply with several notes. Among the first was the suggestion that J.R. should delay the sale to give the community enough time to review the project, especially since a bonus was given to the early investors. He also suggested setting up a board of directors to control the funds, instead of having them go to J.R.'s personal wallet. "You might gain more trust in MasterCoin by removing yourself as a benevolent dictator/point of failure," he wrote.

J.R., under the name "dacoinminster," and Ron, under the name "ripper234," went back and forth in the forum for a bit, but ultimately the sale went ahead as planned, raising over 5,120 bitcoins, or around $500,000 at the time. A foundation was set up after the sale and Ron joined as one of seven board members. This was the first time a blockchain startup had raised funds by selling its own digital token. The crowdfunding mechanism would later be known as an initial coin offering, or ICO, a play on words with initial public offering, or IPO.

In the case of Bitcoin and other cryptocurrencies, digital coins are only created through a network of computers, which must expend inordinately large amounts of energy to confirm transactions (that is, "mining" coins); receiving coins is a reward granted to those who use their computers to do that work. A project that created coins out of thin air like Mastercoin was bound to get criticism from the Bitcoin community. Not only was ownership of Mastercoins concentrated (J.R. owned about 30 percent of the total) but the Mastercoin Foundation was a privileged party, as it was the only entity getting a fee per transaction. For many Bitcoin enthusiasts, this disqualified Mastercoin from being categorized as cryptocurrency.

For Vitalik, Mastercoin was nevertheless better than Ripple's approach. At least in Mastercoin's case, he reasoned, the coins were distributed among the community in the sale and not entirely owned by one centralized party. Also, the funds were managed by a nonprofit foundation, which would better align incentives with the broader community and not be subject to the whims of a small group of people at the top of a corporation.

J.R. had talked about this new fundraising idea earlier that year at the San Jose conference.

"We've talked about what's possible, we should also mention what's stupidly easy. If you wanted to today start a new protocol on top of Bitcoin, you can do it without going to a bunch of venture capitalists and saying hey, I got this idea," he said. "You can actually say . . . Here's who we are, here's our plan, here's our Bitcoin address, and anybody who sends coins to this address owns a piece of our protocol. Anybody can do that."

J.R. wrote in the "Second Bitcoin Whitepaper" that Mastercoin would be a protocol layer between the existing Bitcoin blockchain and the users' currencies, and the software would "contain simple tools which will allow anyone to design and release their own currency, with their own rules without doing any software development." Fundraising was just one of many potential uses for these new cryptocurrencies issued on top of the Bitcoin network. The Mastercoin software would allow users to create so-called smart contracts within the Bitcoin ecosystem. Smart contracts consist of code that self-executes when a set of predefined rules are met.

Nick Szabo, the cryptographer who in 1998 invented the digital currency "Bit Gold," coined the term "smart contract" in the early 1990s. In a 1997 paper, he said smart contracts "combine protocols with user interfaces to formalize and secure relationships over computer networks." The system eliminates the need to pay for and trust third parties like auditors, accountants, lawyers, and notary publics, as the agreements are executed through a computer program. The humble vending machine is a primitive precursor to smart contracts, Szabo wrote in the paper.

Bitcoin also uses this technology, as it transfers value from one person to another when certain conditions are met. Its scripting language allows for other smart contracts like multi-signature accounts, payment channels, escrows, time locks, and others. But it was limited to a few uses, and Mastercoin wanted to change that.

Four months after the July sale, Ron had become director of the project and, as he was telling Vitalik, Mastercoin developers were working on setting up different functionalities that would expand on Bitcoin's. Ron could tell from Vitalik's questions that this young *Bitcoin Magazine* writer had read up on all the documentation and probably understood the tech better than he did. By the end of their chat Vitalik asked if there was anything he could help out with. Ron pointed to the team's open online board, where they kept track of the dozen or so tasks and research projects they were working on. "Just pick whatever looks interesting," he said.

While he was in Israel, Vitalik had also met with Yoni Assia, who led eToro, a platform for stocks and foreign exchange trading, which had started to venture into Bitcoin trading and was collaborating with the Colored Coins team. Similar to Mastercoin, the guys at Colored Coins were trying to attach real-world assets, like stocks, real estate, and gold, to the Bitcoin blockchain. Vitalik had been following the project and making contributions to some of the code since late 2012. When he got to Israel, he asked Yoni if there was any more work he could focus on while he was there. Yoni thought his ability to put complex ideas into words for *Bitcoin Magazine* could be useful, offered to pay him some bitcoins in exchange for writing a new Colored Coins white paper, and told him to come work out of eToro's office if he wanted.

Vitalik made the hourlong trek from Ofir's apartment in Tel Aviv to eToro's building on the outskirts of the city almost every day. He wanted to save the few bucks of bus fare, and also he just loves walking. He arrived at the office, settled in the common area, opened his laptop, and got to work. Yoni didn't have much luck trying to get Vitalik to do small talk, but as soon as the conversation switched to anything technical or crypto-related, Vitalik lit up and chatted for hours, or for as long as Yoni could keep up with him.

Vitalik wrote the white paper in about two weeks and sent it to the Colored Coins Google group on November 13. After briefly introducing how Bitcoin was created and its advantages over existing payment systems (irreversible transactions provide a high degree of security, lack of a centralized authority makes it invulnerable to censorship, public transactions allow for unprecedented business transparency, etc.), he asked, "Given all of these advantages, the natural question is: Is it possible to use the same functionality for other applications as well? The answer, it turns out, is yes," he wrote. The distributed database, secured by cryptographic proof-of-work, "is good for more than just the single limited-supply currency originally envisioned by Satoshi Nakamoto in 2009." The same technology can be used to maintain ownership of company shares, property, bank deposits, basically, anything that can be represented as a digital asset, and is a "rivalrous good," meaning that only one person can own it at a time, Vitalik argued. However, Bitcoin doesn't include the facilities to do this by default. An additional protocol is required, "an overlay network of issuance of distinct instruments encapsulated in a design we call 'colored coins,'" he wrote.

Vitalik went on to explain each use case in greater detail and later specified the code. Many thanked him for his efforts but also asked him to make changes and clear up some doubts. A handful were especially upset that Vitalik hadn't cited previous work.

Yoni, who coauthored the white paper, came to Vitalik's defense and replied, "Vitalik has been working together with everyone involved with this project from day 1, and has done a great job taking a lot of the work done so far and putting into one paper, after the last comment more refs have been added and more will be added too if needed."

Meanwhile, Vitalik was also working on Mastercoin. He had reviewed the research and work done so far and sent an email to Ron and J.R. proposing to write the specification for contracts for difference (a way to bet on the future price of securities). Ron replied that sounded "terrific" and after some discussion with J.R. in a separate email, decided to pay Vitalik $1,000 for his work. Vitalik soon updated them, saying his "generalized financial contracts idea could actually be used to implement CFDs, bets, insurance and trust-free dice all at the same time with minimal protocol complexity (the complexity would be pushed to each individual application). I can get a spec done in a couple of days."

Two days later, on November 13, Vitalik emailed them again.

I came up with something quite a lot more powerful than I thought it [sic] would:

http://vbuterin.com/ultimatescripting.html

It's a lot of description, but don't be intimidated; scroll straight to the examples section and you'll see that it basically replaces almost everything that we've wanted to do in a much cleaner and more generalized way.

In the document, he wrote,

the Mastercoin Foundation intends to integrate even more complex contracts [than Bitcoin or other blockchains], including bets, contracts for difference and on-blockchain dice rolls. However, up until this point Mastercoin has been taking a relatively unstructured process in developing these [*sic*] idea, essentially treating each one as a separate "feature" with its own transaction code and rules.

Instead of adding features to a protocol, Vitalik argued, it would be better to build a flexible layer that would allow anyone to create anything they wanted.

"This document outlines an alternative way of specifying Mastercoin contracts which follows an open-ended philosophy," he wrote in the email. The new approach would "specify only the basic data and arithmetic building blocks and allow anyone to craft arbitrarily complex Mastercoin contracts to suit their own needs, including needs which we may not even anticipate."

Below that introduction was the code and algorithms that would make the protocol work. Ron and J.R. were impressed, but not so eager to ditch their progress and go with Vitalik's alternative proposal. J.R. was particularly concerned about the lack of security in a platform that was so open as there was no way of making sure the code that was written on top of it would be bug-free.

"Whoa, I knew there was a good reason we hired you!" Ron wrote.

It seems this would be a lot more complicated to implement though. This is quite major, and needs to be discussed with the developers. Our key advantage is our momentum. I don't want to hinder us by having developers struggle to implement this spec. Wouldn't it be a lot fast [*sic*] to just implement CFDs/generalized CFDs, and generalize it later?

"This is REALLY interesting," J.R. replied a few hours later.

I shied away from scripting when I wrote the spec, because I was worried that I wouldn't be able to account for all the corner cases and potential hacks and security holes. I figured that whatever scripting I defined, people would come up with "poison transactions" which caused me big headaches later on. Have you given any thought to how this could be abused?

I definitely think that scripting could be an advanced feature that would add a lot of value, if we do it very carefully. I agree with Ron though that doing it now could result in our developers getting bogged down in the details, and slowing our progress a lot. The number of corner cases would (I expect) multiply exponentially, and I'd rather see Mastercoin doing its core functions before we start experimenting with scripting.

Vitalik was surprised by their comments. Why couldn't they get that what he was saying is so much better, Vitalik thought. He considered working on a specific feature maybe for half a second but immediately discarded the idea. That approach was just wrong. The more he looked at these Bitcoin 2.0 projects, the more they felt like a Swiss Army knife. All these people spending so much time making the nail file, the corkscrew, the tiny scissors . . . but what if nobody wants to use any of those things right now, and they just want a knife, or something else entirely different? Why not build the Lego blocks that would allow anyone to make whatever they want?

He got back to work on Colored Coins and took some of the suggestions the team had made to update the white paper. Not everyone was happy with the update and suggestions kept coming in, but Vitalik didn't answer any of the messages in the Google Group.

Alex Mizrahi, one of the most active developers in the project, wrote in the Google group two years later.

The problem was that Vitalik started writing it [the white paper] without prior discussion. He was barely aware of topics which we discussed in this mailing list for ~1 year before he started writing this spec, and he just didn't have time to do it properly, he wanted to complete everything in 1–2 months. I just found it very disappointing that the spec was being written in a haphazard way. As for his ideas, he had a plenty of them; and I actually considered 3 or so color kernels he designed, and they just weren't good. . . . As far as I know, none of the implementations adopted his ideas.

Vitalik had found a welcoming group in online Bitcoin forums when it was hard for him to navigate the real world, but now he was coming up against the limits of the Bitcoin community.

On one of his walks from eToro back to Tel Aviv, he became convinced he didn't need Colored Coins, Mastercoin, or anyone else to do what he wanted.

"Screw it, I'll do it myself," he thought.

PART II

Prelaunch

6

The White Paper

Vitaly Dmitriyevich Buterin's first days in this world were spent surrounded by the bustle of university students. His parents, who were both in their fifth year of computer science programs, took him to live in their dorm room three months after he was born in Kolomna, a midsize city near Moscow, on January 31, 1994. Their small room was one of several on the same floor, all lined up and down a long corridor that led to a common area and a shared kitchen. Natalia and Dmitry would take turns taking care of Vitalik; one would watch their newborn as the other went to class or studied at the small desk by the bed.

They moved to Moscow after they graduated with hopes of finding better-paying jobs in the big city. That was 1995, and Russia was mired in an economic crisis that resulted from the collapse of the Soviet Union just four years earlier. Inflation was soaring at double-digit rates every month, nearly half the population was living in poverty, and productivity had sunk to levels not seen since the aftermath of World War I as many uncompetitive state companies shut down. Everything that people were used to was broken and the whole nation was trying to figure out their lives and pick up the pieces. Natalia's parents lost their lifetime savings basically overnight because of hyperinflation.

Vitalik's parents were relatively fortunate amid the upheaval.

Natalia started working at a travel agency, which paid more than most programmer jobs and allowed her to learn English; Dmitry was a software engineer at a bank. They both moved on pretty quickly and Natalia took a job as an office manager at Heinz, the ketchup maker, and was soon promoted to the finance department. After three years there she went on to work for investment bank Renaissance Capital, also overseeing the firm's finances. Meanwhile, Dmitry started a software company that sold accounting tools for businesses.

While his parents worked, baby Vitalik was looked after by his grandparents from his mother's side, who had moved with them from Kolomna. His unusual talent with numbers was apparent from an early age, and they incorporated math into their games. In the seesaw and on the swing, they threw any arithmetic operation at him and he shot back the answer in seconds. By age four Vitalik's favorite toy was the computer. It wasn't loaded with fancy games. He just loved to experiment with different shapes and colors on Microsoft Paint and would spend entire afternoons punching in numbers and testing formulas on Excel.

By 1998, the limping Russian economy suffered a new blow as demand for oil, its main export, plummeted following the Asian financial crisis. The government defaulted on its debt and the central bank stopped defending a fixed trading band for the ruble, which caused the currency to plunge. Many companies, including Renaissance Capital, slashed expenses to stay afloat amid a contracting economy, and that meant cutting Natalia's job.

The relationship between Natalia and Dmitry was also unravelling. They were so young when they met and had taken on big responsibilities so quickly. They started thinking about moving to a place with less economic turmoil and where they could pursue new opportunities and experience new cultures. Even as their relationship faced its own strains, they agreed they'd move to the same location, even if they were separated as a couple. They wanted Vitalik to always be close to both of his parents.

They researched countries to determine which would be the most hospitable in terms of work visas; their best options were Australia and Canada. They had never been to either but decided on Canada. It was closer, and the weather was a little bit more like Russia's, so they figured it would be easier to adapt.

Natalia moved to Edmonton first, a city smack in the middle of Canada, where she got an accounting degree that would allow her to continue working in finance. Dmitry moved to Toronto with Vitalik one year later and Natalia moved there soon after they arrived. They decided Vitalik would stay with Dmitry so he wouldn't have to go through so many changes.

It was in Toronto that Vitalik went to kindergarten for the first time. Back in Russia, most of the interactions he had were with his parents and grandparents. He had never been much around kids, and it showed as he hit and bit his classmates and snatched toys from their hands. Communication was difficult. While he picked up writing and anything numbers-related very quickly, learning English took him more time.

Dmitry sat with him on the floor surrounded by Legos and, as they played, spoke to him in English. As Vitalik put the colorful blocks together, Dmitry could tell there was so much going on in his brain that he wanted to express, but when he tried to, he stumbled with the words.

It was easier for him to type stuff on his computer. By the time he was seven, Vitalik still wasn't very good at expressing himself in complex sentences, but he wrote a thirty- to forty-page document in Microsoft Word that he called "The Encyclopedia of Bunnies." It was very technical and structured like a scientific paper, with a table of contents and charts throughout. It listed the chemical elements you would find and the math that explained how things work. Dmitry recalls it as his son's first white paper.

Vitalik was placed in a gifted program within Canada's public school system, and even then he wasn't being challenged enough. His parents got him a private math tutor, a former university professor in Ukraine, who gave him more advanced material. He sat in class memorizing the formulas, going through the mandatory readings, and got high marks without putting too much effort into tests or homework, but he couldn't see the point of it all. It was just so boring. When the bell rang for recess and everyone ran off to play sports and gossip, he stayed behind. His shyness made it hard for him to connect with other kids and make friends.

By the end of middle school his parents thought something had to change. Vitalik needed to be immersed in a more challenging environment, one that encouraged him to speak out in class and interact with like-minded people. They decided to enroll their son in a more specialized private school, and Vitalik helped them narrow the options down to four. He spent one day in each of the four schools and decided to go for the Abelard School, with only about ten students per grade.

He was able to take advanced math classes, but also Latin and ancient Greek. He went from hardly speaking in public to joining the debate team. He was still going to his math tutor after class, enrolled in programming school on top of that, and traveled across Canada and abroad to compete in math and debate championships. Trophies from those competitions now fill a shelf in his grandparents' house. Outside of math, programming, languages, and debate, he spent hours playing *World of Warcraft*, where players take roles in a steampunk world populated by dragons and elves. Natalia wanted to incentivize his musical side, too, and put him in piano lessons for a bit, but that was one thing that didn't really stick.

It was during this time in high school, in 2011, that Dmitry mentioned Bitcoin to Vitalik.

"Hey, this is a really interesting concept," said Dmitry, who still had his software company and tried to stay up to date with the latest tech developments. He had come across Bitcoin somewhere online and tried to explain to Vitalik what he understood it was.

"But this does not have any real-world backing, how can it have any value?" Vitalik said.

About a month later, the term "Bitcoin" popped up again as Vitalik surfed the internet. This time he put more effort into trying to understand it. He read the technical materials and scoured Bitcoin forums until something clicked: He wanted to get his hands on some. He wanted to be a part of the Bitcoin economy. But just buying BTC didn't feel like genuinely participating, so he decided to work in exchange for it. He went on BitcoinTalk and offered to write articles and take payment in bitcoin. The guy behind the Bitcoin Weekly blog replied, offering five bitcoins per article, or about four dollars at the time. When he managed to save 20 bitcoin, Vitalik used 8.5 to buy a T-shirt and loved the feeling of having entered a parallel economy where traditional currency and banks weren't needed. He realized you could create a whole world, a new community, that doesn't rely on the existing financial infrastructure.

He came up with a new business model for the Bitcoin Weekly blog, where he would publish the first paragraph of an article and then hold the rest for ransom. If the community managed to send two and a half Bitcoins, he would release the rest of the article. It worked, and he ended up getting something like $20–$40 per piece. The coins were coming in from anonymous users everywhere in the world, and that was another aspect he loved about cryptocurrency. Unlike past technological innovations cooked up in Silicon Valley garages and universities, this innovation was truly global.

In just under three short years, Vitalik had gone from Bitcoin skeptic to writing about Bitcoin to working on Bitcoin projects.

After about six months on the road, his world tour ended in San Francisco. As he climbed up and down the city's steep hills, he continued to refine the idea of a new blockchain that could become the platform enabling any decentralized, censorship-resistant application imaginable. He made his way to Ripple CTO Stefan Thomas's studio apartment, just south of Market Street, where he would stay for two weeks, eager to get to work.

He opened his laptop and started typing, "The Ultimate Smart Contract and Decentralized Application Platform."

He needed a name, so he went to look for science fiction terms for inspiration. He was scrolling through Wikipedia when he saw the word "ether," which he remembered from a childhood science book. Ether is the disproved concept that there's a very subtle material that fills space and carries light waves in the same way that physical matter carries sound waves. That's how he thought of the word "Ethereum." Vitalik wanted his platform to be the underlying and imperceptible medium for every application, just what medieval scientists thought ether was. Plus, it sounded nice.

"Ideally, this should be its own blockchain, but I don't have the technical skills to build this all by myself," he thought.

The obvious option would be to build it on top of Bitcoin, as Mastercoin was doing, but Vitalik discarded that idea as the Bitcoin community was mired in a heated discussion over one of the protocol's features. Developers were getting ready to release an update to the cryptocurrency's protocol that changed the OP_RETURN script, which allowed arbitrary data to be stored in the Bitcoin blockchain. The March 2014 update cut the amount stored in each transaction to 40 bytes from 80 bytes.

This spurred heated responses from teams building on top of Bitcoin, like Mastercoin and a similar project called Counterparty, as they used the script to add functionality to the cryptocurrency—the whole point of their projects. Bitcoin developers argued a limit was necessary to prevent people from taking advantage of the free storage space and bloating the blockchain.

"It is called a free ride," Bitcoin developer Jeff Garzik wrote on the BitcoinTalk forum. "Given that the overwhelming majority—>90%—application for the bitcoin blockchain is currency use, using full nodes as dumb data storage terminals is simply abusing an all-volunteer network resource."

Hundreds more posts were written, open letters were sent, articles were published on CoinDesk. Vitalik decided to avoid the drama. Also, he had no idea whether or not the community would even consider his platform to be legitimate; innovations like what he was planning were often met with skepticism and criticized by the Bitcoin community. He decided Primecoin would be a good fit for his project. It was a smaller blockchain, with fewer political conflicts, where Ethereum could be a larger part of the community.

For about two weeks in late November he only worked on the Ethereum white paper, sometimes from Stefan's studio, sometimes from the Ripple office.

Stefan was working on building a smart contracts layer for Ripple (which he didn't end up releasing), and was excited to share his progress with Vitalik and hear about his experience working with Mastercoin and Colored Coins. But he was a little disappointed that Vitalik didn't talk much and kept mostly to himself. He was putting down on paper all the ideas that had been forming in his head for the past few months, from his time with the anarchist hackers in Calafou to his work with the different Bitcoin 2.0 teams. As he saw his thoughts materialize, it became even more apparent to him how different his platform was from what had been attempted.

"The Ethereum protocol's design philosophy is in many ways the opposite from that taken by many other cryptocurrencies today," he wrote in the closing paragraph, and smiled. Ethereum wasn't just another Bitcoin project. It was the most ambitious cryptocurrency project since Bitcoin.

When he was finished, he reviewed the twelve-page paper once more and drafted an email intended for a select group of people he thought were in the best position to give him thoughtful feedback. It was Wednesday, November 27, 2013, at 10:49 a.m., and the subject was "Introducing Ethereum: a generalized smart contract/DAC platform."

> Hey all,
>
> I would like to introduce the first draft of a whitepaper for a project that I have been working on quietly these last two weeks. The project is called Ethereum; the idea is for it to serve as an all-purpose computational platform for smart contracts and decentralized autonomous corporations, and

to essentially generalize the functions of Namecoin, Mastercoin, colored coins and other such projects that I'm calling "cryptocurrency 2.0." Here is the whitepaper:

http://vbuterin.com/ethereum.html

Essentially, it generalizes all financial contracts and agents into an entity called a "contract" which can automatically send and receive transactions, maintain an arbitrarily large internal state and has internal script code in assembly language that it runs every time it receives a transaction. Sub-currencies, decentralized exchange orders, Namecoin-style registries, financial contracts and smart property will all be easily implementable using this scheme.

This is only the first round of the project, in the form of a whitepaper that I am sending to a small select group of people (around 13). I encourage everyone to give it a read and see what they think and what they do and do not understand. Once I get back comments and suggestions on both the organization of the paper and the actual protocol I will update the paper and send it out to a much larger group of people (and then in round 3 make a loud public announcement), and at the same time I will also start implementing a Python client. If anyone wishes to join the project, feel free to send me an email expressing your interest.

Regards,

Vitalik

He was sure his work would get torn apart. "With an idea this big, there has to be a very good reason why nobody has tried to do it," he thought.

Vitalik wanted to create a new platform that used the blockchain technology that underpins Bitcoin, but with many key differences with the original cryptocurrency. Some of those changes had never been tried before. He expected to get replies smacking down his white paper and explaining why it would never work. But that never happened. Vitalik's email got forwarded and then forwarded again, so what he got instead was a flood of responses from people who were excited about the project and wanted to work with him.

By early December it became clear there was enough interest to make Ethereum its own separate blockchain, instead of an overlay of Primecoin.

Vitalik's vision was much too big to be constrained by another chain. He was thinking about creating a base layer for everything. A computer that could simultaneously live in all the nodes of an enormous global network, which would be able to process anything you threw at it, without downtime or interference, so developers could build whatever they dreamed of, and nobody would be able to stop them or their applications. Like an infinite machine.

7

The First Responders

Anthony D'Onofrio, more widely known by his pseudonym of "Texture," was making the four-hour drive to see his pregnant girlfriend, like he did every weekend. She was living in Sebastopol, California, a small town near the vineyards of Sonoma County, about two hours north of San Francisco, and he was living in Merced, the city known as the gateway to Yosemite National Park, about two hours south of San Francisco. It was the beginning of winter, and the temperature had started to drop.

Traffic was unusually light as Texture relaxed into the seat of his white, 2002 BMW 325i. He had started a weed edibles business and had chosen this "mom car" with the explicit goal of attracting the least amount of attention possible, as it was often loaded with THC-laced candy. He mused on recent conversations he'd had with his former roommate, an active developer in the Bitcoin community, who had been begging him to check out the Bitcoin podcast that was now blasting through his speakers. For months he had refused, figuring Bitcoin was nothing more than fake money that was making a group of privileged "miners" who had access to specific hardware, which burned loads of electricity, richer. It was pretty much the opposite of what he stood for.

He liked to think he didn't care much about money. The edibles business was his first serious attempt at making it after three years of trying different experiments, similar to the Free Hugs movement, where people stood in high-traffic public spaces offering free hugs to encourage selfless, random acts of kindness. In his case, he'd plopped down in New York's Union Square with a box of T-shirts and markers; by the end of the day, thirty kids had come and gone wearing their artistic creation. Then he left New York City to return to his hometown of Little Rock, Arkansas, where he started a "religion" called Smiles Church, premised on handing out Popsicles and providing free hugs.

When he was completely broke, he thought about going back to programming full time, which is what he was doing before these experiments and continued doing on and off, but his wrists and arms were still hurting from bad posture from when he used to sit at his computer for twelve hours straight. Making food was the other thing he was good at, and there seemed to be a gap in the market for quality edibles. So that's what he did.

As he'd embarked on the trip to see his girlfriend, he'd decided to combine the *Let's Talk Bitcoin* podcast with one of his candies. Maybe he needed to open his mind a bit to finally understand what his friend had been going on about. He had been on the road for about two hours, letting words that described the future of money pour into his brain. As he got closer to Oakland, the clouds cleared. His head cleared, too. And then he felt as if *a vision* were being beamed from the sky through his forehead. As he recalls it, the words of the podcast faded as he crossed the Bay Bridge, and it was just him, the stars above, and the water below. He saw the future. It wasn't about Bitcoin. It wasn't about money. It was bigger than that. It was about the fundamental way human society is structured. Communities had been broken, left powerless and at the mercy of an elite group. But that was about to change. Blockchain technology would give people the capacity to rebuild society so that the individual could take control of his property, his identity, his destiny. It was almost . . . biblical.

"I need to talk to the *Let's Talk Bitcoin* guy!" he said to his friend, running over his words, when he got back home. He figured the podcast's host, Adam B. Levine, would be the best person to help him dive further into this strange new world.

"Yeah, I saw the future. I'll explain later, but just help me get a hold of this guy."

"I'm actually flying up to see Adam in Washington," his friend explained. "He's, like, on a family trip with his wife but told me to come over. I think he just had this breakthrough about his company that he wants to discuss."

"No, no, no," said Texture, waving his hands, his finger nails accentuated by black nail polish. A beanie covered his shaved head; sunglasses and hoodies over his stocky frame usually completed his look. "Cancel your flight and get in my car. We're driving there. It's gonna be a blockchain road trip."

They drove twenty hours straight to the spa where Adam was relaxing with his wife, only stopping for gas and talking nonstop about how cryptocurrencies and blockchain technology were going to change the world.

At the spa, they hopped in a hot tub with Adam and continued their futuristic tirade.

They jumped from idea to idea to idea, each one crazier than the previous one. It felt like their brains were continuously being blown as they identified limitless opportunities, while they cycled between the Jacuzzi, the sauna, and the steam room.

"There are so many possibilities opening up with Bitcoin overlays like Mastercoin and even some completely independent blockchains are popping up, like Counterparty and NXT," Adam said. "Everyone is looking to expand blockchain technology beyond peer-to-peer cash."

They were in white bathrobes and slippers, lying on poolside lounge chairs, when the topic of Vitalik's white paper on Ethereum came up.

Texture took some time to read it and said, "So this thing is trying to be a platform for all the token and blockchain use cases we've been talking about, but without having a specific function designed for each use case."

"Right, instead it has a machine that's at its core," Adam said.

"The Ethereum Virtual Machine," Texture said, scrolling through the paper.

"Yeah, which is Turing-complete, so it can process whatever piece of code you throw at it," Adam said.

"Turing completeness" is a concept named after mathematician Alan Turing. Turing-complete machines are able to run any computer code. Bitcoin has a scripting language that supports some computation, but Ethereum's Turing-complete language is designed to support anything a programmer could dream of, and still run in a decentralized way.

"The problem with Turing-complete machines is that infinite loops can break them. Like, for example, you ask the computer to add x + x, as long as the result is less than 5, and you also tell it that x equals 1. It will add x forever and crash the machine," Adam said.

"Oh, so it's easy to attack," Texture commented.

"Yeah, but Ethereum solves this with its internal cryptocurrency ether," Adam replied. "Each computational step has a cost and users pay for it in ether. Whenever you tell the network to run a piece of code, you also tell it the maximum amount of ether you're willing to pay. The machine will stop working if it doesn't get enough money to run the program."

"So ETH isn't just peer-to-peer cash like BTC. It's also used to run the network itself?" Texture said.

"Yeah, that's why Vitalik calls ETH 'crypto-fuel.' It's the gas oiling up the Ethereum network," Adam concluded.

Texture reclined in his chair, his fingers to his temples. His brain was being blown again.

Ethereum is a proof-of-work chain, like Bitcoin, which means miners get ether as a reward for validating transactions. Miners decide if they're willing to process the transaction for the fees offered.

The reason to separate gas and ether is so that computation costs can remain stable even as the price of the cryptocurrency fluctuates with supply and demand in the market. So, for example, a transaction that costs 100 gas will always cost 100 gas, but the amount of ether the sender will have to pay the miners to process it will depend on the market price of ether.

One significant difference between Ethereum and Bitcoin is their record-keeping method. Bitcoin uses the Unspent Transaction Output model, or UTXO. The balance on each Bitcoin account is composed of unspent coins left over from other transactions. One balance usually includes many UTXOs as with a physical wallet, which might contain many denominations of bills and coins. To buy something with your bitcoin, you may have to use a combination of UTXOs, just like you would use a $10 and a $5 bill to buy something worth $12. The $3 left over from that transaction would become a new UTXO.

Ethereum uses the Account/Balance model, which keeps track of the total balance, or "state," of each account. If Bitcoin's UTXO model is similar to bills and coins, Ethereum's model is more like a checking account, allowing for fine-grained control over the amount that can be withdrawn, and making more complex programs easier to implement.

One use case that would be more suitable for Ethereum than Bitcoin, Vitalik wrote in his white paper, would be a hedging contract, where A and B put in $1,000 worth of BTC and after thirty days the script sends $1,000 worth of BTC to A and the rest to B. Because UTXOs are all-or-nothing, the only way to achieve this is through the very inefficient hack of having many UTXOs of varying denominations.

In Ethereum, there are two types of accounts: externally owned accounts, controlled by people's private keys and containing no code, and contract accounts, controlled by their code. Every time a contract account receives a message, its code activates, allowing it to read and write to its internal storage, send other messages, or create new contracts. This leads to another key difference with Bitcoin in what Vitalik called the "first-class citizen" property of Ethereum—the idea that contracts have equivalent powers to external (or people's) accounts. This makes running applications with self-executing code easier, as there's no need for someone to pull the trigger. If the purpose of blockchain technology was to remove the middleman, this concept was ingrained at the core of Ethereum.

All these parts come together to form a foundational layer: a blockchain with a built-in Turing-complete programming language, allowing anyone to write smart contracts and decentralized applications.

Some of the applications that could be created on top of Ethereum, Vitalik wrote, are digital currencies, hedging contracts, a domain-name system, a reputation system, a shareholder-run corporation where decisions on where to move funds can be made by a quorum of investors, "and potentially even the groundwork for a social network." Another example was crop insurance. "How? Simple— a contract for difference using a data feed of the weather instead of any price index," an on-chain decentralized marketplace, and the list went on.

Vitalik wanted to create the rails under which almost any imaginable transaction could work in a peer-to-peer, unhackable, and uncensorable way. He was picturing a world computer that would take power away from bloated corporations and governments, making the world more efficient and fairer. The possibilities would be infinite.

"Other cryptocurrencies aim to add complexity and increase the number of 'features,'" he wrote.

> Ethereum, on the other hand, takes features away. The protocol does not "support" multisignature transactions, multiple inputs and outputs, hash codes, lock times or many other features that even Bitcoin provides. Instead, all complexity comes from an all-powerful, Turing-complete assembly language, which can be used to build up literally any feature that is mathematically describable.

By the end of the white paper, Vitalik's excitement was palpable.

"As a result, we have a cryptocurrency protocol whose codebase is very small, and yet which can do anything that any cryptocurrency will ever be able to do," the paper concluded.

When Anthony Di Iorio read Vitalik's words, he, too, sensed that this could be something very big, even if his technical skills weren't sophisticated enough to grasp the details. He forwarded it to Charles Hoskinson, who was producing some educational programs for the Bitcoin Alliance of Canada.

Charles wears button-down shirts with pens clipped to his chest pocket and looked about a decade older than his twenty-six years in 2013, thanks to a receding hairline and a little chubbiness. No one would ever guess he was born and raised in Maui until he was eight, when the family moved to Colorado, where his mother's big Italian family was based. Life in Hawaii was good. He was homeschooled—his father, Mark, had a bad experience as a minority white student in Hawaii's public school system and didn't want his son to go through the same—so he had more freedom to spend extra time focusing on math and computers. One of his favorite things to do was to take the thirty-minute walk from his house to the library with his mother and brother. He'd pick up sci-fi novels and picture books of the *Titanic*, which had been discovered a few years earlier, and flip through programming handbooks, even though he couldn't understand a word.

When they moved stateside his parents meant to enroll him in a regular school, but everyone was so used to the homeschooling system they never got around to it. Charles didn't mind studying and worked through the summer, which helped him finish school at fifteen. He was too young to get a proper university degree, so he enrolled in a two-year math program at Front Range Community College in Westminster, Colorado. He transferred to the Metropolitan State University of Denver after that, where he studied math and computer science for a year. He finished when he was nineteen and was finally ready to pursue a more long-term college degree.

He originally wanted to be a doctor, in part because he felt the pressure to continue with the family tradition; his father, grandfather, and uncle were all doctors. But now so was his brother, which left him free to do something else. His first choice had to be mathematics. He had already devoted years to it. To him, math was truly beautiful. He looked at all the fields of science and saw that physicists, biologists, and chemists come up with some sort of hypothesis, they prove it, and then a hundred years later somebody comes in and creates an improved model. They pretty much forget everything that was done in the past. It becomes a footnote, and he didn't want to be a footnote. Mathematics is the only field, he noticed, where laws are thousands of years old. He loved that proximity to immortality: once you prove something, it's proven forever.

Charles also loved that there was nothing innately practical about mathematics. Some laws and formulas exist for their own sake, just like poems don't exist to serve a particular purpose, except to be admired and to reveal some deeper truth. Of course, math is full of proofs that can be ugly and complex. But every now and then, there's a formula that's correct and beautiful because it's concise and easy to understand. Charles loved searching for those gems.

So he went to the University of Colorado at Boulder to get a PhD in math. But after three years, he discovered that his idea of solving some important problem that would inscribe him in the holy grail of math for all eternity wasn't compatible with a sustainable career as a professional mathematician. Charles was thinking about increasingly complex problems without actually having any productive output (that is, published articles in peer-reviewed academic journals). He could switch to easier and less interesting problems that would allow him to be more productive and get tenure, or he could do something else in life. This was 2012, and he decided to take a break and figure out what he really wanted to do.

Charles didn't want to be a doctor and he didn't want to be a mathematician. He had also tried to be a political firebrand, and that hadn't exactly worked out—he had taken a few months off in

2008 to volunteer for the Libertarian Party. He joined the Ron Paul crew in their effort to "audit the Fed," as they chanted and wrote on protest signs. The Federal Reserve's financial statements and balance sheet are periodically audited, but the libertarian candidate was pushing for greater oversight. The US central bank wouldn't only have to open its books, but it would also allow review of its monetary policy. This was a hot topic at the time as the Fed was aggressively cutting its benchmark rate and adding economic stimulus to help the economy recover from the 2008 financial crisis.

Hundreds of congressmen got behind the proposal but ultimately not enough for it to pass. Charles had spent months traveling across the country, knocking on doors in Iowa and New Hampshire, giving out pamphlets on street corners and going down endless lists of phone numbers to dial, just to see the bill flop. After that, he just felt tired. He watched the Occupy Wall Street movement get co-opted by social progressives, while the grassroots and right-leaning Tea Party got taken over by hard-core conservatives. All the political movements that were supposed to effect change and bring transparency got adopted by the institutions already in power. He stopped believing he could make a difference or that a system he thought was broken could be fixed. There was no point in trying anymore.

After quitting his teaching job at the University of Colorado, he took a series of consulting contracts doing programming work. They were mostly boring jobs that paid the bills while he figured out what he really wanted to do. He kept drifting until he noticed Bitcoin was spiking. He had read the white paper in 2011 after seeing an article on the website Slashdot. At the time, he thought it was an interesting idea, but its volatility would never allow it to become a widely used means of exchange. To him, there also had to be a lot of infrastructure behind it, like credible exchanges and liquidity, before it could become a self-fulfilling prophecy and work. Those rails just weren't there.

In 2013, when the price shot above $100 for the first time, he took a second look. Unlike a couple of years earlier, there was some professionalization in exchanges (or so Charles thought: the main exchange at the time was Mt. Gox, which dissolved in 2014 after losing 850,000 Bitcoins from its clients). He also saw that some venture capital was being invested in the category, that more merchants were taking Bitcoin, and that a zealous community of advocates and innovators was coalescing around the idea. Unlike what he had seen during his foray into libertarian politics, cryptocurrency revolutionaries weren't asking for permission to change the system. They were already there and anyone who wanted to could use them and ditch their bank. It was the ultimate form of protest. "Bitcoin is here to stay and there's going to be a whole industry built around it," he thought.

He decided to learn everything there was to know about Bitcoin and use his academic background to structure that knowledge into a class that anyone would be able to understand. From his laptop at his home near Boulder, he methodically pored through all the Bitcoin Wikipedia pages, read the source code, and talked to Bitcoin core developers. He put together PowerPoint presentations and videotaped himself talking over them. After a month he had about ten classes ranging between thirty minutes to two hours, and put them all up for free on Udemy, an online platform. The course was called "Bitcoin or How I Learned to Stop Worrying and Love Crypto."

It was Charles's way of making a name for himself in a community where he didn't know anybody, and nobody knew him. Opportunities would come after that, he figured, and soon enough, he was proven right. A few weeks after he put the course up, he had amassed a following of several thousand students and got to meet Bitcoin celebrities Adam B. Levine, Andreas Antonopoulos, Roger Ver, and Erik Voorhees. One of his students was Li Xiaolai, a Chinese English teacher and author who had cashed out shares of the company he was working at when it went public and bought thousands of bitcoin at less than a dollar. By 2013 he was a multimillionaire and had opened a cryptocurrency fund.

One day, Charles got a message from Li that said something like, "Hey, I love your class. I'll invest $500,000 for you to start another crypto project."

Charles thought it was the Chinese version of the Nigerian prince scam and forgot about it. But a few days later, Li messaged him again. This time Charles looked him up and saw that he was an actual person and a supposed heavyweight in China's Bitcoin community.

He responded that he would have to think about what he wanted to do, and messaged his students saying, "I have an opportunity to create a new venture. What do you think are the biggest problems in the cryptocurrency space that we need to resolve?"

One important piece missing in the crypto space was a decentralized exchange, according to Charles's students, as it would allow users to trade crypto without relying on a third party to store funds. By that time, concerns that Mt. Gox might become insolvent were already escalating.

A reliable and liquid decentralized exchange would make cryptocurrencies really hard to kill as there would be no way to shut down trading, he thought. There were already some projects trying to do this, but they weren't gaining any traction and they would all be better off combining their efforts.

He named his new project Invictus and created a thread on BitcoinTalk announcing it: "It is clear a P2P exchange needs to be developed to ensure the long-term survival of all cryptocurrencies. There seems to be a great deal of innovation and different approaches to building a P2P exchange thus I think it is prudent to aggregate those actively working on an exchange into a single project for the purposes of collaborative innovation, funding, brainstorming and also reducing needless replication."

The first to reply a little over an hour later was someone who went by the name "bytemaster," with just two words: "I'm in!" That was Dan Larimer.

Charles contacted him and found Dan was already working on something similar. Just six days before Charles's thread, Dan had posted on BitcoinTalk his proposal for a "Fiat/Bitcoin Exchange without Fiat Deposits."

"I have some capital from a Chinese guy, want to partner up?" Charles said. "I can be the CEO and you can be the CTO."

Dan agreed and Charles flew out to Virginia to set up the company. He arrived at Roanoke airport, which has a small, Y-shaped terminal, with two runways and about sixty flights a day. The building quickly cleared of arriving passengers, and he was left almost by himself, except for a pig farmer sitting nearby, with whom he struck a conversation as he waited to be picked up. Dan finally showed up and they drove out to his home in Floyd, a rural town in southwest Virginia with a population of about four hundred. It was the first time that Charles had met Dan, yet he was on his way to cofound a company with him and live in his house.

Dan, whose half-turned-up smile conveyed a mischievous air, lived with his father, Stan, an engineer who had worked in R&D projects for the defense industry. His increasing interest in cryptocurrencies led him to work with his son on his latest project. They incorporated Invictus Innovations in the state of Virginia on the Fourth of July, with Li as a director and with Li's BitFund as the main investor. The next three months were spent bootstrapping the company and publishing research notes.

The most notable research published was in two articles on Lets TalkBitcoin.com in September, where Dan and Stan presented the concept of a Distributed Autonomous Company, which also came to be known as a Decentralized Autonomous Organization, or DAO— a concept that would change Ethereum's history a couple of years down the road.

A DAO was the groundbreaking idea of creating a computer-run organization. The business's rules would be set in a computer program and executed with as little human involvement as possible. Because the organization would be built on top of a public blockchain like Ethereum, decision making and flow of funds would be fully transparent, uncensorable, and immutable.

Bitcoin, Stan argued, "can be viewed as an unmanned company," as it automatically performs some of the same functions banks do, namely, keeping private books for customers' accounts and transferring credits between accounts upon receipt of a properly signed "check."

But DAOs don't have to be limited to cryptocurrencies: there can be unmanned escrow services, incorruptible arbitration services, governments that can't ignore their constitution, crowdsourced venture capital firms, and many more, they argued.

Invictus soon grew even more ambitious than building a peer-to-peer exchange. They also wanted to make a proof-of-work cryptocurrency, a decentralized identity management system, and an encrypted messaging platform. The idea was to build an ecosystem where users would be able to communicate and transact without having to give out personal information or trust centralized third parties. They called the project BitShares and presented their vision at the Atlanta Bitcoin Conference in October.

But by that time, Charles and Dan had started to fight. Their grand plans required additional funding, and Dan was pushing to raise money by holding a crowdsale like Mastercoin's, but Charles thought it was too risky. He joined the growing group of skeptics who saw these funding mechanisms as undercover securities offerings. Finally, Charles gave up and asked to be bought out.

That's Charles's version of the story. The reasons behind Charles's departure were never publicly disclosed, but posts on BitcoinTalk in January 2014 make at least one thing clear: it wasn't on good terms. After one forum user wrote a laundry list of criticisms to BitShares, Charles chimed in saying, "you forgot to mention the firing of their CEO:)"

"To the extent that he says anything other than that he resigned for personal reasons Charles is violating the NDA or spreading lies," Dan Larimer wrote. "Beware of this shark, he will be your friend one day and plan your destruction in secret the next."

"I never signed an NDA Dan and I haven't lied once here," Charles replied. "I've left this issue mostly alone and my integrity is not in question. You're the sole person who divested me and also received 100 percent of my shares. I don't need to bring you down Dan. I just need to finish what I asked the community to help me do in June. I wish you well and hope for the best."

Charles went back to Colorado feeling somewhat defeated after his first attempt at running a business. At least he had enough funds to keep him afloat as he decided what to do next. In the meantime, he continued working on the Bitcoin Education Project and created content for the Bitcoin Alliance of Canada at Anthony's request. He wouldn't have to wait too long to figure out what his next move should be.

"This thing definitely has legs," Charles told Anthony after seeing Vitalik's white paper.

Anthony invited Charles to get on a call with Vitalik, Mihai Alisie, and Amir Chetrit, who had joined the project after receiving the email with the white paper. They decided on a rough timeline: Vitalik would unveil Ethereum at the North American Bitcoin Conference in Miami at the end of January and hold a crowdsale the week after the conference.

For a few weeks it was just the five of them—Vitalik, Mihai, Amir, Charles, and Anthony—holding regular calls to talk about Ethereum. Soon many others joined the Skype group. Anthony wanted everyone involved to meet in Miami during the conference so they could determine whether they were a good fit and could build a company together.

He rented a huge Airbnb house to accommodate all interested participants; he even bought a plane ticket for a developer with the online name of "Gavofyork," who had quietly been working on an Ethereum implementation in London.

8

The Miami House

Gavin Wood had never seen luxury like what Anthony Di Iorio set up for the Ethereum crew in Miami: an eight-bedroom house—a mansion, really—with almost as many bathrooms, a terrace, a garden by the canal in which people jumped to swim with actual dolphins. There was a dock and canoes for the taking; there was a bar, a pool table, and two living rooms.

Gavin, who has prematurely gray hair, with a narrow face and elfin features, couldn't even afford his plane ticket. Anthony flew him in after Vitalik asked. He had been staying in the spare room of a friend's apartment in London and working at a two-man startup, building a program that used artificial intelligence to read and simplify legal documents.

He and his business partner had set February 2014 as the deadline to decide whether to raise venture capital for their company or do something else. Gavin wasn't sure what that something else could be, just that it would have to involve programming. He taught himself how to write code on the old computer his mother bought from a neighbor when he was about seven years old. The computer had three games. His family couldn't afford to buy more at the electronics store in Carnforth, the small English town he lived in, twenty minutes north of Lancaster, where he was born. He had no choice but to start making his own games.

As he got older, he continued making the arcade-like games of the 1990s, with bombs going off and evil characters running around that the player would have to shoot. He even physically mailed a floppy disk with one of his games to a computer magazine (this was pre–widespread internet days), which wrote a profile on him and the game. He didn't only love making games, he also loved playing them. His favorite one was called *Frontier: Elite II*. It was open-ended, with no pre-scripted missions, and consisted of trading goods and people in a futuristic galaxy with the goal of amassing the most resources possible, legally or illegally.

His fascination with computers increased, if that were even possible, after he saw the internet for the first time as a teenager. He was staying at a friend's farm over the weekend and they started chatting with a Lancaster University student over Internet Relay Chat, or IRC. Them being seventeen years old, the conversation quickly turned to going out. They asked the human at the other side of the chat box if he could help them get into the city's nightclub, which was reserved for university students and those they got on a list. He agreed and just like that, the internet had become a real-life game-changer.

He went to the University of York to study computer science and then did a PhD in music visualization. During university he also started to contribute to the open source movement, writing software on Linux. After university he emailed his childhood idol David Braben, who had made *Elite II*, the game he used to obsess over, and told him he was a great programmer and that he wanted to work for him.

He flew over to Cambridge for an interview and got hired, but he stayed for only one year. He was disappointed they weren't working on the next version of the game and found he didn't enjoy a normal, nine-to-five office job. He went back to university to do his thesis corrections and one day, chatting with his landlady about what to do next, she mentioned she was doing the Camino de Santiago, a pilgrimage crossing northern Spain. He decided that would be a good way to clear his head and went with her. She quit after the first few days, but he stayed and by the end of the trek he had managed to fall in love. He drifted for the next few years, following his new girlfriend to Italy, Norway, Canada, and back to the United Kingdom as she moved around for her research work.

In that time, he continued working in open source projects, did some contract work for Microsoft, and was even a math teacher at a Catholic school in Italy. It reminded him of his own time at the Lancaster Royal Grammar School, where he lived a parallel life to the spaceships of his games as an altar boy in Carnforth's local church. When he was about thirteen, he thought the math and science he was learning at school were clashing too much with what he was learning at church, so he quit church and became a "radical agnostic," which meant he very specifically didn't care whether God exists. He taught kids fractals with the hope that he would open their eyes to the idea that the world is made out of math and rule sets, and that you don't need a high and mighty creator.

In late 2008 Gavin and his girlfriend backpacked around Central America. Gavin remembers hearing about the fallout of the financial crisis on a TV in a bar in Nicaragua. For Gavin, it was more confirmation of what he thought all along: the world is ruled by elites who will seek to maximize their own profit at the expense of others. The solution was decentralization. Computer science made it clear to him that the more centralized a system is, the higher the potential to create critical points of failure. To him, the banking system is one example of these closed systems, so it was only natural that it would fester and rot.

Back in London, Gavin and his friend Aeron Buchanan created a board game called Milton Keynes, which was about gaining political influence to buy plots of land and collect income from real estate (owning the brothel helped you get the highest points). Then he tried to sell the music visualization system he created based on his PhD work to nightclubs, without much success. In early 2013 he cofounded the company to help read and write legal documents. He created an algorithm that went through contracts and made a notification pop up whenever there was a potential problem. He was proud of the code he wrote, but funds were quickly drying up and he had started to consider finding a plan B.

That's when he saw the video in the *Guardian*. It showed the life of a squatter who advocated for the use of Bitcoin as an alternative to the traditional financial system. While Gavin was critical of centralized governments and large banks, he also hated confrontation, which meant he was never drawn to activism. He had read about Bitcoin before, but it was with that video that he understood cryptocurrencies fomented political change by circumventing the establishment, rather than fighting it directly. This technology had an actual chance of rebalancing power in favor of the individual, he thought. The very next day, he looked up the squatter's email and asked to meet.

The man in the video was Amir Taaki, who had recently created open source code libraries and tools for building applications on top of Bitcoin. He's also an anarchist who lives completely off the grid, supports separatist movements, and speaks Esperanto. Amir is the guy who had led Mihai and Vitalik to the hacker community near Barcelona. He invited Gavin over to the abandoned office building in central London that had been taken over by Bitcoin people. Gavin found bare walls and empty rooms stretching across almost entire floors, all the cubicles and ugly ergonomic chairs gone, though you could still see vestiges of bland office life; gray carpets covered the floors and white acoustic tiles buffered the ceiling. The squatters settled there with the few things they had, usually no more than a backpack or two, and would spend hours clawing away at their laptops, sitting on the floor, backs against the wall.

In this tour of the space, they eventually reached a door with the words "Bitcoin Magazine Global Headquarters" scribbled in green marker. There they found Mihai Alisie, the editor in chief, in a makeshift bed of blankets with his girlfriend, Roxana. Gavin also met Johnny Bitcoin, nicknamed for his enthusiasm in spreading the Bitcoin gospel and recruiting new crypto believers.

Gavin decided he wanted to be part of that world. After his visit, he started thinking of ways to build infrastructure for digital currencies and toyed with the idea of designing a decentralized exchange, as he believed that trading decentralized money shouldn't depend on trusted third parties at centralized venues. He also kept in touch with Johnny Bitcoin, who in November sent him Vitalik's white paper for Ethereum.

His initial impression was that Ethereum was an interesting albeit half-baked concept, with inefficient design decisions. He was skeptical, but decided to email Vitalik offering to write an implementation of Ethereum on the C++ programming language. It would be a good way to learn more about how blockchains work.

It said, "Johnny gave me the heads up-I can do C++ (e.g. github/gavofyork). How far along are you with Ethereum?" Vitalik said he wasn't getting much progress with a Python implementation, and was looking for coders who could help.

Gavin got to work right away. He coded all through the end of December and into Christmas Eve. The first "commit," or change to the Ethereum source code, was done by Gavin on December 24. He wouldn't leave his small room for days, ordering two pizzas at a time, just so that he wouldn't have to get up as often. He'd pick up the pizzas at the door and then keep coding late into the night, get some rest, and start again the next morning.

That's when Vitalik invited him to join the rest of the team in Miami. It was the week before the North American Bitcoin Conference in late January 2014. Aside from his brief meeting with London's Bitcoin squatters and his recent foray writing code for Ethereum, Gavin hadn't had any contact with the crypto community. He didn't own any Bitcoin, a fact he was slightly ashamed of as he greeted the men (and maybe one or two women) at the Miami house. He assumed they all knew each other from Bitcoin parties and Bitcoin startups and had all become Bitcoin rich.

Bitcoin was running on its biggest high to date, surging from around $100 at the beginning of 2013 to over $1,000 in November.

It had since given up some of those gains and was back at around $600. But many of the people there had first bought Bitcoin when it traded for a few bucks and were feeling rich. Better than rich, they were feeling vindicated. The rally in 2013 proved naysayers wrong. Also, many alternative digital currencies were popping up for the first time as developers worked to improve on Bitcoin and speculators bet on the next great thing. From 2008, when Satoshi Nakamoto created the first decentralized digital currency, to 2011, Bitcoin ruled alone. But by December 2013, dozens of new coins, also known as alt-coins, had been created, and the speculation around them helped fuel the rally that year.

When the early Ethereum team gathered in Miami, the first alt-coin bubble in cryptocurrencies' short history had just reached its high point. As they schemed and dreamed of greatness, they were also planting the seeds for what would become a much bigger alt-coin boom. But that would be a few years later. That week the only thing people in the house cared about was that they were witnessing the birth of the next Bitcoin as in, the next big thing in cryptocurrencies. Some of them also cared about how to become a part of it, each for their own particular reasons—whether it was stroking their ego, getting rich, or changing the world. Or all of the above.

Gavin joined the small group congregated around an easel. Pie charts mapped out how proceeds of the crowdsale they were planning to hold right after the conference would be distributed. The five cofounders at the time—Charles, Anthony, Amir, Vitalik, and Mihai—were to get a large stake.

"Well, this kind of sucks," Texture said to Gavin, who was standing nearby. By the time he got to the house, the whole Ethereum pie had been more or less carved out on that whiteboard.

Texture didn't think these were the kinds of discussions the team should be having right at the start of the project, when it wasn't clear what each person was going to be delivering or what the concrete goals were.

"Yeah, I thought this was going to be a hackathon," Gavin replied.

But the whiteboard wasn't only used to dream about riches. Charles Hoskinson relished the chance to talk about his favorite topic: numbers.

Yanislav Malahov, a Bulgarian developer who had worked with Vitalik on a project to digitally register and transfer art based on the Bitcoin blockchain, remembers hearing the term "morphic encryption" for the first time as he listened to Charles. Vitalik was one of the few who could keep up. At one point, Charles started testing him, drawing up one complicated math problem after another, and the nineteen-year-old Ethereum creator would instantly solve them in his head and spit them out.

Gavin soon grew tired of this and continued to mingle, or at least try to. He was happy to see one face he recognized. It was Ashley Tyson, whom he had recently met through Yanislav. She had been helping launch a search engine for 3D-printable files with Cody Wilson, who founded a controversial nonprofit that develops 3D-printable gun designs, and got into Bitcoin after PayPal and banks suspended the startup's accounts. She'd met Amir Taaki at a Bitcoin meetup in Berlin and started working with him and Cody on Dark Wallet, a Bitcoin application designed to make transactions more private.

"Are you involved in this thing?" she asked.

"I've been writing up some code for a testnet on the side," Gavin said. In cryptocurrency, testnets are meant to be exactly the same as the live version, except they use worthless cryptocurrency and are used to experiment, making sure the network and/or its apps are working correctly.

"Do you think it can be the next Bitcoin?"

"I don't know. But we can certainly try to make it."

Ashley kept asking what Ethereum would actually be used for and was never fully satisfied with the half-baked answers she was getting about how smart contracts would revolutionize everything, from toasters to banks and governments.

"It will be so powerful you'll be able to build anything that can conceivably be built," Vitalik said. "The inventors of JavaScript never intended for someone to build Gmail, or Facebook or Bitcoin wallets on top of it. We don't know what people will build on top of Ethereum, but the idea is that they will be decentralized and unstoppable applications."

That sounds great, Ashley thought, but she still didn't see *how* they'd do it. Nevertheless, the discussions about technology and the future, the complicated gibberish written on the whiteboard, the fact that there was no music blasting—just excited conversation and the punching of computer keys—reassured her that this group of excitable techies were building something special.

As the sun set that first day in the Miami house, people started pouring beer into their Solo cups more frequently while others lit up cigarettes and joints, as talk about a grandiose blockchain future that had filled the room all day grew louder.

"Gavofyork," Charles said. "Good to finally put a face to an internet name."

"Yeah, same here," Gav replied, staring distractedly in the direction of his laptop.

"You've got work to do or something?"

"Well, actually, I thought we'd all be working on Ethereum," Gav said.

"Sure, but isn't getting to know the team, establishing a common vision and plan, also part of the work?"

"That won't get us very far without building the actual thing."

"Don't know how much work we'd be able to do in just a few days anyways," Charles said. "I think it's a good use of our time to get to know each other."

"One week is plenty of time," Gavin scoffed, and then got a twinkle in his eye. "I'm willing to bet that I can get a rough testnet up by the end of the week."

Charles laughed and said, "You're on! I bet that you can't get an Ethereum testnet by the end of the week. . . . Let's say before Vitalik's announcement at the conference so maybe he can even demo it."

"Done," Gavin said, shaking Charles's hand.

Charles says they bet a nice bottle of wine.

From then on, Gavin devoted most of his time at the house to coding, which was what he'd rather be doing anyway. It's not that he doesn't like people; he just doesn't like new people, or crowds, very much. Every day he monopolized the same spot in the house at the head of the kitchen table, laptop open in front of him, eyes on the screen, fingers on the keyboard. People would bring him drinks and food and leave him to his task.

As he sat alone at the table, typing away on his computer while everyone else socialized, it dawned on him that the Ethereum organization he thought was already a done deal with set roles was actually in its very early days. Everyone was still trying to figure out where they fit. As he watched Anthony, Amir, and Charles loudly talk about the benefits of blockchains and decentralization, he realized he was the most technically sophisticated person in the room, or at least the most technical person who had made any progress on the Ethereum code. To Gavin, that was worth something. As he typed away, those thoughts converged to form three letters: CTO. He should be chief technology officer. And of course, cofounder.

Gavin wasn't the only one writing Ethereum code at that time. While most of the gang was in Miami for the conference, Jeffrey Wilcke decided to stay at home in Amsterdam. Jeff, who dropped out of computer science because he thought the way it was taught at his university was too "artsy," did programming work for various businesses before getting involved in cryptocurrencies. When he first learned about Bitcoin in around 2010 or 2011, he wasn't too excited about it as he saw it only as a way to make digital payments. In mid-2013, his partner on some of his programming work told him he was in touch with the team at a cryptocurrency project called Mastercoin, and asked if he wanted to work for them. Jeff thought it was interesting enough, plus they had no other gigs at the time, so he said yes.

But what got him really excited was reading Vitalik's white paper a few months later. While Bitcoin was digital money, he understood that Ethereum could be digital *anything*. It was a hacker's dream: a decentralized platform that was flexible enough to support any computer program. He wanted to see if he could help it succeed and started writing an Ethereum implementation in Google's Go language. He didn't want to be so openly involved because he was working with Mastercoin, so he joined Ethereum group chats and forums under the alias "Obscuren" and turned down the trip to Miami.

At the time, Jeff was visiting his parents' home in the outskirts of Amsterdam, trying to turn what he thought were interesting ideas in Vitalik's paper into code. He felt a little bad for spending so much time on Ethereum instead of doing his job at Mastercoin, but his gut told him to stick to Ethereum.

9

The Announcement

Time at the Miami house progressed with a stream of conference goers dropping in to meet the new crypto wizards. Beds in the eight rooms were all taken, and many slept on the couches and even on the floor. Pizza boxes were stacked on the kitchen table and beer flowed as the mostly men discussed all the possibilities that this next Bitcoin held. Bloggers and YouTubers came to interview Vitalik, Charles, and Anthony. Amir kept a low profile. He didn't take any interviews and, even though he was one of the cofounders, asked to not be listed as one on the website or anywhere else.

In this open-door house for open source believers, some were too trusting. One of the guys at the house got a few thousand dollars' worth of bitcoin stolen because he had left his laptop open. Everyone rallied behind the cause of finding the lost bitcoin, and for one full day and night the Ethereum team was absorbed in a game of whodunit. They made a list of everyone who could have had access to the laptop and crossed off those who for various reasons couldn't have committed the crime. It was at this point that Joseph Lubin, who had met Vitalik at a Bitcoin meetup Toronto, took the lead. He helped confront the suspect, and the bitcoin was finally returned to the rightful owner.

Joe, broad-shouldered and bald with inscrutable dark eyes, studied electrical engineering and computer science at Princeton. He was also part of the university's squash team and roommates with Michael Novogratz, who would go on to found a cryptocurrency investment firm after the fund he ran at Fortress Investments was shuttered. Joe gave professional squash a go after graduating, but ended up focusing on research about artificial intelligence, machine vision for robots, and autonomous music composition, and held different software engineering jobs at various tech and research firms. He ran a software project at Goldman Sachs's private wealth management division for two years and left to lead software consulting firm Blacksmith's New York office in 2001. He continued his software consulting work at a company called eMagine and then cofounded a hedge fund. The 2008 financial crisis and the September 11, 2001, attacks on the World Trade Center contributed to his interest in cryptocurrencies, which his background in computer science and engineering had already spurred. He was pessimistic and critical about the financial system, which he viewed as easily corruptible and ruled by debt-addicted central banks whose reckless policies are devaluing their currencies.

He thought about dropping everything and waiting out the financial system's collapse in some far-flung South American village, but ended up moving to Jamaica to help his model and actress friend set up a recording studio. He was visiting his family in Canada over the holidays in 2013 when he decided to contact Anthony Di Iorio because of his involvement with the Bitcoin Alliance of Canada. Joe had been following cryptocurrency forums and blogs, including Vitalik's articles, and thought cryptocurrencies could be a way out of the faulty financial system. He joined Anthony at a Bitcoin meetup in Toronto, where he met Vitalik. While his past life at Goldman Sachs aroused some suspicion, his stint as a music producer in the Caribbean made him more likable to the anarchist-leaning hackers in the house. His experience—and bank account—also made him one of the most "adult" adults in the room.

"He could really be an asset," Anthony said to Charles.

By Friday, Gavin had coded a bare-bones version of Ethereum.

The test would be whether the system was able to transfer digital currency between nodes. He set his laptop next to a second machine that was also running an Ethereum node on the kitchen table, right where he had perched himself for the past few days. A small group gathered behind him and watched as he typed up some code. When he hit enter, he wasn't just trying to communicate with the second computer directly, he was relaying the transaction through the entire network. If the test digital coin he had created actually transferred, it meant the groundwork for an actual working cryptocurrency was there. It was like wiring a whole house and then flipping the switch. If the lights turned on, it meant the wiring was done correctly. And after a few seconds of nobody saying a word, and Gavin hardly breathing, the lights turned on. The digital coin was transferred. A thrilled Gavin exchanged high-fives with Charles as Vitalik neatly clapped his hands together and said, "Yay!"

It wasn't in his character to show it too loudly, but Vitalik was thrilled. The blockchain he had dreamed up was actually coming into being, and as he looked at everyone filling up that big house, he could hardly believe most of the people there wanted to keep building it.

After getting an Ethereum testnet up and running, Gavin thought he had earned his place in the inner circle, and he let the rest know.

"I should be cofounder and CTO," Gavin said.

Anthony wasn't so keen on the cofounder part. To him, founders had a fiduciary duty with investors, a responsibility that shouldn't be taken lightly, and Gavin was a newcomer who had just popped up in the Miami house. He hadn't been a part of the early conversations and while he was good at coding and had made some progress, programmers and engineers can be hired to do a job; that work could be outsourced.

Gavin obviously disagreed. To him, this point of view was outrageous, especially since Vitalik was the only one of five founders who came close to having the programming skills needed to get the job done. But he chose to not confront Anthony.

Anthony didn't really change his mind right then, but he may have decided it wasn't in the team's best interest to completely alienate Gavin. That very night Anthony approached him to make peace and gifted him a bottle of Johnnie Walker Red. Anthony doesn't remember this happening, though he doesn't deny that it did. (Tellingly, Gavin still keeps that alleged bottle of whiskey, half full, sitting on a counter in his minimalistic Berlin apartment.)

Vitalik's turn to speak came on Sunday, January 26, the second day of the conference, from 9:30 a.m. to 9:50 a.m. at the Miami Beach Convention Center. He didn't even make it to the main hall of the event and was presented simply as "Vitalik Buterin, head writer at Bitcoin Magazine" in the agenda. Everyone at the house was up early when the day came. The Ethereum procession to the conference consisted of a car that Charles rented and a couple of Ubers packed with jittery developers and entrepreneurs, the star of the show among them.

His speech started off with a top-down view on Bitcoin, a kind of historical summary of what the world's first decentralized digital currency is all about. A black T-shirt with "ethereum.org" written in white across his chest hung loosely from his thin frame and bony shoulders. His hands jerked in quick gestures when he talked. He stammered at times and spoke with a slight lisp. But even so, everyone listened raptly.

A blueish pool of light reflected on a black curtain right behind him, and a single spotlight illuminated the podium, but otherwise the stage was dark as his speech started gaining steam with him going into Bitcoin's limitations. Buzz-cut blond hair framed a broad forehead, his pale cheeks lined with acne scars and punctuated by a pointy chin. But what stood out the most were his narrow blue eyes, which even someone sitting in the audience could see were flickering as his vision for Ethereum played before them.

"Ethereum, instead of having features, tries to be simple. We don't have features, we have the programming language," he said, his words picking up speed. "Out of this one single Lego brick of crypto-currency, you can make pretty much everything."

The whole conference room stood, clapping and cheering when he finished. They swarmed around Vitalik as soon as he got offstage and followed him outside the conference room. He stood against a wall, flanked by Joe and Anthony. Dozens surrounded him, taking turns to ask questions and holding up their phones to take pictures and video as Vitalik continued to explain Ethereum. Dan Larimer, Charles's old business partner at BitShares, was in the crowd and asked tough questions about Ethereum's ability to scale into millions of users and billions of transactions without the network collapsing. Dan later posted the video on YouTube and tried to refute Vitalik's technical and long-winded answers one by one.

Back from the conference, the team stormed into the house. Cups were clashed together; shoulders were squeezed as the talk turned to the millions they'd raise to manifest their dream into reality. The idea was to sell ether in exchange for bitcoin. People from all over the world would be allowed to send funds into a digital wallet controlled by the Ethereum team.

Amir Chetrit was hearing from his contacts in Israel that they could potentially raise several millions more than their initial target of $5 million, which was great, but it also made him nervous. With Vitalik's huge success at the conference, he grew worried that they were attracting too much attention about a crowdsale that looked like an unregistered securities offering.

"Let's calm down a bit here," he told the team. "Let's make sure we're doing this right. We don't want to go to jail."

Joe, who had experience dealing in securities, backed Amir up and eventually everyone agreed they should regroup and think about how to do the crowdsale properly.

That week in Miami was one of only a handful of times the early Ethereum team gathered at the same place. The men who came together in that huge house by a stream of water didn't quite fit in.

They all had a rough edge that meant they had to be jammed into the puzzle of society, or rebel and break free. Their chosen mode of expression, their vehicle to embark on that journey, would be this new protocol.

It was too early to make any concrete decisions, so it didn't matter if they didn't all share the same vision—which they didn't. Peace under those circumstances couldn't last much longer, but at that time, the common goal of seeing Ethereum succeed allowed them to overlook their many differences and paths in life. To this day, they all largely remember their time in Miami fondly.

With the decision to delay the crowdsale made, one by one they gathered their things and caught planes to different corners of the world. The house that fostered so many dreams was shut, soon to be occupied by another Airbnb user.

Gavin was very still, sitting near his gate at the airport, staring into the distance. His thoughts came in and out of focus, a product of his excitement and also his lack of sleep. He felt a surge of adrenaline as the images, dialogues, and feelings of the past few days replayed on the back of his eyes. Outside, the sun had started to set. There was just one possible conclusion. "Fuck. This is like, big. This is really big," he was thinking. "Bloody hell. This is it."

As soon as he landed at London's Heathrow Airport he called his cofounder at the software startup to tell him he wouldn't be working with him any longer; he wanted to dedicate all his time to Ethereum. A few days later he would tell a friend, "I don't know precisely what this is, but I do know that this is the very best chance we will ever get at success."

10

The Town of Zug

How many cofounders should a startup have? One founder is usually frowned upon by venture capitalists, wary of a big ego that goes unchecked. Two founders are more common, three founders are fine, four is stretching it, and more than that is considered unwieldy and chaotic. Not to mention the downside of having to share the wealth (or at least the potential thereof) with others. But these were the old rules, and they didn't apply to the newfangled world that Ethereum would help bring into existence.

In the few weeks after Miami, Ethereum's original group of five—Vitalik, Mihai, Anthony, Charles, and Amir—grew to eight with the addition of Gavin Wood, Jeffrey Wilcke, and Joseph Lubin. Gavin got his wish of becoming CTO, while Charles had been named CEO in the very early days when the group gathered via Skype. A long list of contributors and advisors was also listed on Ethereum's website. There was no shortage of people wanting to be a part of it, and Vitalik was happy to bring everyone in.

Vitalik wasn't thinking about impressing VCs. He wasn't thinking about company equity, either. In this brave new world of token sales, Ethereum could ditch startups' mandatory trek to Silicon Valley's Sand Hill Road. Ethereum didn't need VC money because they could access investors from all over the world without them. Vitalik didn't *want* VC money because, to him, Ethereum should be free and open for anyone to use, not owned by anyone.

Post-Miami, the team's priority was deciding where to set up either a company or a foundation. The question hadn't been decided and two factions were forming. While they discussed different structures, the main ones being seriously considered were a for-profit company supporting and building the application layer for an open source Ethereum protocol developed under a nonprofit foundation, or a nonprofit foundation to support development of the open source network, while the wider community would build applications and infrastructure on top of it. Charles, Anthony, and Amir pressed for a for-profit company the most forcefully, while Vitalik, Jeff, and Mihai were the biggest champions for the nonprofit-foundation-only structure. They had to decide whether in this new phase for the internet that they foresaw they would be Google or Mozilla: a corporation, with centralized management and a predictable revenue stream, or a foundation supporting developers from all over the world to build Ethereum in a more decentralized and organic way.

They put that decision on hold and got to work finding the right place to set up their legal base. The early team had already set up a company in Toronto, using Anthony's Bitcoin Decentral (later just Decentral) as the headquarters, but now they were on the lookout for a more permanent home, somewhere with regulations that allowed for the type of crowdsale they were planning to do, and where their proceeds wouldn't be taxed too heavily. The leading candidates together with Canada were Singapore, the Netherlands, and Switzerland.

Mihai and Roxana volunteered to check out Switzerland. They landed in Zurich on the last day of January and contacted Johann Gevers, a South African who had moved there to found blockchain-based payments firm Monetas. Johann convinced the Romanians they had come to the right place. Switzerland had low tax rates and agreeable regulation; it was a major financial hub in the center of

Europe, not to mention the gorgeous mountains and lakes everywhere. Mihai reported his findings back to the team and after some discussion, they decided to make Switzerland their home. While the structure of Ethereum and the for-profit/nonprofit question wasn't settled, they registered a Swiss company to make administrative steps easier, like renting a place to live and opening a bank account, which, ironically, they still needed to do business.

Johann introduced them to Herbert Sterchi, who made a career out of being the token Swiss resident the local law requires to sit on company boards. But he ended up being much more than that; he provided key contacts and was their guide through Swiss bureaucracy for the following months. Mihai wore the one tie he had to register Ethereum Switzerland Gmbh, a limited liability company, and tried to not give away that he was couch surfing and using up the last of his savings to be there. Under the guidance of Johann and Herbert, they picked Zug, the Swiss canton with one of the lowest corporate tax rates.

The adorable-sounding town of Zug seems to be filled with equally adorable medieval-era houses accented with colorful wooden shutters, tile roofs, and cobblestone streets. But the old city center quickly gives way to modern office buildings with tenants like UBS and Credit Suisse, upscale boutiques, and chain stores.

Most important, its regulators and officials are keen to attract high-tech firms to their region. Zug's officials had witnessed how the local clockmakers went out of business, one by one, as customers started to buy digital watches. So when local regulators and politicians saw Bitcoin taking off and that Swiss hands-off regulation was attracting entrepreneurs to the area, they decided that this time, Zug would embrace change.

Charles, Ethereum's new CEO, came shortly after Mihai and Roxana had arrived. Other team members started trickling in from different corners of the world. Mihai had met many of them at a weeklong hackathon in an abandoned meatpacking factory in Milan, which he joined after his time in Calafou.

Taylor Gerring was trying to build applications on top of Bitcoin in Chicago but he quit that, gave away his dog, broke up with his girlfriend, and bought a one-way ticket to Switzerland. It was a similar path for Mathias Groennebaek, who came from Denmark; Stephan Tual, who came from London; Lorenzo Patuzzo, who had rented out the room for Mihai and Vitalik in Barcelona and decided to jump on the blockchain train; and for the rest of the ten or so early team members. They were web and graphic designers and programmers who gambled everything on what was still just an idea in a white paper written by a nineteen-year-old.

Job titles would be figured out along the way, depending on the project's needs and the person's abilities, and there were no salaries. They were all working for free on the unwritten promise they'd get some of the cryptocurrency raised in the eventual crowdsale, while Anthony Di Iorio's, and later Joe Lubin's, loans paid for major expenses. The big ones were rent and legal fees. Anthony estimated that, between the two of them, they had lent Ethereum about $800,000, though Joe said it was less than $500,000, without providing a more accurate estimate. The rest of the team also contributed as much as they could, working with no salary, depleting their savings, and using their credit cards to pay for daily expenses.

They hopped from Airbnb to Airbnb in the small towns near Switzerland's capital during February 2014. One of the places they stayed at the longest was a two-bedroom apartment in Meierskappel, thirty minutes by car south of Zurich. During the day, they piled around a small table by the kitchen, laptops covering almost every corner of it. They used every available chair in the house, including a small bench they brought over from the living room, and huddled there, elbows touching. They worked on the website and discussed things like the future organization's structure, community outreach, and communications leading up to the crowdsale.

Lorenzo was designing the Ethereum logo. Before they all arrived in Switzerland, Anthony D'Onofrio, aka Texture, had redesigned the Ethereum website and created a logo that combined two sigma symbols and looked somewhat like a diamond. Lorenzo took that as a starting point but wanted to create an image that better represented what he understood Ethereum was: an inclusive platform to be used by all humanity. It had to signal strength, but at the same time flexibility and transparency. The image of a pyramid started to form under his pencil and that evolved into an octahedron, which is two square pyramids joined at the base. The many facets of the shape suggested endless possibilities in the platform. The team later submitted the octahedron to their own logo competition, and it won the online vote.

Mihai and Charles were occupied with administrative work. To incorporate Ethereum as a Gmbh, they had to open a bank account, which is not a trivial thing to do for a cryptocurrency company, as they're often seen as too risky. A few firms shut their doors in their faces but finally PostFinance, a small Swiss bank with no US branches or connections, took them on as a client.

The next big step was to figure out where they stood legally with the crowdsale. Herbert introduced them to Luka Muller and Samuel Bussmann, partners at the law firm MME, which had never worked with cryptocurrency companies but was based in Zug, so knew the relevant authorities. Luka had focused on regulatory compliance and anti-money-laundering cases, while Sammy was the tax guy. On their first meeting, Charles and Mihai had to bring them up to speed about Bitcoin first, and then Ethereum. The lawyers didn't really get it at first. It was their first time looking at digital currencies in any detail.

"Send me everything that's been written on this; you're going to teach me," Luka said.

They sent him *Bitcoin: A Primer for Policymakers*, by Andrea Castillo and Jerry Brito, which had been published a couple of months earlier, and reams of legal documents and papers on digital currencies and cryptography. Luka read every word of it and came back with detailed questions. Vitalik and Joe sometimes traveled to join the meetings. It was a brutal three-month period of complicated legal discussions of what Ethereum is and how fundraising using a digital coin tied to a network of computers should be treated, legally and from a tax perspective.

About halfway through the process Charles woke up in a cold sweat in the middle of the night. It dawned on him that they had spent dozens and dozens of hours with a senior partner at a law firm. "How much are the billable hours going to be!" he thought. Luka said the research part of the process would be on him.

Every bit counted. They were living off their savings and still hadn't found a more permanent place to stay. One day they learned just how precarious their living situation was. The owner of the apartment they were subletting told them they only had a few hours to get out of his place because of some family event that had just come up. The dozen or so early Ethereans gathered their stuff and were left to wander the barren streets of Switzerland in the middle of winter. They turned to Herbert Sterchi, the token Swiss they had hired, for help. He didn't hesitate to invite them over to his place in Lucerne, about nine miles away. Their relief was cut short, however, when Herbert opened the door to a tiny one-bedroom apartment where all of them could barely fit, even when standing up. Someone took the couch and the other ten or so team members slept literally shoulder to shoulder on the floor. Charles slept in a closet in the bedroom. For Charles, worse than that was that Herbert would swing open the closet doors at 5 a.m. and greet him with a melodious "Good morning, Charles!" which he proclaimed at the top of his lungs while standing in his undergarments. They had to catch the train to Zug for more meetings with lawyers and regulators, the very middlemen and bureaucrats Ethereum wanted to someday, somehow, make obsolete.

11

The Spaceship

Landlords didn't love the idea of renting their properties out to a
bunch of unemployed foreign guys who would be using the space to
both live in and create a cryptocurrency company. Herbert got one
of the landlords to accept a full year's rent up front, or about 82,500
Swiss francs including the security deposit, money that Joe Lubin
lent to the venture.

The Ethereum house was located in Zug's suburbs, steps from
the last stop on one of the town's twentysomething bus lines, away
from the lake and closer to the hills. There are some cornfields, and
a stream runs by the road that's right in front of the property, which
is part of a small complex of three identical houses. The house
looked so odd and futuristic, standing tall and geometric, that they
later took to calling it "the spaceship." When they first walked in on
March 5, 2014, if any of the excitement about building this next-
generation blockchain had worn off from sleepless nights crammed
on Airbnb floors, it came rushing back. The place was all open
spaces and light. There was that faintly chemical, new house smell
of paint and concrete, and naked wires hung from the walls as they
were the first ones to live there. There was a basement, then the
first floor had only a bathroom and access to the staircase and the
elevator—yes, the house had an elevator, which infuriated Anthony,
who thought the Switzerland crowd was spending too much. There

were three bedrooms and a family room on the second floor. The top floor had an open kitchen and space meant to be used for the dining and living room, but which they used as the working area. At the end of the room was a big window that opened onto a terrace.

For the first few days, they focused on making the space livable. They got long slabs of cheap wood that they set on top of A-shaped legs to make a large work table and hung colorful halogen lights at crooked angles on the wall. Lorenzo, who after designing the logo had become the de facto handyman, carved an extra bedroom out of the family room on the second floor.

They started settling into a routine, taking turns cooking, bringing groceries, cleaning bathrooms, and sweeping floors. Once the February snow melted and the sun shone on the terrace, they would take a few minutes after breakfast to lounge outside. Most talk revolved around Ethereum and what it could do. As they looked out at the green hills and the slice of lake that poked out in between the buildings in the distance, they dreamed about identity on the blockchain, internet of things, and taking down banks with smart contracts. They would come back inside and usually Roxana had organized chores for the day: Did they need groceries and who would go to the store? What would they make for lunch and who would cook?

This ragtag group of programmers and designers from all corners of the world had just met, yet they were working together, eating together, and sleeping next to each other. They hardly knew anyone else in the small town, so anything they did after work, they also did together. The very concept of "after work" didn't really apply. There were no fixed office hours. Ethereum was their life. It was their family, too.

The guys all had different schedules, so the house was always alive with activity—one group heading to bed while another was settling into another long working session. A main task was building the website for the crowdsale, which wasn't trivial as it had to link with the team's Bitcoin and Ethereum addresses and generate new

Ethereum wallets for contributors to later receive ether, and it all had to be secure enough to protect from hackers. Then there was polishing up the logo and creating the rest of the website design, shooting promotional videos, and running communications with the community, writing blog posts, engaging in social media, and coordinating meetups.

Vitalik, Anthony, and other Ethereum team members based outside of Switzerland would sometimes pop in for a few days, so sleeping arrangements constantly changed. Most of the time, though, three people slept in each room except for Charles, who had claimed the basement for himself and his assistant Jeremy Wood, and Mihai and Roxana, who had their own room.

Even if they had had money, there wasn't much for these bigger-city transplants to do for entertainment in this small town. On weekends or at the end of a long day, a small group would peel off and wander into nature, talking about their progress and as the weeks dragged on, increasingly venting about others. They took breaks and projected YouTube clips on the whiteboard in front of their work table, so the videos they watched played on top of their Ethereum scribblings. They often drank and smoked weed late into the night. They sometimes barbecued on the deck and invited Johann Gevers, the guy from Monetas who had first pitched Zug as the ideal base, and Niklas Nikolajsen, the founder of Bitcoin Suisse, who helped them convert their Bitcoin loans into Swiss francs, to join them. Ethereum, Monetas, and Bitcoin Suisse were the only crypto ventures in Switzerland at the time, so those barbecues gathered the whole of the Swiss blockchain economy on one deck.

Taylor Gerring had met Mihai at the hackathon in Milan back in late 2013 and had later joined the team at the house in Miami. The conference ended on January 26, and by February 9 he was on his way to Switzerland. He had wanted to build cool decentralized applications on top of Bitcoin, but now loved the idea of doing that in a more flexible protocol.

He enjoyed the communal aspect of the house but very soon

small perceived slights started to annoy him. For instance, the groceries. Every couple of days a group would spend an hour or two between shopping and the walk to the store and back. He thought that was a huge waste of time so he proposed they get groceries delivered, but he couldn't believe he was getting pushback on that small extra expense from Anthony and Gavin.

Anthony was suspicious of this group of young guys who he thought had never had money before and were now squandering someone else's—that someone being him. Gavin thought the Switzerland crew was doing pretty peripheral work compared with actually building the network, so it was hard for him to think almost any spending was justified.

"I know that to some people in the project what we're doing here is at the most, just helpful," Taylor said to Mihai. "Why can't they get it's not just helpful, it's necessary. The world doesn't work with just coders and engineers."

He had been fine sleeping on his hammock in Miami. But when months started to go by and they were still using Ikea mattresses thrown directly on the floor, complaints about spending from team members who had their own beds and didn't need to share a house with a dozen coworkers seemed even more jarring.

Mathias Groennebaek's connection with Ethereum also started with the Bitcoin wallet hackathon at the Milan squat. Though there were not many formal titles, he thought of himself as an operations manager. He had worked with major corporations in the consultancy firm he ran and was used to meeting deadlines and having some structure. It started to bug him that he seemed to be stuck with a group of people with almost no real-world experience. Mihai's only work experience, for instance, had been to run *Bitcoin Magazine*. With some exceptions, the rest were also a bunch of computer geeks who had only done freelance gigs here and there, and were used to working on their own. Some carried that same mentality to Zug, burying their heads in their own projects with little regard to how that fit with an overall plan or timeline.

People were going off on strange tangents and on moon-shot projects before the platform was even running, in some cases because they were naive, and in others because they needed to feed their egos. To Mathias, Charles Hoskinson was an example of the latter. Their CEO loved to congregate everyone in front of the whiteboard. Then he would proceed to write out complicated math problems and charts, just for the sake of it, or at least that's what it seemed like to Mathias. One time, Charles spent the day developing a model that would reinvest funds that Ethereum would earn. At this point, it hadn't been decided whether Ethereum would be a nonprofit foundation and Charles was thinking about how the for-profit entity would work. His idea was to create a system that could process investment ideas and decide whether it was worth putting the money in or not. By the end of the exercise, it was clear to Mathias this was probably something that wouldn't be relevant for several months, probably even for years, if at all. "Fucking mental masturbation," he thought.

Taylor couldn't stand those dry-marker sessions from Charles, either. Taylor and Mathias weren't sure what was worse: the times Charles gathered everyone to show off his math skills, or how he would go off by himself to work in the basement. They had picked up that he was trying to broker partnerships with other blockchain companies, yet they weren't exactly sure of the details or what else was going on. If he had to be so secretive about it, it couldn't be good, they reasoned.

A large chunk of Charles's and Mihai's time was spent with MME lawyers, tax authorities, and regulators from the Swiss Financial Market Supervisory Authority, or Finma. They held calls and meetings several times a week. Once they had explained Bitcoin, they were able to explain Ethereum, the world computer capable of supporting decentralized applications that run on the platform's native cryptocurrency, called ether. From there they could start talking about this new way of fundraising, where bitcoin exchanged for ether wouldn't give contributors in the crowdsale any rights or ownership to the platform. Ethereum developers would still be building this platform at the time of the sale, which meant that token owners wouldn't be able to use their ether for a while.

To Charles, though, figuring out the crowdsale was mainly a way to get leverage. He wanted to have this alternative way of raising money, which didn't give away any equity, in his back pocket and use it to get better terms from Silicon Valley investors. He wanted to build Ethereum as a for-profit entity with what some call "smart money" behind it—that is, conventional investors with experience and connections that could help the startup flourish. In his view, there would be a separate Ethereum foundation that could do a crowdsale to distribute ether tokens, but the main fundraising vehicle would be a traditional VC round.

At around that time, Vitalik and Gavin were actually in Silicon Valley visiting VCs, but to them, it wasn't about getting them to buy a piece of Ethereum. They were happy if they wanted to participate in the crowdsale, but it wasn't really about that, either. Even back then, with hardly anything to show for themselves, they thought they were the real deal and wanted to make sure everyone knew it. Gavin says they were "educational meetings," where they visited Google Ventures and other funds. They also wanted to get a gauge on how the market was pricing ventures such as theirs. Charles said they got a sense that they could potentially raise between $15 million and $30 million at a $125 million valuation, which was similar to what Bitcoin software development company Blockstream was raising.

Charles didn't hide his ambition about becoming the crypto Google or his predilection for VC funding, and why should he? In his view, they were creating what would become the biggest company in a new, blockchain-based future. Corporations rule the world for a reason. They're the most efficient way of turning an idea into a reality because the people who make up that company, from the owners to the managers to the employees, have direct incentives to see it thrive and have clear roles to fulfill. To Charles, incentives and responsibilities in nonprofits are murky and because of that, they can never achieve greatness. He wanted Ethereum to achieve greatness, and he knew it could. He was sure Ethereum could become the first trillion-dollar company.

But all this corporate talk made some of the guys in the house nervous. This wasn't what they signed up for. They wanted a new, decentralized world, where they didn't need to ask Silicon Valley investors or Wall Street bankers for permission. They started to escalate these concerns to Vitalik, who started to become concerned that Charles was losing the team's trust. Most of all, he was just frustrated that these internal power struggles were taking away time and energy from work on Ethereum.

For Taylor and Mathias, their doubts about Charles only grew. Sometimes Charles seemed to hint that he was Satoshi Nakamoto, the creator of Bitcoin. Satoshi Nakamoto's identity has been the source of endless speculation, but very few have claimed his identity, knowing they would be met with demands for proof and dogged scrutiny from the crypto community. For someone in crypto, Charles might as well had been saying he was the messiah.

It was early March 2014, the day after they had moved in the Zug house, when *Newsweek* magazine came out with the headline "The Face Behind Bitcoin" splashed across its cover. The reporter on the story claimed Bitcoin's creator, Satoshi Nakamoto, was a Japanese-American engineer called Dorian S. Nakamoto, who was living in a modest town near Los Angeles. Reporters stood guard in front of his door and a flurry of news articles followed. The crypto world buzzed with the news, and soon there were Dorian believers and Dorian skeptics arguing about the merits of the discovery. But that all died down about twelve hours later when an email account linked to the author of the Bitcoin white paper, aka the real Satoshi Nakamoto, resurfaced for the first time since 2009 with the brief message, "I am not Dorian Nakamoto." The message was posted on the P2P Foundation's Ning page, where Satoshi Nakamoto had shared the Bitcoin paper. TechCrunch emailed the foundation's creator, who verified that the email associated with the account was the same one connected to the 2009 post.

Back at the Ethereum house, Mathias saw that Charles had opened Satoshi's message in his laptop and showed it to Richard Wild, one of the designers, with a sly smile on his face and wink in his eye. It may have been an innocent enough act, but to Mathias it was charged with all the hints he had been dropping. There are cryptographic ways to prove whether someone is Satoshi Nakamoto. The Bitcoin creator should have access to the keys that control the first Bitcoins ever mined. Those coins are stored in a few Bitcoin addresses and have never moved, even as the digital currency's price increase has made them worth hundreds of millions of dollars. If someone wanted to prove they were Satoshi, they could sign a message with the key associated with Bitcoin's genesis block and move some of those early coins around.

Mathias sat cross-armed as he watched the exchange between Charles and Richard until he just couldn't take it anymore.

"Just sign something and fuck off," he said.

Mathias, Taylor, Stephan, and Mihai all picked up on these hints and were irritated that Charles seemed to imply, without actually saying it, that he was Satoshi. To Charles, he was just playing along with Richard, who became convinced he was Bitcoin's creator; it was an inside joke between him and Richard. Charles said he thinks it's despicable that someone would seriously claim to be the creator of Bitcoin to gain prestige.

Mathias tossed and turned in his narrow bed at night, trying not to wake the two guys sleeping a few feet away. Had he dropped everything to come to this house lost in the middle of the woods with a bunch of immature dudes and egomaniacs? He needed some sort of cable back to reality to balance out the negativity he started feeling and decided to ask his girlfriend to come. Roxana was here with Mihai, so there shouldn't be a problem, he thought. Things improved briefly for Mathias when his girlfriend arrived, but the rest of the people in the house didn't love the new arrangement. They thought only contributors to the project should be staying in the house. Mihai agreed and after a few days, he told Mathias she had to leave. When he went to drop her off at the train station, Mathias decided he would be back on this very platform very soon. He couldn't stay there much longer.

Meanwhile, MME was finally ready to draft the final structure of the deal. A company would be set up to manage the token sale, which would be considered to be the same as the sale of software. Funds raised would be later controlled by a foundation, which would be created to support an open source platform. A difference between US and Swiss foundations is that in Switzerland, foundations don't have beneficiaries they can transfer funds to. They can only spend donations according to the purpose defined in the foundation deed. Federal authorities make sure these conditions are being met with mandatory audits. In this structure, tokens wouldn't be considered securities and the foundation would pay no taxes for the cryptocurrency it received.

MME read these terms out to the authorities in one of the law firm's conference rooms. In exchange, Ethereum would keep part of the operations in Switzerland and hire twelve Swiss employees. Implicitly, another incentive to allow the crowdsale on those favorable terms was that it would bring a new industry to Switzerland. Johann Gevers from Monetas, who joined many of the meetings, ran with the term Crypto Valley, meaning that Switzerland could be a hub for blockchain development in the way Palo Alto was the hub for internet companies. The Swiss loved the idea. But the legal work was far from over.

12

The White-Shoe Lawyers

Once the team had defined the legal structure in Switzerland, they had to make sure they could legally do the crowdsale in the United States. They knew it was a big risk, as the Securities and Exchange Commission hadn't weighed in on digital tokens, so doing the sale could mean they were selling unregistered securities. But they also didn't want to exclude that entire market and potential user base.

In April 2014, distributed file storage platform Maidsafe, which was built on top of J. R. Willett's project Mastercoin, which Vitalik had contributed to in Israel, raised about $7 million in five hours, prompting the *Wall Street Journal* to say the sale was "manic." Soon after, the SEC issued an alert, warning investors that "a new product, technology, or innovation—such as Bitcoin—has the potential to give rise both to frauds and high-risk investment opportunities."

There was little precedent for what they were trying to do, and regulators were already keeping their eye on these sales. Anthony Di Iorio was organizing the Bitcoin Expo conference in Toronto, and the cofounders decided to meet there to discuss the best way forward. They arrived around a week or two before the event in the beginning of April and worked out of Anthony's downtown office, a narrow, three-story house that gave off a ski lodge vibe with its brick walls and dark brown roof and window frames. A sign that read "Decentral" hung outside. A small sticker on the door read "Bitcoin accepted here," which was true: inside was the first Bitcoin ATM in Toronto. Anthony's Decentral office was used for work on his Kryptokit wallet and to host Bitcoin meetups and other crypto-related events.

It was also a hub for the Ethereum team. Everyone was there, except for Mihai. Even Jeff came down from Amsterdam this time. They all slept in the house's attic, except for a few, like Amir. Amir also came in late, not wearing an Ethereum logo T-shirt like everyone else, and spent part of his time working on Colored Coins, which made some of other cofounders wonder if he even wanted to be part of the team.

That time in Toronto was when everyone met Steven Nerayoff for the first time. Steven is an attorney who quit his job at a fancy New York law firm during the dot-com boom of the late 1990s. He dropped everything and moved to Silicon Valley, where he founded two internet companies to compete with eBay. After the internet bubble burst, Steven needed a break from Silicon Valley, so he moved back to New York in 2002 and started a third company, this time in the health care industry. The firm, Freedom Eldercare, was acquired by a private equity fund in 2008. Nerayoff continued on his founding spree and created an artificial intelligence company, meant to use cameras to alert cities for things like parking tickets, trash collection, snow removal, and crime. Steven also traded gold futures in his spare time and thought "fiat money" was bound to collapse eventually. He says he had half his assets in cash and the other half in gold when the 2008 financial crisis hit, as he had listened to his libertarian friends' warnings that a recession was coming.

When he heard about Bitcoin, the concept immediately made sense to him. He hired Jonathan Mohan, founder of Bitcoin NYC, as a Bitcoin mole. Mohan's job was to be Steven's eyes and ears on the ground, advising him on potential new investments. That's how he'd heard about Ethereum's crowdsale, and so there he was, sitting at a table where the first Bitcoin ATM in Toronto could be found, surrounded by the Ethereum crowd.

Steven explained to the group, some of them reflexively skeptical about newcomers, that if they didn't do the sale correctly there would be legal consequences. He went over some of the basics with them about the different kinds of exemptions the SEC gave for listing securities, basically, procedures that companies and issuers could follow to raise money lawfully. Charles and Joe seemed well versed in the concepts, Steven thought, but the rest of the guys didn't understand a word he was saying. They had no reason to.

"Can you figure out how to do this?" Charles asked.

"Absolutely."

"How?"

"I have no fucking idea."

They all looked at him like he was crazy.

"Maybe I should say, I have no idea, but I'll figure it out. I just need some time," he said, and looked specifically at Vitalik and Charles. "I need you guys to tell me you're going to give me time. If you give me time, I'll figure this out."

They agreed.

On those few days in Toronto, there was also a lot of talk about the unresolved Google versus Mozilla question. Would they be a for-profit company or a nonprofit foundation? By the end of the Toronto trip, that question was still up in the air for some, even though Charles, Joe, and Anthony thought the matter had been settled. To them, Ethereum would be a for-profit software company, which would build applications to run on top of the open source protocol. The Gmbh company that Mihai had incorporated in Zug would be dissolved to give way to a new corporation owned by the eight cofounders. There would still be a foundation to manage the funds raised and give support to the open source protocol.

Back in New York, Steven approached a lawyer named Jeffrey Alberts, a partner at Pryor Cashman, one of the prestigious outfits with big-name clients known as white-shoe law firms. While a few firms had started to specialize in cryptocurrency companies, Pryor Cashman wasn't one of them at the time. But Alberts worked on white-collar defenses so he knew how the SEC tended to see things, and that's exactly what the Ethereum team needed.

The team also managed to get on the phone with Joseph Grundfest, who was SEC commissioner during the Reagan years in the late 1980s and had since moved on to teach at Stanford. They put the question to Grundfest: Do you think this is a security or not?

According to Charles's recollection, Grundfest said that if the Ethereum team really wanted to eliminate all uncertainty, they should ask the SEC for a "no action letter," but it was unlikely that the SEC would issue one, so their best option was to present the facts and circumstances to a law firm and get their answer to that question in writing. They could then demonstrate that their intentions were good, should the SEC ever raise concerns about their offering.

They retained Pryor Cashman and asked the firm for an opinion letter. The firm made it clear that it would write its opinion after independently researching the issue, and that it might very well conclude that ether is a security. If that happened, either Ethereum would have to give up on its token sale and go the traditional venture capital funding route, or they would have to find a way to exclude US investors. The team agreed on those terms and so started a process where they would have meetings and calls with the lawyers and the former SEC commissioner that dragged on for several weeks, as they tried to define what ether is.

It was all Steven could think of. He looked at the few other crowdsales in the cryptocurrency space, but they didn't exactly fit what Ethereum wanted to do. Then he looked at SEC regulations on crowdfunding, but that avenue only allowed for a maximum of $1 million to be raised. Then he studied all the SEC exemptions for securities offerings to find a safe home where Ethereum could plant its flag, but it wasn't fitting neatly on any of those. "Okay, so it doesn't fit any exceptions," he thought. "Great."

Next, he started thinking he could maybe make an analogy to something in the "real world." Something that worked like ether did, that could help him understand where this digital token fit. One key characteristic about ether is that it's not just a digital currency used to transfer value. Ether is also used to pay for that transfer, and for any other operation performed by the Ethereum Virtual Machine using the unit called "gas." To Steven, ether was much like a stamp needed to send a letter, or like the name "gas" suggests, like gasoline needed to fuel a car. He was thinking about these things one day walking along the leafy roads in his Long Island neighborhood when an idea started to form: Nobody would ever think of stamps or gasoline as securities. They're goods, which have market prices, and can be bought and sold. Ether is pretty much the same. It's a good that can be bought and sold. It's made to serve a function on the Ethereum platform, not to be an investment, even if it's sold in a process that may look a lot like an offering.

He met up with Vitalik that night and said, "I had this crazy idea. But I want to make sure I'm thinking about this correctly."

"Okay."

"You have to have ether to send ether, right?"

"Right."

"And you need it to run the code behind decentralized applications."

"Yeah."

"I know you called 'gas' gas for technical purposes, but what if we said gas is legally like gas, the commodity?" Steven went on. "What if we say that what we're selling here is a product or good. It has functionality, it has utility. So, effectively, people are paying for this ability to send ether and eventually for the ability to build dapps and to fuel these dapps."

"That makes sense to me," Vitalik said.

With Vitalik on board, the next step was to bounce the concept off Joe Grundfest, whom Steven saw as a legal godfather to the process, even if he wasn't officially involved.

"So . . . I have this idea," Steven sheepishly said over the phone. He explained the concept of ether as a good, or utility, ready for

Grundfest to say, "I don't know why I've been wasting my time with you, that's the stupidest thing I've ever heard," and hang up.

Instead, Joe agreed. Ether must have utility in the network to steer it further away from the securities definition.

Steven was really taken aback. This thing might actually work, he thought, and brought the concept to Pryor Cashman.

Grundfest said he ultimately gave the Ethereum team two pieces of advice. The first was to try to make ether immediately useful. It had to be code that would be used in a functional environment as quickly as possible. The second was to avoid the United States, because there was the risk that ether would be viewed as a security.

Meanwhile, the developers were getting anxious. The cofounders had a weekly or sometimes twice-a-week Skype call where they would update the group on everyone's progress. Charles and Joe were usually the ones to update the group on the progress with the New York lawyers. When they told them Pryor Cashman was looking into the "utility token" concept, Gavin knew what was coming.

"So another two weeks?"

He was getting increasingly annoyed that there was this continuous pushing back of the sale by two weeks. They had been waiting since February, which had been delayed to get the Swiss lawyers' opinion, and now it was being delayed again to hear what the US lawyers had to say. Meanwhile, they were working on very limited resources and were itching to hire more coders to deliver the platform.

By late January, Gavin and Jeff had finished their proofs of concept for the Ethereum network separately, meaning they had each written out their own versions of the code for the platform and got them to roughly work. But the two versions were running independently and couldn't sync to each other's chain. It's like they didn't talk to each other.

The next step was getting both implementations to work together. They met up in Amsterdam in February to get the job done. They went to a pub and took over a small table in a dark corner for a few hours. There, amid the laughter and chatter of the people around them, and between sips of beer, they established interoperability between Jeff's implementation in Google's Go language and Gavin's in C++. It meant that both versions could get the same outcomes from a given data set.

They hadn't done two separate versions intentionally. It just happened that they both started working on Ethereum at roughly the same time without knowing or talking to each other. It turned out to be a good way to catch problems and come up with more efficient ways of doing things. It was also safer to have multiple clients in case one implementation got attacked; there would always be a backup.

In April 2014, after building the Ethereum proof of concept with Jeff, Gavin published the Ethereum Yellow Paper, a technical specification of Vitalik's white paper. While the white paper described the concept of Ethereum for the first time and included the basics on how it would work, the Yellow Paper dove into the exact details, the nuts and bolts of the Ethereum Virtual Machine, and served as a guide for any developer who wanted to build a software implementation. In Bitcoin, one of these software implementations is the reference for all the rest, while in Ethereum, Gavin's Yellow Paper is the reference.

Gavin also put into writing what he had been thinking the bigger picture for blockchain technology should be. He saw decentralized networks as a tool to build the next version of the internet, or Web 3. Web 1 is the internet of the 1990s, before user-generated content, indexed search, and social media platforms. It lived exclusively in desktop computers. Web 2 is the internet as we know it today, with user-generated content, streaming video and music, and location-based services. It thrives on mobile devices. Web 3 was first coined in a 2006 *New York Times* article referring to a third-generation internet. This new internet is made up of concepts including the "semantic web," or a web of data that can be processed by machines, artificial intelligence, machine learning, and data mining. When algorithms decide what to recommend someone should purchase on Amazon, that's a glimpse of Web 3.

Besides all those features, Gavin's version of Web 3 would allow people to interact without needing to trust each other. It should be a peer-to-peer network with no servers and no authorities to manage the flow of information. Ethereum would be instrumental for this Web 3 vision to become a reality, and much of how the project was defined, with teams focusing on decentralized messaging, storage, and browsers, had the goal of helping shape this next version of the internet.

As they got closer to the crowdsale, Gavin was anxious for the team to focus on delivering the platform, and he identified Berlin as the perfect place to set up a development hub. It was an up-and-coming city, with lots of technical talent, and lower labor and housing costs than other big cities. Gavin convinced his friend Aeron Buchanan, the one he had also done the board game and music visualization startups with, to help him set up an office in Berlin. They packed their bags, including a bicycle, into the back of a car and made their way from London to Berlin.

Back in New York, Steven, Charles, Vitalik, and other Ethereans sat at a bar when they got the long-awaited email from the offices of the Pryor Cashman. At last, their law firm's opinion letter had arrived:

"We are of the opinion that, while there is no guarantee of outcome or result, a court ruling on this issue, under existing reported decisional authority, would more likely than not regard the Ether pre-sale not to be an offering of securities subject to Section 5 of the Securities Act," the draft of the letter said, referring to the section that makes it unlawful to sell a security without registering it with the SEC.

In a supporting document listing the firm's facts and assumptions, the lawyers wrote that they expected that the Ethereum Foundation "will promote the exchange of ether in a manner consistent with the distribution of a product, and not as a speculative investment," and that it won't make any commitments to potential presale participants to continue developing or maintaining the Ethereum platform after the creation of the genesis block.

Finally, the months of work had paid off. The opinion letter meant a big, serious law firm believed they wouldn't break securities laws if they proceeded with their crowdsale. The letter gave them enough protection, or at least perceived protection, to raise the money that would allow them to build the project they were dreaming of.

The framing in that letter, that ether was a product with a specific functionality, opened the door for a whole new way of raising money. Now startups would be able to get funding from anyone who wanted to contribute, all over the world, under what seemed like a safe haven. They weren't selling securities. These weren't shares in any company. They didn't give out dividends that depended on the company's revenue and investors didn't have any rights. They were selling digital tokens, made to be used inside these platforms. They were selling utility tokens.

Pryor Cashman was the first major law firm to put out an opinion letter for a crowdsale to be done by a cryptocurrency company, which other firms saw as a green light. By early 2017, opinion letters such as this one would clear the way for one ICO after another.

13

The Red Wedding

And now it was time to confront that other nagging question: What should Ethereum be?

After all the endless calls and meetings where the cofounders had discussed Ethereum's structure, Vitalik was under the impression that a corporation was a necessary evil. So the Swiss lawyers drafted a document to incorporate Ethereum, which had to be signed by all eight cofounders, plus Herbert Sterchi (their token local board member), in person. They agreed to meet in Zug on June 7, 2014, to make it official.

But other Ethereans had different plans. They had been at the house in Zug for months now, with no pay and little to do other than work, while Charles gave them increasingly tight deadlines. At the top of the list was getting the website ready for the crowdsale, with all the technicalities involved in receiving bitcoin and setting up digital wallets for contributors that would store ether once it was issued. They also weren't sure where they'd stand financially after they raised funds, as each part of the team was vying to get more money for themselves.

Dislike for Charles and his management style had morphed into outright distrust. Some of the hackers, with their inherent suspicion of the established financial system, came to see Charles as the figurehead of an evil corporate mind-set that would corrupt Ethereum's soul. They suspected that Charles wanted to partner with Wall Street banks and Silicon Valley funds instead of using Ethereum to create better versions of those aging institutions.

One night they were all sitting on the floor, some of them smoking weed, and watching *Enter the Void*, an art movie about a French drug dealer living in Tokyo and his DMT-induced hallucinations. One of the hackers turned to Jeremy Wood, Charles's assistant.

"Are you a friend?" he asked.

"What?" Jeremy said, startled.

"Are you a *friend*," someone else repeated, emphasizing.

"Um, yeah, sure, guys," Jeremy answered, and looked away, pretending to be engrossed in the movie.

Suspicions grew into increasingly outlandish conspiracy theories on one of the Slack channels the Ethereum team shared. Steven considered some of the comments to be lightly veiled anti-Semitism. Amir was accused by some of belonging to Mossad, while some suggested that Charles was probably with the National Security Agency (NSA) and would turn Ethereum over to Goldman Sachs.

Vitalik happened to be staying and working from Steven's home in Long Island, as he often did when he stopped in New York, when these messages were sent.

"Hey V, did you see what's going on in the chat?"

Vitalik walked over and didn't answer when he saw the messages, but his face turned red and his usually peaceful eyes lit up with anger. Without saying anything, he got his laptop, stood up, went into another room, and started typing.

"No need for those accusations," he wrote. "Ethereum is user agnostic. If banks want to use it, then that's great."

But it didn't matter how badly Vitalik wanted everyone to get along. A dark undertone kept surfacing in the group chats, and he was getting increasingly frequent calls from Taylor, Mathias, Stephan, and Mihai complaining about Charles.

One night, Taylor and Mihai got on a Skype call with Stephan and Mathias, who had moved to the office in London. It was dark in the Zug house and everyone else was sleeping. The four of them had drinks in their hands, and it wasn't their first glass.

"There are too many factions forming, too many people pulling in different directions, and some have a better claim than others to stay," Stephan said. It was the first time they talked about this openly. "Gavin obviously wants more power, but that's normal. He's the guy who has built Ethereum, probably more than Vitalik. Then there's people with more business experience, people like Joseph Lubin, ex Goldman Sachs . . . you know, he's probably looking at this and thinking 'man, this is a group of children I'm dealing with.' Charles is problematic because of his ego, and some of the things he claims to be. . . ."

"He's clearly lost everyone's trust," Taylor said. "You can't lead a team that doesn't trust you."

"Everyone here has sacrificed everything for this project," Stephan said. "Absolutely everything. I'm broke, I have no money, I'm thinking shit, you know, I'm going to have to go back to a normal job because I'm not getting paid, but I'm still working insane hours. I'm working eighteen hours a day, every day. So I'm picking the side I think has the best chance to win."

"And that's the engineers," Mathias said.

■ ■ ■

Back in New York, Steven had a bad feeling as he dropped Charles off at the airport on his way to rejoin the rest of the team in Zug.

"I think something is very wrong," he said.

"What are you talking about?" Charles said.

"Seriously, I can tell," Steven said. "I'm getting the feeling this is like *Lord of the Flies*. I just don't know who Piggy is."

Charles hugged him good-bye, laughing off his premonition.

But Charles's whole body hurt when he got to Zug the morning of June 7. He had been working every day of the week since December, traveling between Switzerland, Toronto, and New York, fighting over every tiny detail, stressing over the lawyers and the sale, and his body was finally crying stop. Sick and tired, he realized Steven's premonition might be correct when he arrived at the Zug house. The Zug guys were of course there, but Mathias and Stephan had come from London, too, and there were other people there whom he didn't recognize. They avoided talking to him and huddled together, occasionally glancing in his direction.

Taylor had put together a folder that he shared with many of the people in the house, explaining why he believed Charles should not be CEO. Gavin recognized that the lengths to which Taylor had gone to prove Charles should be removed suggested Charles had really lost the ability to lead the group going forward.

"Something's very wrong," Amir Chetrit, who had arrived the previous night, said when he saw Charles. It was the second time Charles was hearing those words in less than a day, and now he believed them.

Anthony didn't understand what was going on, either. He had come to sign papers to formalize what they had agreed on back in April, in Toronto: that Ethereum would be incorporated with the eight cofounders as the owners. "What are all these other random guys doing here?" he thought. Even Joe Lubin's son Kieren was there. This was supposed to be a cofounders' meeting. If he had known all these people would be there, he would have brought his crew from Toronto.

The last couple of days had been a roller coaster for Vitalik. Just two days before, it was announced that he, at the age of twenty, was one of the winners of PayPal cofounder and billionaire investor Peter Thiel's fellowship. That meant he'd get a grant of $100,000 to work on Ethereum. The award was the final push for him to decide what he already had been thinking—he wouldn't go back to college.

But now he was feeling betrayed and confused, with different factions of the group lobbying him to take their side.

He asked everyone to sit around the long work table. It was a sunny spring day outside. Closed laptops and sheets of paper with scribbled notes lay in front of them.

"There's clearly some tension in the team," Vitalik said to the assembled group. "Why don't we go around the table and air our grievances."

Gavin described what followed as the tensest moment in his life. Jeff said he was high on adrenaline, thinking this is the most important thing he had to do—making sure Ethereum didn't become yet another corporation. To Amir, those hours around the table were like the Red Wedding scene in *Game of Thrones*, where the victims had been lured into the enemies' castle to be slaughtered by the hosts. Charles said there was no dignity in that day. Anthony refused to take part in the painful exercise. "The only reason I'm here is to sign documents. I don't even know these people and they're going to air their grievances about me and the team? This is just not fair, it's not right to blindside us like this," he said.

But the discussion went on, with much of the ire directed at Charles. When he argued that Ethereum should have an efficient management structure, he was accused of being an egomaniac who wanted a hierarchy only so he could be at the top. When he said that a company provided the best path to adoption and profitability, he was accused of putting money before everything and being willing to manipulate and deceive to get his way. Charles's voice was drowned out by accusations and personal attacks, some of them lodged at him by people he'd hired himself; some of them came from people he considered friends. He grew quiet and sank deeper into his chair.

Not everyone took shots at him. Vitalik, Joe, Anthony, and Amir didn't have anything negative to say. But they weren't defending him. Gavin didn't say anything critical about Charles, either. He didn't have a problem with him personally, though he did feel that if there was to be a CEO, it could only have been Vitalik. But he turned his criticisms to Amir instead.

"Amir doesn't deserve to be in the leadership group. He hasn't really done much," Gavin said, to the approval of many others at the table. To Amir, that couldn't be further from the truth; he had spent dozens of hours working on all aspects of the project and participating in founders' meetings. Sure, he was still involved in Colored Coins, which took a bit of his time, and maybe that's why the team thought he wasn't as committed, but to him, most of his energy was dedicated to Ethereum.

All the tensions, personal resentments, and suspicions that had been building up in the pressure cooker of the Zug house had exploded.

The room got quiet, and the eight founders stood to speak privately on the terrace, forming a loose circle.

"Some of these guys have been making significant contributions," Gavin finally said. "So yeah, okay, they're not core developers, but they're nonetheless ancillary talent and it's pretty bad if they all seem to be pointing the finger at Charles."

"No, this is ridiculous," Anthony said. "They just don't want anybody in charge. Charles was voted the CEO and we all agreed. So, yes, he's telling people what to do and they don't like it, but a project can't work otherwise."

Charles just stood there, averting his eyes.

"It will be really hard to keep Charles on without losing the rest," Mihai said. "And about Amir . . ."

"Look, I'm happy to step down and focus on better ways to help the project," Amir said. "But we have a founders' agreement in place and I expect everyone to get their share of ETH for the work and time they've contributed so far."

After some back-and-forth, they decided to leave the decision with Vitalik. He could pick the leadership team and decide how to take the project forward.

Seven of the eight cofounders went back inside, leaving Vitalik alone on the terrace. The vision of a world computer had sprung from his own mind less than a year ago and he had welcomed anyone who wanted to contribute to it. It was as if Vitalik had created this rainbow-colored clay that was to be the foundation for his dream, and then he'd shared it with the world, giving anyone and everyone the chance to shape it. But then not everyone agreed on what shape it should take and who should get what portion of it. Like children in a playroom, they started grabbing pieces of the clay for themselves.

Vitalik was only twenty years old and he may have looked like any other young geek in his worn jeans and faded T-shirt covering his rail-thin frame. But few people his age ever have to face what he did that day. He was now responsible for deciding the fates of the men who had left everything to make his idea a reality, and the future of a tech project that was set on raising millions in a legally uncertain sale. He worried about them, but, most of all, he thought about what was best for Ethereum. Stephan saw Vitalik hug a soft, red ball the team kept outside as he sat on the balcony, softly rocking back and forth, as he thought about what to do next.

After what felt like about an hour, he came back inside and everyone gathered around him.

"Ethereum will be a nonprofit and open source project" is the first thing Vitalik announced. "The eight founders will always stay founders and they'll get everything that's due. All your back wages, and all your ether. Going forward there will still be a leadership team of eight. This leadership team will be: Gavin, Jeff, Mihai, Joe, Anthony, Stephan, Taylor, and myself."

With that, he had effectively removed Charles and Amir, and promoted Stephan and Taylor. Amir was out because the team didn't think he had enough commitment to the project—he had also resigned himself. And Charles? Well, even if he ultimately wanted the best for Ethereum, he'd lost the support and trust of the rest of the team. Anthony stayed on but his vision for how Ethereum should be developed was crushed. Joe was already thinking about leaving Ethereum to run the for-profit company building the application layer that he envisioned.

Charles didn't speak to anyone. He went to his room in the

basement and sat on his mattress, his back slumping over his legs. Eventually his assistant Jeremy Wood came down and offered to get him a ticket back home.

"I don't want to go back home yet," Charles said. "Can you just get me a ticket to England?"

"Sure, but why not just go home?"

"I don't want to go home and face my parents and my wife and everybody else. Here I was, talking to Google and going on TV, speaking at big conferences as CEO of this thing that's going to be worth a billion dollars. Now I'll have to come home with nothing. I just can't do it."

Upstairs, the victors partied into the night.

14

The (Non)Investment

This isn't really an investment opportunity for you."

That was Ken Seiff's introduction to Ethereum. It was February 2014, right after the project was announced in Miami, and Ken, like most people, had never heard of Ethereum. Was that even a word? His friend Ashley Tyson had sent him an email with the subject "Bitcoin and things." Ethereum was item number two on the list, right after the Texas Bitcoin Conference in early March.

"They're doing an IPO in a few months," her message continued. "It's one of the most buzzed about things happening in the deep bitcoin community."

Ashley, who had been working with Amir Taaki and Cody Wilson on Dark Wallet, offered to introduce Ken to the Ethereum founders at the conference in March.

The conference was at Austin's race track, Circuit of the Americas. Some attendees joked that the location befit the cryptocurrency's ups and downs, its false starts and surges. Booths displaying Bitcoin-themed art and hardware for mining coins shared the spotlight with a red Ferrari and a yellow Lamborghini parked by the track. A *Bitcoin Magazine* article breathlessly reported that this was the first Lamborghini ever bought with Bitcoin. Three years later, the "Lambo" meme would become ubiquitous in social media as Bitcoin's price surged to thirty times more than the $600 it was trading at in 2014, making many early investors millionaires. Ken was one of a handful of men wearing a button-down shirt, and Ashley was one of the few women who showed up.

"There they are," Ashley said, spotting Gavin and Vitalik. "Come, I'll introduce you."

It was as if Ken were about to meet two matinee idols. Everyone in the exhibit hall seemed to be pulled in their direction, hoping to catch a snippet of conversation and perhaps even hand one of them a business card.

Ken ended up spending the next two days tagging along with Gavin and picking his brain about Bitcoin and Ethereum; sometimes Vitalik joined the discussion, too. Ken was accustomed to hanging out with tech geeks and smart people. He had founded an online retail company that survived the dot-com boom and then went on to do consulting work for divisions of Amazon, Google, and Brooks Brothers. But with Gavin and Vitalik, it was different. Their answers to his questions were so deep and nuanced, he couldn't help but admire their special kind of genius.

Ken returned to New York with one takeaway about Bitcoin that he didn't have before the conference. After talking with Gav, as his friends call him, Ken understood that if he were to use the internet as an analogy, email was to the internet what Bitcoin, the cryptocurrency, was to blockchain technology. He finally got that Bitcoin was both the cryptocurrency and the underlying blockchain and that Ethereum wasn't like email. It wasn't an application. Instead, it was intended to be a base protocol for many projects, like the internet. That led him to believe that if they were successful, Ethereum could actually be bigger than any application built on top of it.

Trusting his gut, he decided now was the time to go all in on Ethereum. Bitcoin already had an $8 billion market capitalization, with little upside for guys like him, he thought. He emailed his investment bank for help, asking how Ethereum tokens should be priced. That was a little ironic because, at the same time, the Ethereum team was going all around Zug talking to lawyers about how they could sell their digital asset without appearing to be selling securities.

"Is there someone at [redacted] who is involved in pricing of IPO securities?" Ken's email to the bank read.

> Confidentially, there is a very interesting deal (called Ethereum.org) that I am looking at in the Bitcoin, cryptocurrency and blockchain world. I think the founders would benefit from understanding how public securities are priced.
>
> . . .
>
> Their investment model is really unusual as they are issuing a currency instead of selling shares—the currency will be the required form of payment to use the platform.

Ken's email goes to show that before Ethereum, when cryptocurrency startups raised money by selling digital tokens, it was assumed that selling tokens was much like selling shares in a project. In fact, these crowdfunding rounds were loosely called IPOs, even though they weren't registered with regulators. It was Ethereum that spearheaded the idea that the digital tokens sold were nothing like securities. They were meant to be assets that had a utility in the blockchain platform; they were not investment instruments.

Ken's bank said it couldn't help, but that didn't dissuade him. He spent the next four to five months bugging the Ethereum team to get updates on the timing of the "presale"—Ethereum's plan to sell digital tokens before they were actually issued, tradeable, and usable. For the first time ever, he was willing to hand a check to a startup and they weren't chasing him down for it. He started to realize it was part of their philosophy. It wasn't about the establishment. This was about making the world decentralized, removing power from governments, Silicon Valley, Wall Street, and putting it back in the hands of people. And that made him even more eager to hand them his money.

Like Ken, a growing number of people were getting excited about

Ethereum. By June 2014, before they had even launched, there were fifty-eight Ethereum meetups in forty-nine different cities, from Toronto to Frankfurt, to Hong Kong, and to Buenos Aires. These were small gatherings of a couple dozen people who got together in bars or coworking spaces to talk about what they would be able to build in this new blockchain platform and to listen to Ethereum team members, who traveled all around the world to explain the project to the new fans.

The crowdsale was the Ethereum team's biggest focus. With the legal questions out of the way, and the decision to be a nonprofit made, they were finally ready. In July 2014, they incorporated a Swiss limited liability company, or Gmbh, called EthSuisse and created the Ethereum Foundation. The company would be dissolved right after the sale and the foundation would then continue managing the funds to support development of the platform and build basic infrastructure. All the code would be open source and free, so developers anywhere would be able to contribute to the platform and build applications on top of it.

The teams in Switzerland, Berlin, London, and Toronto were busy testing the crowdsale website, making sure their multi-signature wallet worked, setting up their so-called cold storage wallet (a piece of hardware to store digital assets offline), and publishing promotional material like videos and blog posts. They published documents called "Terms and Conditions of the Ethereum Genesis Sale" and "Ether Product Purchase Agreement." These were PDFs anyone could download from the Ethereum website and signing them wasn't required to participate in the sale.

The documents might as well have said in big block letters over and over again, "this is not a securities offering, ether is not a stock, you are not an investor, and we are not liable for anything bad that may happen to you as a result of buying ether." A key innovation compared to other crowdsales was that participants were told they were buying software from a Swiss company and that the software was the "fuel" for applications built on Ethereum. While the documents were meant to clarify that ether is not a security, they read a lot like stocks and bonds prospectuses.

"The following Terms and Conditions ('Terms') govern the sale of the cryptographic fuel—Ether ('ETH')—that is required to run distributed applications on the Ethereum open source software platform ('Ethereum Platform') to purchasers of ETH ('Purchasers' collectively, and 'Purchaser' individually)," the document started.

Further down it stated that "the Genesis Sale constitutes the sale of a legal software product under Swiss law," and that the sale of the product was being conducted "by EthSuisse, a Swiss company, operating under Swiss law. It is the responsibility of each potential Purchaser of ETH to determine if the Purchaser can legally purchase ETH in the Purchaser's jurisdiction." In an effort to further dispel any connection between ether and money or investments, the terms also said that developers building the Ethereum platform are volunteers who will receive "gifts of ETH in acknowledgement of their dedication."

The sale terms and conditions and the purchase agreement were peppered with all-caps warnings about how volatile and risky cryptocurrency investments are and that only "experts" in "cryptographic tokens and blockchain-based software systems" should participate.

The legal hand waving revealed just how much the team was aware that they were stepping into a regulatory minefield. It also showed how much confidence they had in themselves. They had gone to such lengths because they imagined that, if they got very big, this first sale of more than $10 million dollars of crypto would be heavily scrutinized. It turned out they were right.

The legality of Ethereum's Genesis Sale would be a matter of debate for years to come. Those arguing that the sale constituted a securities offering in the United States often point to the famous Howey Test, created by the Supreme Court to settle a case back in 1946. The test says that an investment contract "is a transaction or scheme whereby a person invests his money in a common enterprise and is led to expect profits solely from the efforts of the promoter or a third party." In the case of Ethereum, buyers of ether were expecting to profit from the increase in value of the digital token as demand to use the platform grew, thanks to the efforts of developers and others working for the project.

Those arguing that ether is not a security maintain that the cryptocurrency wasn't designed to represent value in a company or enterprise, but to be used to run applications built on the platform and reward those maintaining the network. There is no common enterprise supporting Ethereum, they contend, but rather it is developed and run thanks to a decentralized group of people writing code for the platform, building applications, and maintaining the computers used to validate transactions and computation steps. They'll argue that even if the Ethereum Foundation disappeared, Ethereum would continue running.

The team had lengthy arguments over whether they should exclude US buyers to avoid any issues with the SEC, but Vitalik was of the strong opinion that Ethereum should be used by everyone. How could they become the "world computer" if they were to exclude the world's largest economy? In the blog post where he announced the sale launch he wrote, "We are not blocking the US after all. Yay."

Anyone buying into the sale had to grapple with this regulatory uncertainty, but also with the high risk of investing in a project before it was even live. At this point, all that existed was a bug-ridden testnet. Add to that the fact that the founders would get a portion of the tokens created and it was enough to send the already paranoid cryptocurrency community into a tailspin.

Mircea Popescu, who operated a cryptocurrency exchange and is rumored to be a large holder of Bitcoin, was offering to sell ether at about half of the presale value in eight months, to effectively short Ethereum's cryptocurrency. He was betting ether's value would drop even below what he was selling, so he would profit from the difference.

"Fuck them, whatever they ask for is too much," Mircea said in an online chat.

One thread in the BitcoinTalk forum posted at the time of the sale was titled "[ETH] Ethereum = Scam." The first post said, "it simply is NOT fair and safe or possibly even legal what these guys are doing and if regulation is looming and imposed without warning you people out there supporting crap like this could wound [*sic*] up waking up tomorrow with charges laid against you." It added, "Bottom line it's a dumb idea and it's an IPO and IPO's in crypto are ALL scams."

Farther down the thirty-page thread someone wrote, "Ethereum is a ponzi scheme ran [*sic*] by a few wealthy investors who think throwing bags of money to a coin will attract subsequent bags of money from subsequent investors."

Some went for personal attacks on the cofounders. Joe Lubin's connection with Goldman Sachs was brought up as a reason to be wary, while a more vicious user wrote,

Anthony is some Oliver Twist–esque Fagin character and Vitalik is an anointed coding genius that is utilized to play the role of lead dev. Bitcoin decentral is like an ethereum cult where "utopia" is used every other word and questioning the credentials of people like Anthony or Vitalik [is] absurd. . . .

Of course, some came back with posts like,

If Vitalik Buterin is involved, it's not a scam, as simple as that. Enough for me to think Ethereum is real Bitcoin 2.0. Are you aware what kind of expert he is? On par with Satoshi probably, if not better.

15

The Ether Sale

The sale started on July 22 at midnight in Switzerland. The website they put together for the sale had a real-time counter of the amount of ether sold, and the team watched with relief as the numbers ticked up. More than 7 million ether, or about $2.2 million, were sold just in the first twelve hours. It had been a long, hard wait since December and January, when most of them started working for the project. Everyone was worn out, and most were broke.

"We have been promising that the sale would arise in two weeks for six months, and many team members have endured substantial hardships because of expectations that we set regarding when we would be able to provide funding," Vitalik wrote in a blog post announcing the sale. "We certainly miscalculated the sheer difficulty of navigating the relevant legal processes in the United States and Switzerland, as well as the surprisingly intricate technical issues surrounding setting up a secure sale website and cold wallet system."

At the start of the sale and for fourteen days the price was set so that one bitcoin bought 2,000 ether. At the end of the fourteen-day period the amount would decline linearly to a final rate of 1,337 ether, which meant that one ether was worth 0.0007479 bitcoin or about 30 cents at bitcoin prices in September 2014.

While prices for the sale were fixed, the amount that would be issued was not, so purchasers could buy as much ether as they wanted to. When investors sent their bitcoin to the EthSuisse wallet address, though, they didn't immediately get ether in return. They got an Ethereum wallet and password that would allow them to access their ether when the platform launched. It was a way to reduce the speculative nature of the sale, and have the token be traded only once it could be actually used.

The Ethereum network launch was targeted for the (Northern Hemisphere) winter of 2014–15. The Ethereum team would create ether according to the amount raised in the sale when the first block in the Ethereum blockchain was mined. There was a second pool of ether that would be issued for the cofounders and other early team members, which would be 9.9 percent of the amount raised, and a third pool of ether of the same size would be created for the Ethereum Foundation.

This type of cryptocurrency issuance is known as a "premine," as the coins are created before the network is generating tokens on its own, like Bitcoin does to reward its miners. The concept is controversial, as some enthusiasts will argue Satoshi Nakamoto gave anyone who was interested the same opportunity to gain bitcoin when the network was launched, as he announced when mining would begin and published the software beforehand. In the case of Bitcoin, the total supply of coins is created by miners. Ethereum and other projects that premine their coins are criticized because control of the cryptocurrency's supply is potentially more centralized among "insiders" who participated in the presale and could manipulate the price or influence governance decisions. Before Ethereum, almost any cryptocurrency project that had a premine would be quickly written off as a scam. Ethereum didn't entirely change that, and it's still criticized because of it, but it did help legitimize the concept.

Podcast host and Bitcoin enthusiast Matt Odell brought up these criticisms in October 2018 and Vitalik responded on Twitter, "I personally am really proud to have helped set the precedent of small premines being legitimate. It's an appalling idea that people operating boxes burning huge piles of electricity are somehow the only ones who should be allowed to gain from crypto seignorage revenue."

The sale documents said that once the Ethereum blockchain launched and the premined ether was issued, miners would generate new ether initially at an annual rate of 26 percent of the amount of ether issued in the crowdsale—the issuance rate isn't fixed and is capped at 18 million ETH minted per year. That means that the supply of ether would grow over time but at a decreasing rate. The increasing supply means that large holders' stakes will gradually decline relative to the total supply and ownership will tend to be more decentralized, while a declining growth rate avoids flooding the market with ether and pushing down its price. An uncapped supply for Ethereum also ensures that those supporting the network will always be rewarded with new ether. That's another difference with Bitcoin, which is designed to have a fixed supply of 21 million.

The Ethereum documents and Vitalik's blog posts said that they give no guarantees of ether's future value but the chart they showed in the terms-and-conditions document, with a downward sloping line to represent the ether supply growth rate, surely gave prospective buyers reason to be hopeful.

Bitcoin continued to trickle in, and on the seventh day of the crowdsale, Tuesday, July 29, Ken decided to make the plunge. He had moved back to New York from San Francisco just four days earlier. He and his wife were staying at the Ludlow Hotel in the East Village while the moving trucks were on their way from the West Coast with their belongings, and their children were staying at their grandparents' in Florida to avoid the majority of the move.

He was working at one of his venture fund's investor's offices until he got his own place. It had been a fairly typical day. He had been in meetings with investors and portfolio companies since the early morning and had come back to his borrowed desk in the evening to return calls and get to his outstanding emails.

Bitcoin was about $580 that day, and each bitcoin purchased

2,000 ether, making the cost of 1 ether about $0.29, Ken calculated. Used to thinking in venture capital terms, Ken equated Bitcoin to a later stage, Series D investment, while Ethereum was a seed investment. That meant ether had more room to grow, but also a higher likelihood of failure. Ethereum, with its ability to support all kinds of blockchain applications, also had the potential of being even bigger than Bitcoin, Ken thought.

He had gone through these arguments many times in his head, but he revisited them as he went to the Ethereum.org white and gray website. At the center was the amount of ether sold so far. To the left of that number was the amount of days left in the sale and to the right was the amount of days left at the current price, an interface that not so subtly said "hurry up and give us your bitcoin." Below those numbers was a black button that said, "Buy Ether," along with links to the terms and conditions, the purchase agreement, the white paper, and the intended use of revenue. He had already gone over those documents but he skimmed through them once more. "Ownership of ETH carries no rights . . . purchases are non-refundable . . . cryptofuel . . . distributed applications," he read and took a deep breath. "Okay, let's do this."

His heart beat faster, and he had no idea what to expect when he clicked the "Buy Ether" button. A new page with a three-step process appeared. Step 1, the website told him, "Enter the amount to purchase in either Bitcoin or Ether." The minimum was 0.01 bitcoin and the maximum was 500,000 bitcoin. The cap was in place to prevent buyers from owning a disproportionately large stake of the total ether sold and the terms and conditions said "EthSuisse will restrict any single entity, person, corporation, or group from controlling more than 12.5% of the total ETH sold by the end of the Genesis Sale"—but it's unclear from the documentation exactly how they'd be able to keep track, since all that was needed to buy ether was an email address. Also, EthSuisse would be dissolved right after the sale.

Ken wasn't planning on giving up 500,000 bitcoin, but it was a substantial amount of his personal wealth that he had decided to bet on Ethereum. He typed in the amount. Step 2 was to type in his email address, and Step 3 was to create a passphrase that would be used to encrypt and access his wallet. He checked everything a million times and clicked on "Continue." Step 4 told him to "move his mouse around the screen to generate a random wallet, and once you're done you will be moved on to the next screen." "This is so weird," he thought, as he complied, his anxiety surging when he realized there was no back button. Next he clicked on a button that downloaded an Ethereum wallet to his computer, and then there was a Bitcoin wallet address and QR code for him to send his bitcoin to. He went to his Bitcoin wallet, copied the address—a jumbled-up string of numbers and letters—and letting out a muffled scream, "Aaaahhh!" he clicked send.

And just like that, he had parted with half of his perfectly good bitcoin, which were now traveling into some cryptographic maze. "Into the ether!" he couldn't help thinking. This was one of the scariest moments of his life. There were no charge-backs in block-chain. If he copied the wrong address, or messed up one of the steps, there would be no way of getting his bitcoin back. In the world of crypto, there was no arbiter (that was the whole point), and when the roughly ten minutes it takes to confirm transactions in the Bit-coin network were up, the transfer would be permanent and virtually immutable. He sat back, and just stared at his laptop screen for a while. It was done.

Thousands of other people must have been thinking the same thing as they sent their bitcoin into what seemed like the dark void of the Ethereum sale. It's hard to say exactly how many, but the block-chain shows more than 6,600 transactions going into EthSuisse's Bitcoin address. The total number of people who participated is likely much smaller, though, as big buyers probably split their purchases into several different wallets.

By the end of the sale, people behind those jumbled addresses had bought more than 60 million ether, which at around 30 cents per coin, amounted to $18.3 million. It was a huge success. There had been only five similar crowdsales done by cryptocurrency projects before Ethereum's Genesis Sale and the second-largest raise had been by Maidsafe for $6 million. It was also a success compared with crowdsales in general. Seven months later, Mihai would publish a blog post that said, "according to Wikipedia, Ethereum is rated as the second-biggest crowdfunded project in the history of the internet—sitting proudly next to the first occupant that raised over $70 mil, but over the course of years, not 42 days."

Mihai had turned twenty-seven during the sale, on July 25, and the Ethereum team that was still in Zug decorated the house with colorful banners and took the chance to celebrate both Mihai growing older and the bitcoin that was flowing in. All the laptops in the house had the website permanently open, so that as they had their drinks and ate birthday cake, the big number at the center of the page that showed the pile of ether they had sold was quietly and steadily ticking up.

"I have to admit that we all had high hopes, but no one was anticipating that in 24 hours we would surpass any previous initiative in the space. In any case, it was one of the most fulfilling birthday presents ever and proof that we weren't crazy—or that there are many other crazy people out there and we'd found each other," Mihai wrote.

The Ethereum team had actually written down what those high hopes were. In a document called "Intended Use of Revenue," they included three scenarios: one in case they got $9 million or less in the sale, $9 million to $22.5 million was the second one, and more than $22.5 million was the third. The very worst case for them already meant beating all other previous cryptocurrency crowdsales. In all cases, $1.8 million was allocated to expenses incurred before the sale and $1 million was to be set aside for a legal contingency fund. Of the rest, 76.5 percent went to the developers, 13.5 percent went to communications and community outreach, and 10 percent went to research.

The total supply of ETH started out at 72 million as 5.9 million (the stipulated 9.9 percent of the 60 million raised) was created for eighty-three early contributors and an equal amount was issued for the foundation. Vitalik got the biggest share of the contributors' endowment at about 553,000 ether. Stephan Tual, who was leading communications in London, would later make a big stink with an angry post on Reddit, leaking information about how much specific people had gotten, especially when he didn't think they'd contributed much to the effort.

Vitalik had designed a whole system for calculating allocations based on the date individuals had joined the project and the hours they contributed to it. The foundation wasn't allowed to invest in the crowdsale, so that it wouldn't get a disproportionate stake and raise the centralization red flag, and it could only withdraw 5,000 bitcoin while the presale was running to speed up development. The limit was put in place to avoid any suggestion that the foundation was reinvesting the bitcoin it got to inflate volume.

But there was no rule about the endowment recipients buying up more ETH in the sale, as long as they didn't break the rule of owning more than 12.5 percent of the total supply. Still, there was no way of enforcing that limit. There was a big incentive for cofounders to buy more in the sale, as the amount they would get as part of the endowment depended on the total raised. Put simply, whatever money they put in they'd essentially get more free money back. Those who had lent money to Ethereum also got paid back their loans plus 25 to 50 percent of interest, depending on when they were made. Vitalik had lent more than half the money he had to the foundation and didn't have many funds left to put in. Joe Lubin is rumored to be the biggest holder of ETH to come out of the crowdsale, though he says that's not the case.

Critics in the BitcoinTalk forum and elsewhere didn't go quiet when they saw Ethereum's success. With no proof to support their claims, they posited that that volume was being manipulated by the foundation and the Ethereum team to draw in more buyers. How else to explain why Ethereum's volume was so much higher than other crowdsales?

Preston Byrne, an attorney focusing on early-stage companies and cryptocurrency businesses, published an April 2018 blog post stating that "most of the Ether sold in the 2014 token pre-sale in exchange for Bitcoin may have been paid out to one person or, more likely, a handful of close associates working in concert," because the chart showing the flow of bitcoin was unnaturally even, and almost exactly the same as the chart of a mathematical power function. Something so perfect, he suggested, signaled the work of a bot. Byrne said it was highly suspicious that "the initial two week-period of the Ethereum pre-sale looks more than merely typical, there's very little randomness in it—it looks *perfect*," and, "unless Vitalik subtly managed to telepathically hack everyone's brains so buyers would participate in the pre-sale in an organized fashion," it's likely that enough ether to move markets is concentrated in not a lot of people. Research firm Chainalysis later confirmed the suspicion that ether distribution is concentrated. Only 376 holders control 33 percent of the circulating ether supply, a May 2019 report found.

One anonymous cryptocurrency researcher who goes by the online name of Hasu did further analysis of the sale after Byrne's post. He found that the two bumps in demand during the sale, one at the beginning and one at the end of the forty-two-week period, are an expected consequence of people buying right before the ether price increased. Still, like Byrne, he didn't find an explanation for "why the graph looks so damn smooth."

While Vitalik hopes there was no manipulation by insiders, and says he didn't engage in such practices, he says ultimately he has no way of knowing whether some may have done it. As for himself, he barely had enough money to invest as he had spent most of it bootstrapping Ethereum.

Incentives for early contributors to participate in the sale and get others to do so, and the unnaturally even chart patterns, point to possible manipulation during the ether sale. But the amount of money raised was also a reflection of an intensely anticipated project led by a teenager hailed as a genius coder, building the next-generation blockchain.

A whole new financing model had been tested. One where a ragtag group of feuding hackers with no business plan and no live product, let alone users or revenue, could raise millions of dollars from thousands of people from all over the world. Before, anyone who wanted to buy stock in big tech firms like Facebook or Google would need a US bank account; things got even more complicated for those who wanted to invest in startups that hadn't gone to the public markets to raise funds. Now anyone could be an investor in one of the most cutting-edge technology companies out there. All they needed was an internet connection and at least 0.01 bitcoin.

Ken followed up with Gavin in January to see how the launch was coming along. They had promised the platform (and therefore Ken's ether) would be live around that time.

On January 3, 2015, Ken Seiff <[redacted]> wrote:

> Hey Gav,
> Happy new year! Hope you have an amazing year.
> How is it going? Still planning for a Q1 Launch?
> > Best regards,
> > Ken Seiff

On January 6, 2015, Gav Wood <[redacted]> wrote:

> Hey Ken,
> yeah you too! Was a fairly amazing year as far as they go:) Going fairly well,
> looking forward to a release more or less on schedule, depending on the
> outcome of our external security audit, which is beginning right now. We're

looking at an incremental roll-out rather than a big-bang release as originally planned, so there should be various news and improvements coming out over the year.

Gav

—Never put down to incompetence that which can be adequately explained by self-interest.

On January 6, 2015, Ken Seiff <[redacted]> wrote:

Haha. Can't tell you how many times I have seen that exact change in plans. Welcome to startup hell. That which doesn't break you makes you stronger.

Very excited to see what you guys deliver over the coming few years.

It's going to be massively disruptive.

PART III

Launch

16

Takeoff

Aurel, tall and thin, with buzz-cut hair that contrasted with his long, curly black beard and Dali-like mustache, in 2013 had sold all the shares in the IT companies serving hospitals he owned to go full Bitcoin. He wasn't sure exactly what he wanted to do; buy it, trade it, mine it . . . so he did a little bit of all of those things. It wasn't going well amid a bear market, but he was sure he would rather spend time on this new technology than with old doctors and bored secretaries, telling them to try turning their computers off and back on again. He thought he might be too late coming to Bitcoin to make a killing, so he was looking for the next big thing.

This was around February 2014, and Ethereum had just been announced. Aurel, based in Bucharest, was friends with Mihai's cousin, who offered to put him on a Skype call with Mihai. Aurel was a true believer by the time the call ended. But he felt his hands were tied. He knew he had stumbled onto something great when it was just starting, but he didn't have the coding skills to contribute. He asked Mihai whether he could still come to the house in Zug if he brought along the best developers he could find in Romania. Mihai accepted. The guys he had initially contacted bailed on him at the last minute, so he spent the day before his flight scrambling until he could get two guys to come with him to this Ethereum house with only a day's notice.

One of the developers he brought with him turned out to be instrumental in building the website for the crowdsale and ended up staying. Aurel tinkered a bit with some basic code for the site, too, but left after three weeks when he saw there wasn't much more for him to do. Back home, he stayed in touch with the project, organized Ethereum meetups, and created an Ethereum Romania website to build a community.

At one of his meetups, Aurel went around introducing himself and answering questions about Ethereum and cryptocurrencies, as usual. He noticed one guy who was clearly not into it. He stood at the edge of a small group, looking intently at his drink and planning his exit.

"Hey, what's your name?" Aurel asked.

"Paul," he said.

"Do you want to hear more about Ethereum?"

"Why not."

Aurel tried his most impassioned pitch, but Paul looked like he was trying hard not to nod off. Suddenly, something caught his attention.

"What's that?" he asked, pointing to the Ethereum mining machine Aurel was trying to put together. It was a mess of computer hardware and jumbled-up cables.

"Oh, I'm building an Ethereum mining machine. Want to get a few ready for when they finally launch."

"Why? What do they do?"

"Remember when I told you the Ethereum blockchain, same as Bitcoin, relies on computers to confirm transactions? Well, this would be one of the computers helping in that process. It will receive ether as a reward for putting its computer power toward securing the network."

"This thing will mint cryptocurrencies?"

"Yes. I know it looks bad, but I can do better."

For the first time that evening, Paul perked up. Three days later, he came back to meet with Aurel, waving his phone to display a photo of an industrial-style building with smoking chimneys towering over massive brick and concrete blocks.

"Our new office," he said.

They flew out to set up their mining operation in a Romanian farm. The industrial plant in the photo was located there, in the middle of a forest and next to a hydroelectric plant that drew its energy from the Danube River. From his previous job, Paul knew the factory had a lot of spare space. They calculated it was enough to house about 1,500 GPUs, or graphics processing units, which are used to mine cryptocurrencies because of their speed. It was perfect. They would rent out the space and get cheap, green energy from the power station nearby.

Less than a week later, in May 2015, they were living in a small inn close to their brand-new factory. Aurel threw in all of his meager savings, while Paul put in most of the investment needed. A lot of people probably thought they were crazy. After all, Ethereum's network launch had been delayed by several months so there still wasn't anything to mine.

In the time since the sale, back in July 2014, developers stationed mainly in Amsterdam and Berlin had cycled through a handful of proof of concepts, each one improving on the last one as they focused on shipping the first live network. The team was also growing. Jutta Steiner joined in Berlin to lead the security audits. Alex Van de Sande focused on user interface based in Rio and was building an Ethereum wallet and browser with Fabian Vogelsteller, who had joined in Berlin. Felix Langue and Peter Szilagyi joined Jeff Wilcke's Go Ethereum, or Geth, team. Christian Reitwiessner and Liana Husikyan were building a native developing language for smart contracts called Solidity, together with Gavin. Vlad Zamfir was doing research on ways to improve Ethereum's inner workings and Piper Merriam was building tools for smart contracts and developers. The Ethereum community, as measured by number of meetups, had grown to 115 of these groups all over the world, about double the number of groups at the time of the crowdsale. As the Berlin hub grew, the Zug house emptied out now that the crowdsale was over.

One of the bigger milestones was cutting the block confirmation time to twelve seconds from sixty seconds. That was a massive improvement from Bitcoin's ten minutes, but still far from legacy payment systems like Visa and MasterCard, which process several thousands of transactions per second. The plan was for Ethereum to go through five different stages—Olympic, Frontier, Homestead, Metropolis, and Serenity—over the course of the following year. By the time they got to Serenity, the network would have moved from energy intensive and wasteful proof-of-work into a different consensus mechanism called proof of stake, which relies on the number of coins held by each node instead of on computer power. There would also be a host of different technologies implemented to help Ethereum support a greater number of transactions, in other words, to solve the ever-present scaling problem.

But when Aurel was setting up his mining farm by the Danube in early May, Vitalik had just announced the Olympic release, Ethereum's ninth and last proof of concept. In this stage the Ethereum Foundation dedicated a 25,000-ether fund to reward the community for testing the limits of the blockchain during the prerelease period. People were encouraged to basically try to break Ethereum. The launch would happen shortly after the testing phase, provided there were no major bugs or setbacks.

It meant the Romanians were on crunch time. They wanted to have the mines ready for the moment the network went live in anticipation of getting lots of ether quickly, before mining difficulty increased. But getting the specific hardware needed wasn't trivial. They searched all over the internet, called up different providers, and all they could get were just thirty GPUs. Eventually they got them shipped directly from factories in Poland and the Netherlands. Finally, when they were able to get suppliers for all the different parts—the graphics cards, the central processors, a motherboard to set up the machines, the cables to link it all up, memory cards, the fans needed to cool everything off—the boxes started coming in by the hundreds.

It was a team of six unpacking for a near-industrial size operation. Pretty soon, they were surrounded by cardboard, wrapping paper, and Styrofoam, all towering over computer parts scattered on the floor of the empty factory room.

"How the hell are we going to pull this off?" Aurel wondered.

"We'll just have to," Paul said.

They spent every day for the next two months putting the so-called mining rigs together. Each CPU, or central computer, was plugged to six GPUs, a motherboard, and memory cards. The computer had to understand it was connected to six graphics cards instead of one, and run Ethereum's mining algorithm. They installed the operating system, downloaded the Ethereum mining code, and compiled it for each miner. They were among the first testers of the mining code, so it was no surprise that a few bugs and quirks still hadn't been resolved. Aurel was in constant communication over a Skype group with the Ethereum developers.

By early July, Ethereum had gone for a full month without the developers finding any bugs, the network had withstood the heavy use of the testing phase, and the security audits had concluded successfully. The next step was to freeze the code for two weeks before the launch to make sure it was stable. They decided the launch date should come by consensus, from a hash of a block in the testnet. Because the network was growing at a fairly predictable rate, they were able to calculate what blocks would be created on July 30, after the two-week code freeze ended. They estimated that it should be around 5 p.m. Berlin time when they hit that block number, so most developers would be awake to see it. They settled on block number 1,028,201. Why that specific one, out of all the blocks expected to come in at around 5 p.m.? In true nerd fashion, they picked it because it's a palindrome and a prime number.

"Ethereum is not something that's centrally 'launched,' but instead emerges from consensus," Stephan Tual wrote in a July 22 blog post explaining the steps for developers who wanted to join the main network. "Users will have to voluntarily download and run a specific version of the software, then generate and load the Genesis block to join the official project's network."

This phase of the Ethereum network was named after the American frontier, where there were vast opportunities for settlers, but also high risks. Frontier users had to first generate, then load the Genesis block into their Ethereum client. The Genesis block was pretty much a database file containing all the transactions from the ether sale. When a user input it into the client (the software used to access the network) it represented their decision to join the network under its terms. Then it would be a matter of waiting until block number 1,028,201 appeared on the Ethereum testnet. When that happened, the block would be given a hash (meaning all the block's information would go through a cryptographic hash function, which would spit out a fixed-length alphanumeric phrase), and that would be used as a key in the Genesis block that would tell it to join the live network.

As Ethereum developers, all scattered around the world, worked on the baffling code involved in getting the network to start running smoothly, the Romanian miners were scrambling to get the machines working on time. They worked nonstop in a forty-eight-hour marathon. Aurel collapsed and slept on the floor for only a few hours.

Meanwhile, a small group of dreamers and misfits in an office building in Brooklyn were also preparing for the launch.

They were holed up in two cramped rooms on the ground floor of a coworking space in Bushwick, the Brooklyn neighborhood for those who think Williamsburg is getting too expensive and gentrified. The dozen or so of them had come from different areas of corporate America, finance, and tech, and were busy building Joe Lubin's new startup, ConsenSys.

The company, which was financed by Joe's own money, had the goal of building the applications that would run on top of Ethereum's open source protocol layer. It would do that by investing in startups, incubating companies of its own, advising bigger corporations on how they could incorporate the technology, and generally preaching the Ethereum and decentralization gospel.

Jeff Scott Ward was one of the first hires. The 2008 financial crisis had broken out while he was at school, studying graphic design at Queens College. He struggled to find work and took a low-paying coding job upon graduating. He felt like he'd been robbed of his future while greedy corporations and banks had gotten out of the whole mess unscathed. He thought, "I didn't do this, my generation did not do this. This situation we're in, where we can't get a better life than our parents, is unbelievably unfair."

He went to Occupy Wall Street on the first day of the protests and immediately walked away. Standing around and self-righteously raising his fist wasn't going to change anything, but he did think of what would. The very next day, he bought as many good Java-Script textbooks for beginners as he could find and started learning to code. He had no idea what he was doing, but he was certain that if he was angry and determined enough to white-knuckle it, he would beat the crisis and come out ahead.

With his new knowledge, he was able to get a job doing user interface development for a marketing company. After that he went on to do the same thing for the New York Stock Exchange and then for a company that was trying to become the Bloomberg Terminal of digital assets, called TradeBlock. It was around that time in mid-2014 that he started following the Ethereum project. To him, Ethereum was trying to mimic JavaScript's programming features but for cryptocurrencies, which seemed like the obvious next step needed in technology. He was ready to fly off to Switzerland or Toronto, or wherever they were, but he was a front-end developer and couldn't really help with the protocol layer, which was where the most work was needed.

When he came across Joe Lubin's profile on LinkedIn, he cold-messaged him saying how excited he was about Ethereum and asked what he was up to. Joe told him about ConsenSys, and soon after, Jeff was on a subway train heading to Bushwick, hoping to get hired. Jeff got the distinct feeling he was about to meet Morpheus. He had seen videos of Joe talking and it gave him the sense he was this powerful and mysterious bald man who knows about the future and holds the key to the door that would get him out of the Matrix.

By the time he got to the coworking space he had gone over his pitch in his head several times, psyching himself up until he finally faced Joe. He talked fast and long about how he had finally figured out "we don't need banks, or governments. What crypto is enabling is this opportunity for people who didn't have an economic opportunity to begin with. For those who don't have access to global markets, who are not public companies or accredited investors, basically, the large majority of people." He went on a tirade against the culprits of the 2008 crisis and he painted his vision of how Ethereum would be the JavaScript for cryptocurrencies.

"Is it going to be like *Fight Club* where the buildings come crashing down? No. Is there an opportunity to mitigate against systemic risk? Absolutely, and I think that is almost guaranteed over the long term. It's just a better way of doing things." He also raved about Vitalik, who had recently been awarded the prestigious 2014 World Technology Awards, beating out Mark Zuckerberg, who was also nominated. "He's like, the next Alan Turing!"

Joe didn't say much during Jeff's pitch/rant. He just stood there, cross armed, with a bemused look on his face. He offered Jeff the job while in transit to an Ethereum meetup later that day.

Jeff held out initially because he wanted to see the terms of his contract before officially accepting the position. He was expecting the typical terms of an early-stage startup—some equity in the company and a salary. He kept asking for a contract, but weeks went by and it just didn't come. Finally, he decided to join anyway. He didn't want to miss the boat.

The ConsenSys office in early 2015 was an eclectic group of no more than a dozen developers, designers, and engineers, all heads down, building the very basic foundational infrastructure needed to later raise an Ethereum empire. Software program editors, code libraries, digital wallets, storage systems, an app store. All the pillars that most developers would take for granted had to be built from the ground up, and it was all being done using profoundly different architecture. Most of it was open source, and programs worked in the same execution environment, which meant every piece was interconnected and could serve as bricks to be built on by other developers in different companies.

At some point they started receiving calls from companies, governments, and central banks that had heard about blockchain technology and wanted to learn more. The ConsenSys team was reaching out to institutions, too. Andrew Keys, Joe's first business hire at ConsenSys, went down a Fortune 2000 company list and contacted their CTO or engineers. The goal was to get a call or meeting where the ConsenSys team could explain what blockchain technology and Ethereum are. Hopefully, there would be a second meeting and they could take it forward from there.

Whenever they had downtime, conversations generally gravitated to the Ethereum launch and how amazing it was that real ether would be minted and tradable for the first time. At some point, someone proposed they should buy mining rigs. They would contribute to the stability and decentralization of the network, plus, they'd be able to get cheap ETH. Details were discussed a bit frantically as they realized they didn't have much time. They agreed it would all be done with personal money and not associated with ConsenSys.

Jeff immediately got on it. He went on Craigslist and found a guy who was selling about fourteen old Bitcoin miners with four GPUs each, in East Hampton. Bitcoin miners now used ASICs cards as difficulty had increased, and the GPU-based miners had become obsolete for bitcoin, but perfect for ether. A small ConsenSys contingent drove out in small sedans, stacked the miners in trunks and backseats, and brought them back to the office. Most people took them back to their apartments, and a few were installed in one of the two rooms they used at the coworking space, making the office even more cramped, and when they started running, a lot hotter. Separately, Joe and a friend of his set up a mining operation in response to a rumor that an astrophysics lab manager was going to mine empty blocks with tens of thousands of GPUs, which would have compromised the security of the network. That effort faded fairly quickly though, as they never upgraded the initial hardware purchase.

Vitalik flew to Berlin when it got close to the launch date to be with the developers. The office was an open floor in an old building in Berlin's Kreuzberg neighborhood. Gavin and Aeron Buchanan had found the place and decked it with a mix of office chairs and thrift store furniture, including a row of stained and frayed yellow velvet movie theater seats. They were about a dozen or so coders, mostly in their twenties, who had come from different places mostly in Europe and the United States to work on the Ethereum clients and the base protocol. The Berlin office had been the venue for Ethereum's first developer conference, or Devcon0, in November 2014—they made sure to start counting their annual gatherings at 0; why would they leave out such an important number? About thirty people, or the core developers, designers, and marketers, filled one room of the Berlin office. They sat in folding chairs and listened to talks about the long-term vision and current state of the project. Speakers didn't even use microphones. They just stood in front of the small group and talked, almost like someone making a toast or announcement at a family gathering. Gavin Wood had opened the five-day conference saying that "progress has led to the concentration of power" so Ethereum's "mission therefore is decentralization."

When the day of the launch came, on July 30, 2015, they set up a big TV that displayed a monitor for the test network. Under a dark background, green and yellow letters and numbers showed information like the node names, the gas price, and importantly, the latest block number. Every sixteen seconds or so, another block would be added and that number, displayed bigger than the rest at the top of the screen, would tick up. By the end of the day, Vitalik and Gavin congregated around the TV and the rest of the developers followed. Some cracked open a beer as they stood together watching the block number tick up.

In Romania, Aurel and his team had finished putting together the last mines that very day. Their hands were sore as they had hurried to have all the hardware and software ready and running before the launch. When the time approached, they all gathered around a small laptop screen with the network monitor up.

Meanwhile, a countdown was going on in the group chat for the Go Ethereum team.

"250 blocks to go!!!!!!! half an hour!!!! nothing can stop it now, muahahah!:P," wrote one of the developers.

Somebody sent around a link to a Google hangout that had been set up so Ethereans around the world could celebrate the occasion, but hackers seemed more comfortable in the chat.

"Nobody is speaking. Hehe."

"Too many techies," one of them replied.

"Aw. sing a song!:D," Jeff Wilcke said.

As launch time approached, coders congratulated Jeff as shipping became imminent. "Team effort," he replied. Others sent GIFs of rockets launching and Dr. Evil memes. When there were ten blocks left before the launch, whenever a new block was mined, a couple of people would chime in, creating a countdown until the test network hit block 1,028,201 at 4:26 p.m. in Berlin.

"launch all systems are go! repeat, all systems are go!" one of the developers wrote.

"we have lift off!" someone else wrote.

The code had been set up so that anyone who had downloaded the Genesis block to their client would now be plugged into the live chain. Before, whenever someone opened their Ethereum software, they'd see several lines of code updating with information about the test network. Now they would see something similar—the difference was that the chain was live. To an outside observer, it was hard to tell what had changed, but for those watching from the Ethereum developers' hub in Berlin, there was a bit more fanfare. When the test-net hit the predetermined block, a meme of Ron Paul popped up on the monitor, his arms raised in jubilation, surrounded by green laser beams, with white block letter that screamed, "IT'S HAPPENING."

The group in Berlin "woohooed" and popped champagne bottles. Vitalik stared at the new chain that was forming and laughed.

It was past 11 a.m. in New York and Jeff, from ConsenSys, had slept in. He woke up when Ethereum had already launched and realized he had forgotten to turn on the two miners in his living room. Once he did, after frantically fumbling with them and calling a friend for help, the Telegram robot he set up to alert him whenever he got ether started going off. With the "Ding! Ding! Ding!" sound in the background he got on the ConsenSys Slack channel and watched the flood of celebratory messages come in. It was real! Here was some shred of proof that he wasn't completely crazy for betting everything on this fledgling technology.

The event didn't make any headlines outside a couple of trade websites. That day, the world was thinking about debris recently found in the Indian Ocean and whether it could be linked to a Malaysian Airlines plane that disappeared on its way to Beijing. Others were outraged about an American dentist who killed a lion called Cecil in Zimbabwe. India hanged the man responsible for the 1993 bombings in Mumbai while Rio handled reports of contaminated waters ahead of the Olympics to be held the following year. Hardly anyone was thinking about Ethereum.

Only a year and a half ago, Vitalik had written down the basic structure for what he thought could take cryptocurrencies further, and Gavin had refined the concept in his Yellow Paper so that it could be put into the language of computers. Dozens of developers, designers, and bloggers, and then hundreds of speculators around the world had come together, in many cases dropping whole carriers, uprooting themselves, leaving personal lives in shambles, living off savings, to make that moment possible. The launch meant they could finally get started. Developers could now start building applications on top of this new blockchain. Ether from the Genesis sale was transferred to each contributors' wallets and one by one, new blocks were getting published on the network comprising forty or so nodes. The real Ethereum was coming together.

Developers started peeling off but Vitalik stayed to watch the chain grow for a while longer. He went to sleep that night feeling giddy and opened his laptop as soon as he woke up the next day. The Ethereum blockchain was still going.

Ken Seiff hadn't been keeping up with the project's development. He wasn't in any of the different group chats or online forums, much less in GitHub, where he could have seen progress on the code, and the team didn't communicate with ether buyers. He had more or less written the whole thing off. But some eight months after the launch, he finally checked in with Gavin.

On March 18, 2016, Ken Seiff <[redacted]> wrote:

Gav is there a value to Ether? And is there a liquid market? Can you buy and sell them? Thanks in advance for answering this.

Best regards,

Ken Selff

On March 18, 2016, Gav Wood <[redacted]> wrote:

Hi Ken,

the present value of Ether is $10.25-you can track it here:

http://coinmarketcap.com/currencies/ethereum/

You can buy and sell fairly easily on a few of the exchanges; there's a decent amount of liquidity for Bitcoin and it's not too bad for fiat either. I'd recommend Kraken (www.kraken.com) and Poloniex (poloniex.com).

Gav

—Never put down to incompetence that which can be adequately explained by self-interest.

On Saturday, March 19, 2016, Ken Seiff <[redacted]> wrote:

> Gav,
>
> When I bought the Ether, i thought i bought [redacted] ether with Bitcoin. But at $10.76 for ethereum that doesnt make sense. That would mean it has gone up 30x or 40x or so. Is that possible?
>
> I am sorry to bother you but how do I figure out how many Ethereum I own?
>
> Best regards,
>
> Ken Seiff

On Saturday, March 19, 2016, Gav Wood <[redacted]> wrote:

> Yes that's right. It was 2000 ETH per Bitcoin. If you spent [redacted] BTC then you'll have [redacted] ETH.
>
> You can check fairly easily with any online block explorer if you just have the ether address.

Ken's ether holdings suddenly made him a wealthy man, at least on paper. He went to the block explorer and posted his ether wallet address as Gavin had suggested and confirmed it. It was the best investment he had ever made, or even dreamed of making. It didn't feel real. It had been a huge risk, and he'd gotten his huge return.

Gavin emailed back, "Feel free to buy me a beer with your profits:-)"

17

The Shrinking Runway

Ming Chan hurried into the MIT Media Lab for a conference and saw there was space at a table near the back, next to a young man typing on a laptop. The talk was about to start. She was in the final round of interviews for a director-level job at the famous university—which she attended herself some twenty years ago—and heard from her work partner Casey Detrio there was a blockchain conference there. They had been designing and developing applications for Apple's iOS, and after completing the app they had worked on for four years, were finally free to explore other interests, a big one being blockchain tech.

During a break, she introduced herself to the man sitting next to her. It was Gavin Wood, the cofounder of one of the most promising cryptocurrencies out there, Ethereum. He showed her an Ethereum dapp demo (this was early 2015, so launch was still a few months away), and she took out her iPad and showed him the iOS app she and Casey had designed.

Gavin praised the front-end design on her app and commented that it was something Ethereum would definitely need to focus more on. While not interested in a designer role, Ming made a mental note to research what other opportunities there might be for her at this exciting, cutting-edge tech project.

What Ethereum needed the most was an executive manager.

Ethereum leadership at the time was in disarray. Charles and Amir were both gone, and Mihai had also left to start his own company, called Akasha. Joe Lubin was busy running ConsenSys and Anthony Di Iorio was now building the digital wallet Jaxx. The only ones left to run the show were Vitalik, Gavin, and Jeffrey.

But there was tension growing between Gavin and Jeff, who were each building the most used Ethereum client implementations. Communication between the two of them started to break, and their teams became increasingly closed within themselves as they fought for primacy. Rising tribalism and competition were quickly driving them apart.

Tension was also building between the developers and the business and communications side of the project as each area fought to get more funding for themselves. Aeron Buchanan, who after the sale oversaw finances at EthDev, Ethereum's development arm, noted that while the amounts had been agreed to beforehand, once the bitcoin was in, everything was on the table again. Negotiations opened up and each area of the project wrangled over how much they should receive.

All that bickering stressed Vitalik, who tried to lead seeking consensus and including everyone's opinion. It was also exhausting for him, as he was ultimately more comfortable doing research for ways to improve Ethereum than managing people. Gavin and Jeffrey also wanted to be left alone to code. They decided they would hire a manager for the Berlin office and a director for the Ethereum Foundation. Kelley Becker was brought on to manage operations for EthDev and help Aeron, who was burned out from being pulled in different directions, constantly flying between London, Berlin, and Zug, all of that with the added uncertainty of not knowing when and if he would receive agreed-upon funds (which he did always get, albeit sometimes at the very last minute).

Three board members were also hired. The middle-aged, corporate men didn't exactly mesh with the typical Ethereum developer. Lars Klawitter held a high-level job at Rolls-Royce, Vadim David

Levitin ran business development for Fortune 500 companies, and Wayne Hennessy-Barrett was founder and CEO of 4G Capital, a mobile money fintech business based in Kenya.

Kelley had worked with art nonprofits in San Francisco before moving to Berlin and started work at Ethereum in February 2015 with the goal of creating standards and bylaws for the foundation. But she realized very early on that there were more urgent matters. Cash was drying up. Still, she didn't have the power to make the required decisions herself.

With tensions boiling, Ming's application for executive director came in. After a six-month application process that included several interviews, she stood out to Vitalik among other candidates as someone he could trust, and he advocated for her to be hired. The board members accepted his recommendation, and she took the job offer in March 2015 but, because of Swiss regulation, had to wait until July, just after the launch, to officially start.

Ming knew she was about to dive into a complicated project. The answers she received to questions about the foundation were not always consistent, and she got a sense that everyone had their own particular vision of the Ethereum Foundation and how it should be organized. The Ethereum Foundation had been managed like an early-stage startup in its first year of existence—and that's what it was—but the project was growing. The foundation was hiring twenty or so contractors, and it was sitting on several million dollars' worth of cryptocurrency. It needed to get its act together and start behaving like the serious organization it was becoming. Ming was there to make sure that happened.

The term "house cleaning" is sometimes used in corporations, but for Ming it was quite literal. She went to the house in Zug, which had been largely vacated by then, to start the process. She asked to see the paperwork, expecting to find some sort of semi-organized file system. Instead, she found stacks of financial, legal compliance, audit, and tax documents, which had been stuffed inside kitchen cabinets and piled in loose boxes in the big dining room that had been used as a work space. Some of the information was also stored in hard drives, USBs, and laptops. And then some of it just lived in Vitalik's head.

"It's fine, I remember down to each number and letter," he said.

"Maybe you have photographic memory, but three months, six months, a year from now, are you going to remember every single detail? Also, that's not how it works. We need to be keeping organized records," she said.

She told him it should be a priority to get all the documents in order. They used the house in Switzerland as the base, where she went down the Kafkaesque path of making sense of all the different accounts and legal entities, their employees, tax treatments, and cash flows. But even before they could finish, they would have to figure out how to cut back spending. The Ethereum Foundation was in jeopardy of running out of operating funds just months after the network had launched.

The price of bitcoin had steadily declined all through the Ethereum crowdsale, from over $600 at the start of fundraising on July 22, 2014, to almost $500 when it ended forty-two days later. The problem was that all of the money received in the crowdsale had been in bitcoin, except for the share of ether the foundation got from the premine.

Some on the team, particularly Gavin and Aeron, were pushing to sell at least part of the bitcoin; that way they could make sure they had enough cash going forward. Others, like Joe, thought bitcoin would recover soon and that they would make more money by keeping the crowdsale funds in the digital currency. In the end, with Charles gone and so many people in charge of making decisions that nobody had the final say, almost none of the bitcoin was exchanged.

During the crowdsale, there was speculation on Reddit that Ethereum was selling its bitcoin and pushing down the price. Vitalik jumped in to clear up those rumors and in an August 14 post said, "Less than 100 [Bitcoin have been] sold by the organization," and that they planned on keeping their funds in the digital currency going forward.

"We will hold BTC primarily because (1) we think it's more likely to go up than down, (2) it's easier to pay employees in BTC, and (3) if it does go down hard then that's a partial indicator that the crypto space as a whole has become less appealing so our project is less useful anyhow," Vitalik wrote.

A year later, Vitalik would regret that decision. Bitcoin continued to fall through 2014 and dropped below $200 at the start of 2015, which meant that the $18 million in bitcoin that Ethereum raised was worth about half as much when the platform launched. Ether was also falling. It traded at just under $3 when it first got listed on Kraken and Poloniex, some of the first exchanges to support ether soon after the July launch, but quickly plunged to around 70 US cents by the end of September.

"It is indeed true that the foundation's finances are limited, and a large part of this was the result of our failure to sell nearly as much of our BTC holdings as we were planning to before the price dropped to $220," Vitalik wrote in a blog post in September 2015. "As a result, we suffered roughly $9m in lost potential capital, and a hiring schedule that was meant to last over three years ended up lasting a little under two."

The Ethereum Foundation was spending about 410,000 Swiss francs per month, Vitalik wrote in the blog post, and Ming saw it spent as much as 700,000 Swiss francs in one month. The goal was to cut expenditures to 340,000 Swiss francs starting October, and further cut to 200,000 Swiss francs in the medium term. At the 340,000 rate, they had roughly until June 2016, maybe December 2016, Vitalik wrote. By that point, the intention was for the foundation to secure alternative revenue sources, for example, from developer workshops, conference tickets, and donations.

The situation was dire, but the intention was for more of the work to shift from the foundation to outside entities. The shrinking resources was part of the reason, but the scope of the project had grown well beyond its earliest days, when it was envisioned as a mere improvement of Mastercoin.

At the time, the foundation was holding 200,000 Swiss francs, 1,800 bitcoin ($430,000 at then prices), and 2.7 million ether ($1.7 million at then prices), plus a 490,000 Swiss francs fund reserved for the event they had to use a legal defense, Vitalik wrote, saying he was disclosing those numbers as he wanted the foundation to be "maximally transparent."

Ming got rid of the big house in Zug and rented a smaller office space almost immediately. She also started the process of winding down and reducing all legal entities under the Ethereum Foundation. These units had popped up wherever there were developers, creating more expenses and confusing paperwork. One of the biggest cuts was the London communications office, run by Stephan Tual, and under which Texture also worked.

Tough decisions like these naturally create enemies, but the way Ming was making them didn't make it easier. She got involved in all aspects of the foundation, down to the small details, from finances to chat room etiquette, and she tended to pull people into intense phone conversations of several hours, when a short email could have sufficed—or at least that's what many of those on the other end of the call thought. Most of the time, her intention with her constant clarifications and reminders was to reduce regulatory risk for the foundation down the line.

Taylor Gerring, who was part of the early team in the Zug house and had led the creation of the crowdsale website, was becoming increasingly tired of these exchanges. The relationship between Taylor and Ming deteriorated, and Taylor was finding it increasingly hard to get his proposals reviewed and emails answered. At the end of 2015, his contract wasn't renewed, which he learned from Ming's brother-in-law, a Hawaii-based attorney who was doing work for the foundation along with Ming's sister.

The problem wasn't only that their funds were depleting quickly, but also that Swiss regulators had concerns about the foundation's use of its ether holdings, and until the first week of November 2015, it was unable to use ETH issued in the launch of the network. Ming had to keep providing the foundation's explanations to regulators on how this "genesis" ether was created, how they would use it, and even how the Ethereum blockchain works and what the difference between premined and mined ether is, until regulators were satisfied. The day she received the letter resulting in the EF's ability to use its ether, she was so relieved and overjoyed, she fell asleep that night clutching that letter.

As Ming got deeper into the Ethereum files in 2015 and 2016, she started to find there were missing documents and information discrepancies. Separately, hundreds of thousands in cash was not accounted for. Months of teamwork resulted in the return of most of the cash and missing company documents. Access-related security measures were made.

On top of all that, Anthony Di Iorio was claiming he was still owed 525,000 ether from the loans he made to the project early on. After months of providing documentation attempting to show all disputed amounts had been paid, the foundation finally stopped receiving legal correspondence from him. While he wasn't satisfied and still thought he was owed millions of dollars' worth of ether, he decided not to pursue further legal action.

It was tedious, stressful, miserable work. Ming brought in lawyers, auditors, and tax specialists to help her wade through the mess, and slowly, things started to fall into place. Still, many of her days ended with a cry on the office couch where she often slept, too.

Ming had brought it upon herself to almost single-handedly organize the Ethereum Foundation. The board had met only once in person since the new members came in and in those few months they realized there was actually not much for them to do, because Vitalik had three votes, versus their three votes, plus a tiebreaker vote. They started to become concerned that if they ever saw something they disagreed with, they'd effectively have no way to change it, and they would still be held personally liable. Vitalik explained that past developments within the foundation had persuaded him to structure governance that way. Lars understood that Ethereum was Vitalik's brainchild and that he didn't want to risk the foundation to be steered in a direction he disagreed with. Still, he didn't feel it was right to remain on the board if there was nothing for him to do. By the fall, the three "adults in the room" decided to resign.

Meanwhile, Gavin was growing increasingly frustrated by the foundation's push to reduce disbursements for EthDev, where he led the development team. Tensions further grew after he created a UK limited liability, for-profit company called Ethcore in September 2015, to pursue his own vision for Ethereum development. From conversations he had with Vitalik, Gavin thought Vitalik would eventually join him in this new company, where they would continue to build Ethereum and Ethereum infrastructure together.

But as soon as Ethcore was established, Ming was made aware of it in emails and other communications from people in the Ethereum community saying it was a conflict of interest for Gavin to be a full-time employee of EthDev Berlin, an entity funded by the foundation, and also run a for-profit startup in London. After receiving close to two dozen inquiries, Ming felt it was her responsibility as executive director to do something. Gavin, though, doesn't have any recollection of Ming mentioning a conflict of interest and said conversations around his departure focused on the foundation's unwillingness to continue funding the C++ client.

"Gavin, we cannot continue in this manner, paying you and all your employees, having you keep your full title and, in essence, bootstrap a for-profit entity that's separate from the foundation," Ming would say over several Skype conversations.

"We had an agreement with Vitalik that I would retain an unpaid position in the foundation to consult on platform architecture and lead development for the C++ client," Gavin said. "He should honor it."

"I just can't do it, Gav," Ming insisted. "Please, try to understand. I support you and your new venture; I think you'll be hugely successful and maybe even more valuable to the community that way. But you can't do it and stay at the foundation at the same time."

"I've done more than anyone, maybe even more than Vitalik, for Ethereum. I basically built it from the ground up," he said. "And you're kicking me out of the foundation? Does that seem right?"

"We're not kicking you out. I would like to give you the opportunity to frame your departure your own way," Ming pleaded. "You write the announcement."

"You've got to be kidding me."

Gavin tried to get Vitalik to intervene, but his emails and messages went unanswered. In the end, he accepted he was no longer part of the organization he helped build. Yes, he was angry, but mostly he was sad. Ethereum had been his life for the past three years. It also made him sad that Vitalik hadn't come to his aid, but he also got it. He knew Vitalik had made the decision to let Ming handle the bureaucracies of running the foundation and once he gave her that power, he wasn't going to interfere. He eventually stopped arguing, but it didn't make it less hurtful. Even his @ethereum.org email got temporarily revoked.

He spent some time in December 2015 depressed and hardly leaving his Berlin apartment, until he decided he wouldn't dwell on what happened for any longer. He would just get on with doing what he loves, which is building technology.

His good-bye post cited Pink Floyd, "The time is gone, the song is over, Thought I'd [have] something more to say," and announced he was leaving "with no small amount of sadness," to start a new venture and make his Web 3 dream a reality.

Before the year was over he was dedicated full-time to Ethcore, the company he had cofounded with Jutta Steiner, who had worked on Ethereum's security audits. He took Aeron and most of the C++ developers with him and created a whole new Ethereum client on the more cutting-edge Rust language. They called the client Parity and later the company adopted that same name (Parity Technologies), scrapping Ethcore. By April 2016 the new venture had secured $750,000 in a traditional equity funding round led by Silicon Valley–based Blockchain Capital and Shanghai-based Fenbushi Capital. His old friend Ken Seiff also got a stake.

He was drawing a line in the sand. "You can kick me out of the Ethereum Foundation, but you can't kick me out of Ethereum."

18

The First Dapps

Funds were running out and leadership was in turmoil, but the first green shoots were budding in the Ethereum garden. People were starting to build their own applications on the platform, just like Vitalik had dreamt.

Joey Krug, an Illinois native, learned to code on the Apple II his dad got him on eBay when he was ten. In what felt like a natural transition from programming and playing computer games in all his free time, he also started mining Bitcoin. He saw it as a way to essentially make free money using just his desktop computer. He moved to Southern California to study computer science at Pomona College in 2013 but dropped out a year later to build a Bitcoin business.

Next he moved to San Francisco and rented a basement. Frustrated with the idea that Bitcoin was just digital gold, he joined efforts to build applications on top of the Bitcoin protocol. As is usual with crypto projects, he came together with like-minded coders scattered all over the globe but brought together on the internet. He came across academic papers that talked about decentralized prediction markets but found that nobody had tried to implement them. Joey loved that he could potentially build a parallel financial system where anyone could create derivatives contracts on essentially anything—from speculations on the price of gold to who would win the US presidential election. Unlike past centralized experiments, these couldn't be shut down. Jack Peterson, who was working on his own blockchain startup and whom Joey had met in a chat group online, was excited by the same idea. They decided to go for it together and called their project Augur. It would be one of the first decentralized applications built on Ethereum. These so-called dapps, which would later proliferate, are programs that use blockchain technology to reduce the inefficiencies of centralization and/or to avoid third-party censorship.

But they started out building Augur on Bitcoin, and it was a challenge. The protocol has a limited scripting language and so they had to build custom functionality for everything they wanted to do. They eventually realized it was just not possible to build on top of Bitcoin itself, and that it would have to be a whole separate chain. Joey had read the Ethereum white paper a year earlier, in 2013, but back then, he didn't understand why you would need a blockchain that supported smart contracts. Tired of struggling, he finally took Vitalik's advice and switched his attention to building his dapp on Ethereum. They were able to build on Ethereum in twenty-four hours what had taken them over two months to build on Bitcoin. This was still before the network had even launched, and the only people using it were core developers and a few other enthusiasts like themselves.

They released a test version in 2015, a couple of months before Ethereum's Frontier mainnet launch. Augur works with its own internal token called Reputation, or REP. Users can place bets on future events—for example, will Donald Trump win the 2020 election?—and receive cryptocurrency-based shares depending on the outcome. To keep the system fully decentralized, the correct outcome needs to be defined by consensus, and that's where the REP tokens come in. Holders will stake their REP to an outcome, either before or in a brief period after it happens. Those who staked their REP tokens to the correct outcome get their tokens back plus a portion of the fees users paid to participate in the process. All trading and payouts happen through Ethereum smart contracts.

So when Joey and Jack were thinking of fundraising to continue developing the protocol, a crowdsale of their REP tokens made more sense than going to venture capitalists. A crowdsale would distribute tokens among potential users and raise funds. They also didn't want a handful of venture funds to control the protocol. On August 17, two weeks after the Ethereum network launched, Augur started the first Ethereum-based crowdsale. It lasted forty-five days and they sold 11 million REP tokens for 60 cents each, or $5.3 million, to about 3,000 digital addresses distributed across the globe, without the help of banks or funds. Joey, Jack, and other developers kept 20 percent of the funds. This new method of funding open source protocols had proven successful once more.

Augur was also the first to build their REP coins using the so-called ERC20 token standard, which would become almost synonymous with Ethereum token sales. The idea had been proposed by Vitalik two months earlier, in June 2015. He called it the "Standardized Contract APIs."

"Although Ethereum allows developers to create absolutely any kind of application without restriction to specific feature types, and prides itself on its 'lack of features,' there is nevertheless a need to standardize certain very common use cases in order to allow users and applications to more easily interact with each other," he wrote on GitHub.

He went on to list the code for a dozen or so common functions for currencies, decentralized exchanges, registries, and data feeds, and the post was discussed on Reddit under a thread called "Let's talk about the coin standard," where Ethereans pitched in with their thoughts.

At around that time, Martin Becze had quietly been building a JavaScript client for Ethereum while living in a camper in his parents' backyard in Indiana, until he'd been hired by the Ethereum Foundation as a contractor. He'd decided there needed to be a more formal process for proposing changes to Ethereum. So he copied Bitcoin Improvement Proposals (BIPs) and programming language Python's

Enhancement Proposals (PEPs) and created Ethereum Improvement Proposals (EIPs), a document designed for anyone to propose changes for Ethereum, which had to include a technical specification and the reason why it's needed.

So in November, Ethereum developer Fabian Vogelsteller took Vitalik's initial token standard draft, wrote a proper specification explaining each function and action, and created an issue on Ethereum's GitHub EIP repository. He called it "ERC: Token standard." ERC stood for Ethereum Request for Comment, and followed a common practice among internet engineers and researchers who use RFCs, or Request for Comments. The standard was later known as ERC20, because it was the twentieth issue being discussed.

It was a very simple document consisting of just six commonly used functions for tokens, and two events to trigger after certain functions are invoked. Because it was so simple and because developers were very interested in deploying tokens on Ethereum, it quickly became popular with developers, who started using it as a blueprint they could just copy and paste for any token. If you've ever tried to create a website, you'll know how much easier it is to just take a template off the shelf instead of creating your own. ERC20 did something similar for tokens.

■ ■ ■

Rune Christensen, a Danish student who had been teaching English and running a recruiting business in China, was also one of the few building an Ethereum project. Excitement for the technology and the potentially lucrative upside led Rune to Bitcoin in 2011. He shut down his recruiting business and started heavily investing in the cryptocurrency. He made a lot of money in the 2013 spike, and then lost it all when it crashed a year later. That gut-wrenching volatility is what got him thinking about stablecoins, which Charles Hoskinson's former company with Daniel Larimer, BitShares, was building. He became a BitShares enthusiast but eventually grew tired of the internal drama in the BitShares crowd as well as all the political talk, which was getting extreme, even if he was now too a libertarian believer. Rune felt the drama and politics got in the way of improving the product, allowing competitors to jump ahead of the project.

The budding Ethereum community seemed to be the exact opposite. The drama and politicking within the foundation and among cofounders had been kept out of public view; those outside the inner circle were an optimistic bunch of mostly millennial developers. They had been influenced by Vitalik's penchant for T-shirts adorned with cats and unicorns. They cultivated the aesthetic, which became particular to Ethereum, featuring rainbows, cute animals, mythical creatures, and internet memes. To grossly simplify the two cultures, if Bitcoiners were typically hard-core libertarian and carnivore, Ethereans leaned more liberal and vegetarian.

After spending time in the Bitcoin and BitShares forums, Rune found it was refreshing that the Ethereum community was focused primarily on building innovative tech, rather than on any particular ideology. Back home in Copenhagen, he decided to start an Ethereum-based stablecoin. He didn't know how to code, but taught himself the basics in two weeks and was able to get a bare-bones system running, which he announced in a March 2015 Reddit post.

"Introducing eDollar, the ultimate stablecoin built on Ethereum," he wrote. "As someone who's been obsessed with pegged cryptocurrencies for the past 6 months, I was delighted to find out that even with just my meager programming skills, developing for Ethereum is so incredibly easy that I've been able to come up with what I believe is close to being the perfect design for a stable cryptocurrency."

The first to reply to his post on eDollar, later renamed Dai, was Vitalik, who goes by "vbuterin" on Reddit. He gave Rune a technical suggestion, which Rune's project, called MakerDAO, ended up implementing. Rune says the system would have probably been hacked and a total disaster if he had released it as it was, but at the time, he was part of a cohort of Ethereans who believed smart contracts were invincible and unbreakable. "Build unstoppable applications," the Ethereum.org website would later say. Not only that, but many believed anything was better if it was decentralized. The thinking was, if you picked any business idea and somehow added blockchain technology, it would be an instant success. It didn't matter if a distributed ledger was actually needed. Decentralization was hailed as a goal in itself, rather than a tool.

The purpose of Rune's stable cryptocurrency was that people would be able to interact with Ethereum applications without having to worry about the crazy volatility of ether. It would be pegged to the dollar in value, meaning 1 eDollar would be worth 1 US dollar. The difference with BitShares was that rather than having a single asset as collateral it would use multiple cryptocurrencies on the Ethereum blockchain to be more decentralized and stable.

The system would be managed by a Decentralized Autonomous Organization, or DAO, called Maker. As mentioned earlier, Dan Larimer and his father, Stan, proposed the concept in September 2013, and Vitalik followed up with an article in *Bitcoin Magazine* just a couple of days later. In 2015 DAOs were all the rage in the blockchain world. They fit perfectly into a futuristic, cypherpunk vision where digital money and blockchain-based platforms would replace old, dusty banks and all human intervention would be minimized. Blockchain technology would take people out of the equation as much as possible and leave decision making to computer programs. The rules of an organization would be put into code and computers would execute all the decisions openly and predictably. The decentralized network would ensure that no single party could modify the code or shut down the program. The idea was that people can be corrupted, they can cheat and deceive, but code can't. It was pure crypto-anarchy, because to some of its proponents, these DAOs would presumably be outside of the law.

DAOs "don't need regulation, you don't want to regulate them, and happily you can't," Stan Larimer wrote. The only laws a DAO would be subject to would be the market's.

Developers were starting to build on Ethereum, even as the network was still in beta. That would change on March 14, 2016, or "Pi Day," as Jeff Wilcke announced in a blog post. That's when they launched Ethereum's first production-ready version, called Homestead. The upgrade fixed some flaws found in the previous versions, and would make the network faster and more reliable. It meant that Ethereum was no longer in test mode and was finally ready for serious companies to build on. The network had grown considerably by the Homestead launch. It had about 5,100 nodes, compared with Bitcoin's about 6,000, and was processing about 25,000 transactions a day, or about 10 percent of transactions in the Bitcoin blockchain.

The growing activity on Ethereum and the recovering broader cryptocurrency market pushed the price of ether higher. It got back to more than $1 in January 2016, crossed $5 in February, and climbed above $10 in March. The price jump meant the foundation was more flush.

Later that month, a project called DigixDAO raised $5.5 million in one day. It claimed to be the first DAO to do a token sale. The Singapore-based team wanted to back their DGX tokens with gold bars stored in a vault, where one token equaled 1 gram of gold. A separate token, called DGD, would be used to vote in the DAO and DGD holders would be rewarded in the gold-backed DGX.

Augur, Maker, and Digix were some of the biggest projects in the budding Ethereum community. Developers were also hacking away to create the basic infrastructure needed for this world computer to work. Embark and Truffle were frameworks to develop, test, and deploy decentralized applications, or dapps. Ether.camp and TradeBlock were block explorers, or tools to track the evolution of the network. EthereumWallet.com and MyEtherWallet were digital ether wallets, to store, send, and trade ether. Mist was an online browser and MetaMask was a browser-based wallet, which served as an interface and way to connect with decentralized applications. And so on.

As all this was happening, J. R. Willett, the creator of the first cryptocurrency crowdsale with Mastercoin, recalled what Bitcoin core developer Gavin Andresen had said about Ethereum when it was just starting out. "I suspect they're trying to do too much— 'complexity is the enemy of security'—and will end up either radically reducing the scope of what they're trying to do or will get tired of playing whack-a-mole with security and DoS vulnerabilities," he wrote in a 2014 blog post, referring to denial-of-service attacks. But seeing the progress in 2015 and early 2016, J.R. started to regret not letting Vitalik build his idea on Mastercoin. And yet it was probably for the best. Now the world had Ethereum.

19

The Magic Lock

One of the most ambitious projects was Slock.it. Christoph Jentzsch, a German theoretical physicist, had been working on testing and checking the compatibility among the different Ethereum clients. Christoph was known for being very good at his job, obsessive and meticulous, so when he jumped into a new venture, people paid attention.

"With Uber, Airbnb, and others leading the way, we have to ask ourselves, 'Is this how we want to build the sharing economy?' Monopolistic companies that take extraordinary fees and have full control of the market?" said one of Slock.it's blog posts.

Slock.it cofounders, including Jentzsch's brother, wanted to make it possible for people to rent, sell, and share their property without having to use intermediaries. Instead of going to platforms like Uber and Airbnb to get matched up and pay, the whole process would be done through a lock placed on each item. The lock would be connected to the Ethereum blockchain and all transactions would be automated with smart contracts. This was at a time when not even digital wallets, the most basic interface for Ethereum users, were intuitive enough for nontechnical people, so it was still a long way off before something like Slock.it could work. But Ethereans were nothing if not optimistic.

"Because of the rules in the Ethereum protocol, [the Slock.it smart contract that allows users to interact with each other] will always do exactly what it is programmed to do and cannot be cheated," a December 2, 2015, blog post said.

Here is how the system would work. Imagine someone has a bike she only uses on weekends, while her neighbor wants to bike to work on weekdays. The bike owner would place a Slock.it lock on the bike and set a safety deposit amount and a rental price. Her neighbor would pay that deposit through a transaction to the Ethereum blockchain (without having to pay Slock.it) using his smartphone, and the payment would open the lock. The deposit would be locked in the network until the user returned the bike. He would then send another transaction to the Ethereum blockchain and get the deposit back minus the price for the rental, while the money for the rental would be sent to the bike owner.

In November 2015, Christoph explained the project at Ethereum's Devcon1 conference in London. He did a live demo using a lock attached to a kettle, which automatically turned on when he opened the lock after sending ether (the transaction was live for everyone to see in a block explorer), and steam started coming out of the spout as he talked. Slock.it became the star of the show. In a prescient comment on YouTube, someone wrote the words of a common *Futurama*-based meme: "Shut up and take my money!"

As Slock.it's community manager, Griff Green was one of the most visible faces for the project. Griff had grown up in Spokane, in Washington State, studied chemical engineering at the University of Washington, and got a job in the field, which he left after two years. He was a left-leaning kid who turned into a self-proclaimed socialist as a teenager. But then 9/11 conspiracy videos got him to distrust governments and the banking system, and that got him into Austrian economists. He read Ludwig von Mises's laissez-faire magnum opus *Human Action: A Treatise on Economics* twice. After dabbling in the extremes of the political spectrum, he finally just defined himself as a "hippie anarchist." And that doesn't jibe with an office job.

He sold everything he owned and bought physical bars of silver and gold coins to store his savings so that he could rely as little as possible on banks. He backpacked around South America, Southeast Asia, and India for two years (but always made the trek back home for Burning Man), and financed himself thanks to a friend who was selling his precious metals and transferring the cash.

One day his friend thought of using Bitcoin to make the transfers. Griff loved the idea of currency that wasn't issued by any government and exchanged his real gold for digital gold. He went back to the United States to live with a girlfriend in West Hollywood, where he worked as a massage therapist—he was using the skills he picked up in Thailand—but he couldn't stop thinking about Bitcoin. One day he decided to break up with his girlfriend, take the gains from his crypto investments, which at that point were worth several thousand dollars, and move to Ecuador. His plan was to become a cryptocurrency evangelist, create a Bitcoin ecosystem for the South American country out of the hippie, expats-filled town of Vilcabamba, and retire there. Six months after he moved, it became clear the Ecuadorian government would make Bitcoin illegal, so he left.

Back on the road, he continued studying to get an online master's degree in digital currencies from the University of Nicosia, said to be the first university to offer such a thing, and decided to code up an Ethereum smart contract for a homework assignment. He had recently stumbled into the Ethereum Reddit page and posted the contract and a blog post explaining it, to get feedback. Griff seldom participated in the Bitcoin and altcoin forums because he felt they were too negative and critical, so he was amazed when nobody ridiculed his amateurish code. Ethereum developer Alex Van de Sande even took the time to edit it.

"This is home," Griff thought.

He immediately looked for work in the Ethereum community and asked to join Slock.it, what he thought was one of the most exciting crypto projects out there.

After designing the system and building the prototypes, Slock.it needed funding. The obvious option was a token sale. They coded up a crowdfunding contract, but then decided to take it a step further and created a smart contract that gave token holders the power to vote and decide what Slock.it should do with the funds. Still not happy, they took the concept even further, and created a true Decentralized Autonomous Organization, which would control the funds. This meant that token holders would decide where to allocate the money, and Slock.it would be just one among other proposals vying for it. It would effectively work like a decentralized venture fund. This structure was unprecedented, but the Jentzsch brothers and the rest of the Slock.it team believed in the DAO revolution and wanted to take the lead.

Christoph authored a white paper describing how it would work. At the core of the paper was the desire to make crowdfunding through cryptocurrencies, a mechanism that was growing in popularity, safer for investors. On the one hand, Christoph wrote, presales have made it easier for entrepreneurs to receive funding and for anyone to invest in large tech projects. On the other hand, "small investors remain vulnerable to financial mismanagement or outright fraud," and they "may lack power to identify problems, participate in governance decisions, or to easily recover their investment." As a solution, the paper proposed giving participants direct and real-time control of their funds, and formalizing and automating governance rules.

The DAO code is written in the Solidity programming language and is meant to be deployed on the Ethereum blockchain. After the code is launched, ether is sent to the DAO's smart contract address; the code creates tokens in proportion to the ether sent and sends those tokens to the accounts that sent ether. Tokens are divisible and can be freely transferable and traded. The DAO can store and transfer ether, but it doesn't do much else.

Token holders can submit proposals to use the ether collected in the DAO, and they're given a window of time to debate and vote on them. They have voting and ownership rights in proportion to the amount of DAO tokens held. When a proposal is approved, ether is transferred to a smart contract that belongs to the winning project.

Projects can then send ether, for example from their profits, back to the DAO so it can be used to fund other projects or distributed among token holders, like a dividend.

In the paper, Christoph proposed a way to prevent the "majority robs the minority attack," where an attacker with 51 percent of the tokens is able to change governance and ownership rules, or simply propose and approve to send all the funds to themselves. The solution, which stemmed from a blog post by Vitalik, would be for the minority to always have the option of retrieving their funds by allowing the DAO to split. If someone disagrees with a proposal and wants to withdraw their funds, they can create a new "child DAO," where they can move their ether and leave the rest to spend their own ether as they please. But there's still the problem of voter apathy. Someone could be unaware of the situation and fail to act. That's why the figure of the "curator" was created as a last safeguard against 51 percent attacks. Curators, who can be voted in and out, control the list of addresses that can receive ether.

The white paper was put into open source code by the Slock.it team, and just like Christoph had tested the Ethereum clients, he also ran several tests on each piece of the code. Still a bit nervous about releasing it, he got an audit with Seattle-based Deja Vu, the same company that audited the Ethereum code. With the okay from the audit, Christoph felt he had done everything he could to make sure there wasn't anything wrong and released the framework in April 2016. From this protocol, the DAO was born. It can be a little confusing, but they called the actual fund governed by a DAO, The DAO. The reason for the unimaginative name is that Slock.it didn't want to be the one to name the fund, since the idea was that they didn't really own it. They decided to leave The DAO as a placeholder and the community would vote on another name later.

The DAO had become the only thing the Ethereum community talked about. It was the biggest, most ambitious project attempted and so eleven of the most distinguished Ethereans came on as curators, including Vitalik Buterin, Gavin Wood, Alex Van de Sande,

Vlad Zamfir, Fabian Vogelsteller, and Christian Reitwiessner. They all either had been or were currently part of the Ethereum Foundation.

With that, a four-week fundraiser started on April 30. Fabian, the Ethereum developer who created the ERC20 standard, was really into it. He was excited to see the first completely decentralized, autonomous, community-run fund. He bought some DAO tokens, thinking it had to catch on. Still, his most optimistic estimates had The DAO attracting $20 million. But after the first fifteen days it had already attracted $34 million, and he cheered on as it surpassed $50 million. When it crossed $70 million and kept climbing, he started to get worried, especially considering he had some degree of responsibility over the funds under the curator role.

Christoph was also getting worried. Suddenly millions of dollars were being poured into an experimental piece of code he created. What if something went wrong? To make things worse, the project started attracting attention, and he was getting constant calls and emails from journalists. It got to a point where he couldn't handle it anymore and stopped answering emails. Griff, who was staying at Christoph's mother's house in the Mittweida region in Germany, went with him on walks to help him calm down.

By the end of the crowdsale on May 28, 12 million ether (at 100 DAO tokens per 1 ether) had flooded into an untested smart contract built with the new Solidity programming language. With ETH at around $12, that was $150 million. Ethereum's crowdsale had been groundbreaking with $18 million raised. This was on a different order of magnitude.

PART IV

Lunar Orbit

20

The DAO Wars

It was sunny in Berlin. Young couples and families lay on the grass at Görlitzer Park (Görli to locals) in the bohemian Kreuzberg district, where, one week after the DAO fundraiser had ended, Christian Reitwiessner was holed up reviewing the Solidity language he helped create. The language governed all Ethereum smart contracts, including The DAO's, but he was working on something unrelated to the mammoth project when he noticed a flaw that could potentially be used to drain funds from some contracts. He went on GitHub, a place for developers to discuss and store their code, and under the name Chriseth, alerted other Ethereans about it.

It seemed harmless, so much so that the issue had been sitting in open source code for everyone to see and yet no one had caught it. The problem was with how some contracts were set up to send funds. The code did what it was supposed to, but the order of the commands made it possible for someone really clever to withdraw more funds than they actually had. The glitch was that the computer was told to decrease the user's balance only after sending the funds. And in between sending funds and updating the balance, a new call to the same transaction could be initiated, which would also send funds first before updating the balance. And this so-called reentrancy bug could keep repeating until almost all of the gas in the original transaction was depleted. This meant someone could ask for money multiple times before their balance was updated and before the computer noticed their account didn't have any money left. The example that's often used to explain this is a faulty ATM that only updates your balance at the end of the session, so you can just keep making several withdrawals, and by the time the machine knows your money ran out, it's too late—you've already absconded with illicit cash!

Christian caught this on June 5 and on June 9 another developer, Peter Vessenes, wrote a blog post about it.

"Chriseth at github casually pointed out a terrible, terrible attack on wallet contracts that I had not considered," he wrote. "In Brief: Your smart contract is probably vulnerable to being emptied if you keep track of any sort of user balances and were not very, very careful."

This was the first time the potential loophole was shared outside of GitHub. As Ethereum developers scrambled to figure out which contracts were at risk, the vessel the hacker would use to attack the mother ship had already been created. Back when The DAO's crowdsale had just ended, token holders started tinkering with the split function—this is what allowed members of The DAO to create child DAOs, where they'd be able to send their funds in case there was a 51 percent attack or if they disagreed with a proposal. Dozens of people started testing out this function. They called their child DAOs things like "split me baby one more time" and "banana split."

The fifty-ninth child DAO to appear was called "lonely, so lonely." After a child DAO was created, there was a seven-day waiting period before the owner could pull their ether from the main DAO, and an additional twenty-seven days before they could withdraw those funds from the child DAO. In the initial one-week period, others could also jump on board, and that's just what the attacker did with the "lonely, so lonely" split—or, as it would be later be known, the "dark DAO." The countdown for the "dark DAO" to be able to pull funds from the main DAO had started on June 8.

Ethereans had no way of knowing they only had a few days to fix the bug Christian had spotted.

Three days after Peter's blog post, the MakerDAO team discovered their code was vulnerable and used the hack themselves to drain their smart contract of the $80,000 that was stored in it and secure the funds.

"Today we discovered a vulnerability in the ETH token wrapper which would let anyone drain it," they wrote in their Slack channel. "We successfully executed the attack ourselves. . . . Everyone's tokens (both ETH and MKR) are safe, as far as we know."

One day later, on June 12, a developer who goes by Eththrowa online spotted the same bug in the rewards section of The DAO code, where projects' profits were meant to be sent for distribution among token holders.

The bug "is also present in the DAO code—specifically here in the withdrawRewardFor function DAO.sol," they wrote. "This would allow a user to drain many times his entitlement by calling the contract recursively."

"Wow Great catch!!" Griff replied.

Of course, there weren't any funds yet in the rewards section of The DAO. That led to a post by Stephan Tual, another Slock.it cofounder, which would later become infamous for its bold headline: "No DAO Funds at Risk Following the Ethereum Smart Contract 'Recursive Call' Bug Discovery."

The framework was patched within hours, but the actual code of The DAO couldn't be changed so fast. Christoph and the rest of the developers started the cumbersome process of updating the code. Because of the governance rules, which had been hardwired into the code, this would require a two-week voting time and a majority of the token holders to vote.

Whether two weeks or two days, it didn't matter to the attacker. The specific vulnerability he/she/they planned to exploit—the recursive bug in the splitDAO section of the code—still hadn't been caught.

Someone else had also come close. Emin Gun Sirer, a professor of computer science at Cornell University, had been looking into The DAO for some time. Back in May he had even called for a "temporary moratorium" on the project. In a blog post authored with researchers Vlad Zamfir and Dino Mark, he described at least nine different ways the voting mechanism was faulty.

Emin was scouring the code for places where this recursive call loophole could be exploited and on June 11 he emailed his smartest student, Phil Daian.

"I'm pretty sure I know how to empty out The DAO," Emin said, and they both continued to poke at the code.

The next day was a Sunday and he was in bed trying to recover from a cold, but kept digging. Finally, he thought he found something.

"I still think that splitDAO may have a vulnerability," he wrote to his student. "It violates the withdraw pattern by not zeroing the balances[ ] field until after the call. So I think it may be possible to have it move rewardTokens to a splitting DAO multiple times. This is happening on lines 640 to 666 (hah!) of DAO.sol. Am I wrong?"

Phil spent a few hours going through the lines of code and concluded there was no way to trigger the vulnerability. He replied to Emin and with that, the professor trusted his student and went back to bed. Stephan published his "no DAO funds at risk" post that day. The attacker could have been rubbing his hands together, rightly concluding that, despite that ominous red flag in the "666" line of the code, nobody was on to them.

Vitalik was in Shanghai staying at a friend's apartment when at around 3 p.m. on June 17 he got a message saying something like, "I'm not sure if this is an issue, but it looks like The DAO is being drained."

"That's weird," Vitalik thought. "No money is supposed to be able to come out of The DAO yet."

He went to look at the contract and saw about 100 ether was disappearing from it every second. At this point, the ether price had climbed so the total held in the smart contract equaled about $250 million. As he forwarded the message to Ethereum core developers and the Slock.it team, he didn't want to believe this was malicious but very soon there was no other way around it. The biggest project ever attempted on Ethereum, a treasure chest that held roughly 14 percent of all ether, was under attack. If the hacker was successful, he would kill not only this project, but could also kill Ethereum.

The first thing Vitalik thought of doing was spamming the network to slow down the attack, while he and other developers tried to pin down exactly what was going on. A few hours later Christoph, Simon, and Griff had turned the Jentzsch dining room into a war bunker. As Christoph's five kids ran around getting ready for school, the developers got on calls with other devs, fielded dozens of messages and emails, and dove into the code to figure out how the funds were getting drained, who the attacker was, and mainly, what they could do to stop it.

By the time Alex Van de Sande, known to most by his internet name Avsa, was waking up in his Rio de Janeiro apartment, the flood of messages had escalated and were now coming from exchanges and security researchers. People were calling for markets to be closed, trading to be halted, and emergency code to be deployed.

George Hallam, the Ethereum Foundation's spokesman, said in a chat room with heads of different cryptocurrency exchanges, "ALL EXCHANGES: please pause ether trading as soon as possible." Some exchange CEOs asked if the measure was absolutely necessary. Bill Shihara from Bittrex said stopping trading would prevent the attacker from liquidating funds, but it would penalize legitimate traders, too. Vitalik, who would usually favor a hands-off approach, was so worried about what the attack could do to Ethereum that he swayed toward asking exchanges to intervene too. "Ok can you guys stop trading," he said. "And deposits and withdrawals." Some trading venues complied.

Alex couldn't believe what he was seeing.

"Honey, remember that giant pile of money I was talking about last week? The one kept safe by unhackable code?" Alex, still glued to his smartphone screen, said to his wife.

"Yes?"

"Well, it was hacked."

By that time, most token holders had heard the news. Rather than create their own child DAOs and wait seven days to withdraw their money from the main DAO, like *Titanic* passengers in nightgowns diving into the first lifeboats they could find, they were jumping into whatever child DAO had an approaching deadline. Alex also tried to do this but when he pressed the button on his Ethereum wallet, he got what's known as one of the most annoying messages on earth. "Wrong password."

"Wait, this can't be happening, I know this password, it must be some bug," Alex thought, cursing whoever had built the application— and then remembering it was him.

He stopped thinking about the hack and started debugging the issue. By the time he fixed it, the deadline for the lifeboat he wanted to jump on had passed. He opened Skype and started typing a message for Griff. "Hi Griff, I've got 100,000 DAO tokens, how do I get my money out?" But he immediately felt ashamed and deleted his message. He knew everyone involved in the creation of The DAO, and he was even a curator. He realized he should be helping, not just thinking about himself.

"Hi Griff, I've got 100,000 DAO tokens, how can I help?"

"Hi Avsa! We are all still figuring it out! But thanks for the offer!" said Griff, who had hardly left the chair in Christoph's dining room all day.

Christoph was trying really hard not to have a nervous breakdown. The past few weeks had already been extremely stressful. He had left his job as tester for the Ethereum Foundation and, five kids and all, had taken on the Slock.it project with no salary. All the excitement around The DAO had felt like a whip on his back, as everyone just wanted the thing to be done and he felt pressured to deliver as fast as possible. It hadn't felt right when all the millions started flowing in, and now that initial discomfort in his gut wasn't letting him breathe.

Developers for the Ethereum protocol, its software clients, and applications had all dropped what they were doing and gathered on Skype, Gitter, and Slack chat rooms trying to figure out what to do. Maybe they could try to replicate the attack and drain money from the attacker. Or they could drain the money that was still in the main DAO into a safe place. Another option was a so-called soft fork, where miners wouldn't process transactions aimed at withdrawing money from The DAO or any of the child DAOs, effectively preventing the attacker from stealing the funds.

This last option was tricky. Public blockchains were supposed to be censorship resistant and changes should only be made if there's consensus among most participants. Arguably, a small group advocating to block a specific action went directly against that. To Vitalik, the soft fork was a relatively quick fix and he believed the proposal had gained enough support from the developers, so he made it public.

"CRITICAL UPDATE Re: DAO Vulnerability," was the blog post headline. "An attack has been found and exploited in the DAO, and the attacker is currently in the process of draining the ether contained in the DAO into a child DAO."

He explained that even if no action was taken, the attacker wouldn't be able to withdraw any ether for at least about twenty-seven days, and that, while the issue affects The DAO specifically, "Ethereum itself is perfectly safe."

"A software fork has been proposed," he wrote. "Which will make any transactions that make any calls/callcodes/delegatecalls that reduce the balance of an account with code hash 0x7278d050619a624f 84f51987149ddb439cdaadfba5966f7cfaea7ad44340a4ba (ie. The DAO and children) lead to the transaction (not just the call, the transaction) being invalid."

Another even more drastic and controversial option had started to surface: a hard fork, or a modification to the Ethereum protocol itself. In this new chain, everything would stay the same, except The DAO smart contract would be modified so that it only allowed token holders to withdraw their funds.

"Worst nightmare for Ethereum. Hope this doesn't cause calls for a hard fork," someone posted on the Ethereum page on Reddit. "It'd ruin ethereum's legitimacy as a platform."

Later in the day and for some unknown reason, the attacker stopped draining money. He had siphoned 30 percent, or 3.6 million ether, of the 12 million ether into his child DAO, while the rest remained in the main DAO.

"I believe we figured out how the attacker did it," Griff said in a message to Alex, and explained the mechanics of how the attacker had used the recursive call feature (the one where you make multiple, successive withdrawals) and managed to take more money than what they had.

"I think we can replicate the attack. We can drain The DAO ourselves," Griff said.

Alex joined Griff and other developers including Fabian Vogelsteller, Jordi Baylina, and Lefteris Karapestas in a private Skype group. Others would jump in and out of their discussions, but they would be the main participants. They were preparing for a nonmalicious counterattack, or what's known as a "white-hat" attack. They wanted to steal from The DAO to redistribute the money to its rightful owners, so the name Robin Hood Group emerged.

It was midafternoon in Brazil and already dark in Europe when they had their first call. The white-hat hackers had successfully replicated the attack on a testnet and felt technically ready to do it.

"But the question remains, should we do it?"

"Well the problem is, if you figured it out, how many others have figured it out too?"

"We are surely not the only ones."

"So anyone could do it at any moment now?"

"Yes, it's a matter of time. We don't actually understand why the original attacker stopped."

"Maybe he thought he had enough and could get away with stealing only 30 percent."

"Or maybe his attack wasn't as good as ours. We believe he might have burned his tokens while doing so."

The attack required DAO tokens to request ether from the main DAO. The sequence had to be executed quickly, moving tokens from one account to another, to avoid the computer program in the main DAO from taking the tokens.

"If we have 600,000 tokens we might be able to drain the remainder of the funds in only a few minutes."

"But again . . . should we? There are other solutions."

"Everyone's talking about doing a soft fork, or even a hard fork."

"Doing a white-hat attack would be a good preventive measure, wouldn't it? If the other solutions don't work then we'd lose the opportunity to do this. If they work then this attack will be reverted anyway so it won't matter."

"We still can't do it right away. We need to infiltrate The DAO first."

"So let's do it!"

"But we don't know the legal ramifications of this, no one knows. I wouldn't want to implicate our companies."

"Or the foundation."

"No, this is all on ourselves. But it still matters who pushes the button."

"We have to announce we are doing this the moment we do it. It's not like we could do it in secret, otherwise it wouldn't be a white-hat attack, just a normal dark-hat one."

"Also, it would crash the market if no one knows what's happening."

Ether was already crashing from $21 before the hack to around $15. The cryptocurrency had lost about a third of its value in one day.

"So, who should press the button?"

There was a long silence. Everyone wanted it to be done, but no one wanted to be the one to do it and they had this circular discussion for a while, until Alex said he could be the one to press the button. He had volunteered his 100,000 tokens, so the attack could be traced back to him anyway.

"I can do it. You'd have to teach me how. But I can do it."

"Okay. When's the next window?"

Remember, someone who split from the main DAO had one week before they could withdraw their funds into their child DAOs. Crucially, in those seven days, other token holders could decide to join them in their vessel. The Robin Hood Group, as they were already widely known, could use this to their advantage and infiltrate escape pods that had already been created. They had to do this with two accounts, one human user and one robot, which would allow them to automate the attack. They also had to know who the owner of the vessel was to coordinate with them and make sure the money they "stole" would be rightfully returned. And they had to pick child DAOs with approaching deadlines to reduce the chances an attacker jumped in with them.

Griff started reaching out to people in the community, asking who the owners of the child DAOs were, and as word got out that there was a group planning a counterattack, people started volunteering to help. Finally Griff found the perfect candidate, someone who owned a child DAO with time running out for outsiders to join. They were ready.

They all got on a call. The hackers started guiding Alex through the process: create a new account with a tough password and move DAO tokens into the account. Next, they sent him a piece of code to deploy from that account. That was the robot that would join him on board the child DAO, where they would proceed to drain the mother ship, hoping they got to the funds before the attacker. They had to wait until the last possible moment, so as not to alert the attacker of what they were doing. With thirty minutes left, they started a new call, and at twenty-five minutes Alex deployed the robot and fueled it with the required tokens. At twenty minutes left, it was time.

"Let's go rob a bank!" Alex said, adrenaline spiking as he pressed the button.

But nothing happened. He waited a few seconds, then a minute, and still nothing.

"There's something wrong here, the transaction is not being picked up," he said, but at the other end of the call, there was silence. He was disconnected. Skype was offline. He opened Google. His computer was offline. After trying to turn his modem on and off, with still nothing, he got back on Skype using his phone connection.

"Guys my internet is offline! Can someone take over?"

"Let me try!" Griff said.

While Alex frantically called his internet service provider, Griff connected to the Ethereum blockchain, but he had to wait until he was in sync with the latest block.

"I see we have an internet issue in your neighborhood!" a robotic voice at the other end of the call with Alex announced. "If the connection doesn't come back in three hours then we can schedule a visit. Press one to schedule it anyway."

"Ahh!!" Alex screamed to himself as he punched in the options. He felt like the future of Ethereum lay on his shoulders and all he could do was schedule an appointment with his ISP. With a heavy feeling in his stomach, he saw the deadline fly by. Griff hadn't been able to connect on time.

"When is the next opportunity?"

"Tomorrow morning. But by that time, it's likely that all the money will be gone."

"Maybe the attacker thought $30 million was enough?"

"I doubt it. He can get all of it."

"Let's reconvene tomorrow."

In the meantime, more and more people had piled on to argue about whether to soft-fork, hard-fork, or just accept that The DAO had been hacked and let it die. To many, Ethereum would have failed in its core values if they did anything about it, as it would signal some projects are too big to fail and deserve a bailout, just like big

Wall Street banks in 2008. What was the point of cryptocurrency if they went down the same paths they were trying to escape in the first place? It didn't take long for the cypherpunk term of "code is law" to emerge as a fundamental principle that shouldn't be broken.

Others argued that code is a tool to help people, not the other way around. If developers knew how to fix the issue so that money could be returned to its rightful owners, then they should do it; otherwise, they're not much better than the thief. Some said faith in Ethereum would be lost if the reset button was pressed; others argued faith in Ethereum would be lost if it wasn't. The survival of the entire project was at stake in practical terms, and its core values were also being questioned. What did Ethereum stand for if its code wasn't immutable and uncensorable?

Between all this soul-searching, some token holders just wanted to get their money back. Bitcoiners who had been skeptical about Ethereum from the start took this as the perfect opportunity to gloat. The level of hostility spurred conspiracy theories that a prominent Bitcoin company had deployed robots made to spam social media with anti-Ethereum comments. The Ethereum Foundation started to get dragged down in the mud as some commenters said the only reason a bailout was being discussed in the first place was that foundation members had invested in the project and were curators. There was so much blame and fear being thrown around that anyone who spent time in those threads would have to come out feeling dirty.

In the very early hours of Saturday, June 18, the second day after the hack started, Mircea Popescu, the guy who thought Ethereum would fail and had offered to sell ether at half the price of the crowdsale, posted a letter in his blog. The author of the letter claimed to be the attacker. But because the author didn't correctly identify themself in the encrypted signature, it was more likely an attempt to vex the Ethereum community—troll, in internet speak—in one of its most difficult moments than to actually come out as the DAO hacker.

"To the DAO and the Ethereum community," it began. "I have carefully examined the code of The DAO and decided to participate after finding the feature where splitting is rewarded with additional ether. I have made use of this feature and have rightfully claimed 3,641,694 ether, and would like to thank the DAO for this reward."

The letter went on to state that a soft or hard fork would amount to "seizure" of his legitimately earned ether, and would "further damage Ethereum and destroy its reputation and appeal." It then threatened legal action against anyone who attempted to seize or freeze the funds and ended in a note that must have unnerved any Etherean reading it: "I hope this event becomes an [sic] valuable learning experience for the Ethereum community and wish you all the best of luck. Yours truly, 'The Attacker'"

The attack still hadn't resumed. The Robin Hood Group decided to reconvene and try their counterattack again. They had one hour before they could join the next child DAO and they hadn't been able to identify the owner. They had all just reconnected their machines to the Ethereum network, and yet again, it was taking too long for them to sync to the last node. They missed the deadline again. If only they had woken up early on a Saturday. On the other hand, they had hardly slept the night before.

The next day, they went through a similar process, but this time Alex was up at 5 a.m. and his computer was ready for action. Together, with Griff, they figured out when the next closing child DAO was and jumped on with both the human account and the robot, without a glitch. They were in. It felt good but also a bit anticlimactic. They sent a couple of celebratory emojis and then Griff went to bed.

But Alex had the whole day ahead of him and thought, why stop here? He could join all the other "escape pods" right away. They hadn't done it before to avoid calling attention to themselves and alerting the attacker to their plans, but it had been two days and the attacker still hadn't reemerged. Also, as details of the hack continued to come to light, it was easier for others to figure out how to exploit it, so all the child DAOs became vulnerable. Alex thought he might as well preempt the dark-hat hackers.

He told the group what he was doing and used the same process to infiltrate every single escape pod scheduled to leave the mother ship in the next three days.

But was any of this legal? Sure, the Robin Hood Group was planning to do their hack in the open, and their intention was to return the funds to their owners, but would good intentions alone stand up in court? Executing their plan would still mean stealing millions of dollars from a smart contract they didn't control and hadn't even written.

Also, others were pushing, and developing the code, for other alternatives. Most in the Ethereum community wanted to avoid a hard fork if possible, so the soft-fork idea continued to gain traction as the lesser of two evils.

The Robin Hood Group convened for the next couple of days, discussed whether they should deploy their warriors, and then decided against it, until on June 21, four days after the first attack, they detected some movement in the main DAO, the mother ship.

"I think the attacker is back on the move," one of the Robin Hood hackers said on the Skype chat.

Everyone went on high alert. Funds were being drained, and they hurried to check whether it was a token holder legitimately reclaiming their ether or an actual attack.

"Confirmed, it's a reentrancy attack. It can be the original attacker using a new identity or a copycat, but it's clear that it's an actual attack."

"So, are we counter attacking?"

"Yes. Definitely."

If they'd had any doubts about unilaterally taking funds before, now they felt the attacker was forcing their hand.

"Are you still okay doing it Alex?"

Everyone's hearts started pounding, eyes glued to the computer screen. They were all sitting in unremarkable settings—makeshift home offices, desks crowded with soda cans and junk food—but they felt they were in the middle of a high-risk mission in some far-flung galaxy. Alex imagined the backdrop was a chaotic space station the size of a small city, where hundreds of vessels were docked to the mother ship. Many captains had asked to take off with their spacecrafts, and they were all queued up and ready for launch. A member of the Robin Hood Group was on board every one of them with two agents, a human and a robot.

The last step before takeoff was doing the intergalactic exchange of DAO tokens held by their spacecrafts, for ether held by the mother ship. For the attack, the agents had to be fueled up with tokens. Together, the Robin Hood hackers had pooled together 300,000 tokens. When it was their turn to go, the robot would present the tokens to the mother ship and ask for the equivalent amount of ether. The next step would normally be for the mother ship to hand over the ether and take the tokens. But in the attack, the robot had been programmed to repeatedly ask for funds. The mother ship's computer would count the tokens and, since it still hadn't taken them away, would send the full amount of ether again. The process would be repeated until the robot reached a limit of operations it could perform. The robot would then send all their tokens to the human operator so that the mother ship wouldn't take them away, and then they'd start over.

Alex pushed the button. They waited for the few minutes it took for the entire Ethereum network to confirm the transaction and the block to be recorded and then . . .

"It worked! Holy shit it actually worked! $100 were moved to the split account."

"Yeah but at this rate we'll never be able to empty it! The other attacker also moved $20 and we need to overtake them."

They moved the tokens back to the contract and started again. The human-controlled account would move the tokens back the robot, which would take a few seconds and then the attack would resume, but with $100 million in the mother ship, it could take all week. They scrambled, asking friends and acquaintances they knew had invested in The DAO to donate their tokens, too, which added up to 800,000 tokens.

Their robots loaded with extra ammunition, they were able to take a few thousand dollars every minute. Suddenly, a second attacker started to drain the system, too. The wider community noticed and the Robin Hood hackers realized they had no other choice: They had to come out of the shadows even if that meant alerting even more attackers. Alex decided to make the announcement on Twitter. Growing up, one of his favorite books was Douglas Adams's *The Hitchhiker's Guide to the Galaxy*, the first of a series of sci-fi novels. The yellow block letters that yelled "Don't Panic" on the back cover made a big impression on young Alex. So when he was composing his tweet, he took the chance to reference his teenage space heroes.

"DAO IS BEING SECURELY DRAINED. DO NOT PANIC," he tweeted.

Not everyone got it.

"NOTHING SAYS DO NOT PANIC LIKE ALL CAPS," someone replied.

The attackers were upping their game, so the Robin Hood crew needed to move even faster. Alex handed his keys over to Fabian, who wrote a script and was able to further automate the process. Everything was going fine but then: "My transactions aren't going through!" Fabian said. Each transaction on the blockchain has a stamp that serves as a counter, called a nonce, and the system will ignore transactions that are in the wrong order. When Alex handed over his keys, they messed up that counter and no transactions were getting through as the system was waiting for the right nonce. The attackers could overtake them at any moment. When Fabian understood what was going on, he felt he was in the middle of a car chase on the blockchain. He quickly set the nonce manually, all the pending transactions got executed in one go and they continued the process.

Soon the white hats were back to withdrawing thousands of dollars every second, and now an Ethereum whale—meaning someone with an unusually large supply of tokens—offered to contribute a few million tokens to the cause.

Now they had 6 million tokens, and with that, the Robin Hood Group's smart contract was draining about $30,000 every few seconds. A third attacker and then a fourth one joined the race for ether, but they were only able to steal a couple of hundred dollars each time. This went on for a few more hours, until their program was trying to take more money than what was available. Fabian and the others kept refining the code until they were able to drain the very last cent from the mother ship. About 70 percent of the funds were recovered, with 30 percent still in the original "dark DAO" where the attack had started, plus a few ether in the hands of other dark-hat hackers. The good guys now just had to wait a few days before they could withdraw the funds and give them back to their owners.

For the first time all week, the white hats were able to get some sleep without worrying about the possibility of waking up to a completely drained DAO. But that feeling would be short-lived. They weren't alone in their spaceships.

After draining the mother ship, they came to the unsettling realization that an unknown someone or some*thing* had joined them. They rushed to check their spaceship's passenger list and verify whether this new presence was a friendly one, and with a sinking feeling saw that among the plain human accounts there was one robot. The attack had to be executed with a human account and a robot, so that piece of code in their spaceship could only mean an attacker was on board with them. And he had infiltrated every single "spaceship" they had jumped on. They thought they were about to fly into safety, but an alien was lurking among them.

There wasn't much they could do at that point. After the seven-day period for others to join child DAOs, its members had to wait an additional twenty-seven days to withdraw the funds into a separate account. But once they did that, the attacker could join them again and stop them from taking the funds. Then they'd have to go through another buffer period before they could withdraw the money, which the attacker could also block, and so on. They could be locked in these galactic DAO Wars forever.

21

The Fork

The only way to recover the stolen funds now seemed to be the soft fork, where miners wouldn't process transactions aimed at withdrawing money from The DAO or child DAOs. Peter Szilagyi, who had become Jeff Wilcke's right-hand man in the Go Ethereum team, was leading the effort so that the Geth client would allow for this option. The version of the Ethereum software client that enabled it was called "DAO Wars."

"We've released version 1.4.8 of Geth (codename 'DAO Wars') as a small patch release to give the community a voice to decide whether to temporarily freeze TheDAOs v1.0 from releasing funds or not," Peter wrote in a June 24 blog post. "If the community decides to freeze the funds, only a few whitelisted accounts can retrieve the blocked funds and return them to previous owners. A similar mechanism is provided by version 1.2.0 of Parity too."

For the soft fork to be adopted, most miners would have to update their software with the "DAO Wars" version. As days progressed toward June 30, when the patch would be implemented, most miners had signaled they were on board with the update. But once again, it wasn't so easy. Two days before the planned soft fork, Emin Gun Sirer, the Cornell professor who had spotted flaws in The DAO before, and two students announced that the update opened Ethereum to potential denial-of-service attacks.

The soft fork would make miners ignore transactions that helped attackers withdraw funds from The DAO. But an attacker could "flood the network with transactions that execute difficult computation, and end by performing an operation on the DAO contract," the researchers wrote. "Miners running the soft fork would end up having to execute, and then subsequently discard, such contracts without collecting any fees." That could jam up the network.

With that, the soft fork was off. The very next day the Geth team released code to undo the changes that went into the "DAO Wars" soft-fork release. In keeping with the Star Wars/DAO Wars theme, the new software release was called "The Network Strikes Back." That's what happens when computer geeks are running the show.

The only options left were not doing anything or doing a hard fork. Discussion on the Ethereum Reddit page and Twitter escalated with people arguing the pros and cons of a hard fork for days. Should Ethereum follow the "code is law" crypto dogma, where what's inscribed in smart contracts and in the blockchain protocol can't be tampered with? If developers make this change now, how could anyone be certain they won't do it again in the future? But what if following this principle threatens the very survival of the platform? Should emergency action be taken in extenuating circumstances?

Because of Ethereum's balance account model, a hard fork would be different than a Bitcoin hard fork. To change the Bitcoin blockchain, the entire network history would have to be rolled back to the point in contention. In Ethereum, no transactions are rolled back. Instead, the specific contentious account balance is modified. Some argued that this made a hard fork less intrusive, while others said the ability of developers to arbitrarily tweak the blockchain at will made it worse.

The soft fork was canceled on June 28, leaving them only until July 21 before the attacker could withdraw funds from the "dark DAO."

As with the soft fork, developers for the software clients wrote a version that would give users the option to hard-fork, which would start a new Ethereum chain where The DAO funds would be restored to their owners. But a decision had to be made: Should the hard-fork option be the default, giving miners the ability to opt out? Or should it be the other way around, asking miners to opt in?

"The Hard Fork is a delicate topic and the way we see it, no decision is the right one," Jeff Wilcke wrote in a July 15 blog post titled "To Fork or Not to Fork." "As this is not a decision that can be made by the foundation or any other single entity, we again turn towards the community to assess its wishes in order to provide the most appropriate protocol change."

A voting tool on a website created by developers outside of the foundation was used to gauge where the community stood. Votes were weighed by ether held in the participant's digital wallet. Voting lasted one day, and holders of just 5.5 percent of the total ether supply participated. About 80 percent voted for the opt-out option, meaning the hard fork would be the default. One quarter of the opt-out vote came from a single address. The vote wasn't representative of the entire community, and neither were the informal Twitter polls and Reddit threads leaning for a hard fork, but lacking a better alternative, Ethereum software client developers chose to take them as confirmation that the hard fork would be the default in the software upgrade.

On July 20, the day of the Ethereum hard fork, Vitalik sat in a cafe overlooking the running track at Cornell University in Ithaca, New York. It was the day the platform he had built would irrevocably change. Some warned it would be destroyed because of it. Vitalik hoped it would come out stronger. He was there for a blockchain bootcamp led by Emin, the professor who kept pointing out flaws in The DAO, and developers and researchers including Alex, aka Avsa, of the Robin Hood Group; Vlad Zamfir; Casey Detrio; and Martin Becze, who introduced the Ethereum Improvement Proposals. Some of them were now crowding around Vitalik's laptop as they waited for block number 1,920,000 to hit. That's when the hard fork would be implemented, unless most miners opted out.

The blockchain monitor showed the Ethereum chain chugging along, with a new block added every few seconds. It looked like a long and narrow Lego tower was being built from the side of the screen. But suddenly, the next block was placed to one side of the tower, instead of directly on top.

"It's happening!" Alex said as Vitalik laughed in amazement.

The new blocks continued to get attached to the new chain, and the old chain stopped growing. It meant most of the miners supported the new chain, where The DAO funds were safe. The hard fork had worked without a glitch.

Even those who had been torn about the decision to hard-fork, including Vitalik, were relieved.

Emin strongly believed there was no reason to let the ether thief get away with it. He didn't buy the whole "code is law" argument. "Code is not law," he said. "The law is the law. We are not going to tear down an entire financial system and build a new one only to be enslaved by the algorithms that we have come up with. Monetary systems have to serve the people and if they don't serve the people, people will find a way to replace them."

Trying to settle the issue, Emin said to Vitalik, "I'm going to ask you a question and I want you to answer truthfully. I'm not going to judge you. Just be completely honest. Are you serious about building this world computer? Or are you trying to appeal to illegal money flows, the drug dealers, the illegal gamblers, and whatnot?"

"No, that's not what this is about," Vitalik answered. "We want to build the next generation of applications."

"Immutability is paramount if you want to appeal to this illegal money crowd," Emin said. "If you don't, then it's completely reasonable to do a fork."

Vitalik believed in the value of immutability, but he also believed this was an exceptional situation, where Ethereum itself was at risk, and so extreme measures were needed. As the network grew, it would become increasingly unlikely that a vulnerability in one single project would compromise the entire chain, like The DAO had. As the community continued to expand, it would also be even harder to get rough consensus around a change of similar magnitude. He wanted to at least give Ethereum the chance to grow to that point.

Later on the day of the hard fork, the Cornell researchers brought a bottle of champagne into the classroom they were using to discuss consensus algorithms. They had changed the label to one that displayed something more appropriate for the past events: a fork. They clinked their glasses—or whatever sound plastic cups make—but as usual, the celebration didn't last long.

A few hours later, the old Ethereum chain everyone there thought was dead emerged from the grave. It suddenly continued to grow, side by side with the new chain.

"What's going on? Someone is actually losing money, mining an unprofitable chain? What for?" Alex said.

For the old chain to keep growing, someone had to be connected to the old network and spend energy to confirm blocks on a blockchain with a worthless cryptocurrency.

The old chain was like a parallel universe where pre-fork Ethereum was left intact. Everyone's accounts held the same amount of coins they had at the time, and funds were still stuck in the "dark DAO." But the cryptocurrency held there wasn't ether. It was this parallel chain's own cryptocurrency. Ether was only mined on the new chain.

Blockchains are supposed to work on economic incentives, but in this case, the old Ethereum chain, which was later called Ethereum Classic, emerged from people who ignored immediate economic incentives and instead spent time and money to make sure an immutable Ethereum chain survived. Maybe the chain's cryptocurrency would later gain in value and they would be compensated.

"We believe in decentralized, censorship-resistant, permissionless blockchains. We believe in the original vision of Ethereum as a world computer you can't shut down, running irreversible smart contracts," the Ethereum Classic website said. "We believe in a strong separation of concerns, where system forks are only possible in order to correct actual platform bugs, not to bail out failed contracts and special interests."

Others supporting the survival of the old chain were Bitcoiners who wanted to make a point: Ethereum is a silly little alt-coin with sycophantic followers bowing to their supreme leader, Vitalik Buterin.

As he tried to make sense of what was happening, Vitalik got a message from Gregory Maxwell, a prominent Bitcoin developer. He wanted to buy Vitalik's coins on the old chain. With his offer, he was signaling his support for Ethereum Classic. Basically, he was "taking off his glove and slapping Vitalik across the face," Emin said.

Soon anyone who wanted to buy Ethereum Classic or sell the coins they got for free (anyone who held ether got the equivalent number of Ethereum Classic) would be able to. Even the DAO thief would be able to cash out. On July 24, four days after the hard fork, cryptocurrency exchange Poloniex would be the first to list Ethereum Classic, with the ticker ETC (ether's ticker is ETH). Two other exchanges, Kraken and Bitfinex, followed suit a couple of days later. Coinbase added ETC the following week and with that, the cryptocurrency could be traded in most major exchanges, while it continued to gain hash rate (mining power). By the end of August, ETC was trading at a little over $1 and ETH was at around $13, with a market capitalization of about 10 percent of Ethereum's.

A few days later, Griff Green arrived in Zurich. With the DAO Wars alive in the Ethereum Classic chain, the Robin Hood group was now holding 7.2 million ETC, or about $15 million at the time, in their child DAO. They had to make sure they could keep the ETC in their possession safe and return it to their owners.

Not all the Robin Hood hackers were part of this new group—notably Alex Van de Sande, or Avsa, who had a big role in the original Robin Hood Group, was absent. This new team would later be called the White Hat Hackers, and they were freaking out. To clarify, the Robin Hood Group were "white-hat hackers," or nonmalicious hackers. This new group was, too, and they just came to be known as the White Hat Group. They had received threats of legal action from multiple DAO token holders who were demanding they hand over their money. That had been their goal from the start, but they wanted to do it without breaking any laws. They hired a Swiss firm called Bity SA, which had also advised Slock.it, to "protect, secure and later distribute the funds equitably under an independent Swiss legal structure," Jordi Baylina, one of the White Hat hackers, wrote in an August 11 post on Reddit.

Before the trip to Switzerland, the White Hat Group had to redo the hack on the Ethereum Classic chain while no one was paying attention. Whoever the attacker(s) was, they didn't try to block them from removing funds from the child DAO, like they had feared they would in the Ethereum chain. It could have been that the attacker was distracted by the fork, or maybe he was happy with his earnings so far. The speculation is that they probably profited more from short positions on ether, which plunged after the DAO hack, than from the actual attack.

The White Hat Group was able to recover the funds. They could have simply returned the equivalent in ETC to their owners, but after discussing the matter with Bity, they decided they should return the funds in ETH. To Griff, the investments had been made in ether, so they should be returned in ether. There was also some general animosity toward Ethereum Classic. Griff referred to Ethereum Classic as "deadETH." They just didn't believe ETC would have any value going forward. They also viewed the chain as one that was supported by so-called Bitcoin maximalists who wanted to see Ethereum fail; they didn't want to contribute to its success by distributing ETC to DAO investors. There were also technical concerns. The biggest one was the threat that transactions on the Ethereum Classic chain would be "replayed" in the Ethereum chain. This means that, because both chains are equal up until the time of the fork, there is a risk that transactions can get mixed up and coins can get lost.

But dumping 7.2 million of ETC onto the market overnight

wasn't easy. The White Hat Group and Bity were able to trade about 14 percent of the funds for ether and bitcoin before crypto exchanges Poloniex and Kraken froze Bity's accounts to review the transactions. Bity pleaded for the exchanges to release the funds, but days went by with no clear resolution and the money was now split between ETC, ETH, and BTC.

"These developments have put us in a position where safely providing the salvaged ETC as ETH to the DAO Token Holders is becoming much more costly and complicated than distributing directly in ETC," Bity said in an August 13 statement.

By early September the White Hat Group had been able to get the ETC back. At least they were able to make some additional money for the DAO investors. They had sold ETC in early August, when it was around $2, and bought it back in September, after it had fallen to around $1.2.

At around that time, on September 5, the original attacker had withdrawn his booty from the "dark DAO" on the Ethereum Classic chain. It was 3.6 million ETC, or about $5.5 million at the time. Giving Ethereum the middle finger once more, they then donated 1,000 ETC to the Ethereum Classic development fund.

As the DAO thief was running off with his ill-gotten bag of cryptocurrency, Griff Green was making his annual pilgrimage to Burning Man, the weeklong, crazy, happy, hippie gathering in the middle of the Nevada desert. Amid art installations and spontaneous musical performances, Griff, decked out in a red Santa hat and Santa-like jacket over a green T-shirt and shorts, took the stage to proselytize about decentralized autonomous organizations. He was still pitching his vision for DAOs as enthusiastically as ever.

He told the audience of about twenty sunburnt and dusty festival goers sitting on the floor and on pink sofas that he had just participated in a project that "allows people with money and a desire to change the world to connect directly to the people with the plan and the time to implement that plan to change the world. There's nothing between the two groups except computer code. No lawyers, no bankers, no accountants, everything is outsourced to the block-chain."

"Our project unfortunately was not a success, it ended up getting hacked," he said before taking questions. "We were eventually able to hack the hacker and give everyone their money back. Despite this hack, no one lost a single dime."

Not everyone in Ethereum was so optimistic. The DAO and hard fork had been a punch to many Ethereans' stomachs. They were left trying to regain balance and gasping for air.

Rune, the founder of the MakerDAO stablecoin platform, one of the most promising Ethereum projects, had decided to retreat to Thailand for the next few months.

The Maker team supported the hard fork when there weren't other better options left, and continued to build its project on the Ethereum blockchain, but Rune was conflicted. He was attracted to cryptocurrencies because of his deeply rooted libertarian beliefs. He loved the lack of centralized control that blockchains allowed and believed in a potential future where governance would be automated and dictated by computer code. To him, if humans messed up the DAO code, they should be left to assume the consequences. Also, the whole vote was a sham, he thought. Of course people with money in the DAO had a bigger incentive to vote. To him, Ethereum's hard fork felt like a slippery slope that could result in the end of blockchain.

"I got into Ethereum expecting that if you write some code, it would stay and work like it's supposed to," he said to a team member at MakerDAO. "But now it's like, 'oh no, we lost money, now we're going to change the rules on you.' That sounds exactly like, you know, any freaking political system, right? Where the rules apply differently based on how much money you have."

The realization came to Rune and many others that Ethereum wasn't all rainbows and unicorns. Before the fork, the community only recognized the benefits of blockchain technology, revering it as almost magical. But they were blind to the potential dangers and downsides.

Open source code could be prone to even more breaches than in centralized, private applications because it was open for everyone to see. That meant it could be reviewed and fixed by anyone, but bugs could also be exploited by malicious actors for their own advantage. And blockchains didn't fix everything. They made everything slower, and harder. It made sense to use them only in very specific situations. Smart contracts didn't make invincible applications. They're difficult to code, and the use cases weren't so obvious anymore. Suddenly, after the reality check of the hard fork, Ethereum didn't feel like a magical, happy revolution. More and more, blockchain technology just seemed like some boring tool for businesses.

"Like, fuck, where does this thing actually work? Like, where are the use cases? There doesn't seem to be any freaking use case right now!"

"What about our stablecoin?"

"That relies on other Ethereum projects becoming successful. I believe there are use cases for blockchain, but there's so much crap right now. They're just taking blockchain and applying it to something random they can easily hype. It's all bullshit," said Rune, who was in Thailand at the time. He decided he'd stay there for a while longer, take some time off from the project, and travel in Southeast Asia. "I'm out."

22

The Shanghai Attacks

A ringing phone awoke Martin Holst Swende in his Shanghai hotel room at 4 a.m. on a Monday. It was his first day as security lead for the Ethereum Foundation. Technically, keeping the system attack-free had been his responsibility for all of four hours, so the words he was about to hear sounded like a bad joke.

"The network is under attack."

Martin had flown over from Stockholm, his home city, the previous day. Like many in the Ethereum community, he was there for the third annual Devcon. Martin had quit his job working at Nasdaq's information security department to join Ethereum. He had been informally participating in the online chats with the core developers for the past three months.

"Very funny," Martin said, sitting up on the bed. "Messing with the new guy."

"Um, no. Not a drill. Get over here!"

"Shit."

He joined Peter Szilagyi, Jeff Wilcke's right-hand man leading the Go Ethereum implementation, and a handful of other developers including Nick Johnson, Piper Merriam, and Vitalik in what was intended to be the press room for the biggest Ethereum conference so far. Jeff had stayed home in Amsterdam because his son had just been born, but was online with them. About eight hundred people would flood the event space in a few hours. This was September 19, two months after the hard fork, and Ethereans had just started to recover from the trauma. Devcon2 was the big family reunion where they could hug it out and focus on the cool things they were building.

Except someone was dead set on not letting that happen. They wanted the first words on the Shanghai stage to be "Welcome to Devcon2, Ethereum was just destroyed." A message in German was embedded in the attacker's transactions. It said, "Go home."

■ ■ ■

The issue was in the Go Ethereum, or Geth, software implementation, not in the Ethereum protocol itself. Geth developers had tried to make the system faster by keeping some memory on caches, rather than on the hard drive, and that's where the attacker had found a vulnerability to exploit. He found a way to make the system keep reading data repeatedly until it ran out of memory space and crashed. All the nodes using the Geth client, or about 90 percent of the network at the time, went belly-up. Ethereum was able to keep running thanks to the Parity client, the software implementation led by Gavin Wood's company.

Martin, with thick-rimmed glasses and a low tone of voice that helps to punctuate words he delivers in a slow cadence, had been one of the developers trying to catch bugs in exchange for ether in Ethereum's proof of concept before the mainnet, or Frontier, launch in 2015.

Like Martin, most of the bug catchers had focused on consensus flaws, not on denial-of-service attacks. The thinking was that the need to pay for gas would make such attacks expensive and less likely to cause real damage.

As dawn came in Shanghai that Monday, they realized just how wrong they were. Sure, they were angry at the attackers, but the prevailing feeling as they scrambled to find a solution was that this was a test. It was a pain, but ultimately a good thing because someone was forcing them to iron out flaws they hadn't been able to catch. Ethereum was supposed to withstand exactly these sorts of attacks, and if it wasn't, they'd better fix it fast.

They came up with a solution in a couple of hours. It was rough, but it got the job done. They called the patch "From Shanghai With Love."

"Geth 1.4.12: From Shanghai With Love, hotfix for recent DoS issues. Please update!" Vitalik posted on Reddit at 5:37 a.m. in Shanghai, prompting an outpouring of praise from the community.

"Parity is rock solid, kept the network alive during a major crisis," one commenter wrote. "The Geth developers are nothing less than unreal. The time it took them to respond and deliver couldn't be matched even by the likes of google or apple."

"I think most non-devs don't get how extraordinary it is to have such a fast and committed response from devs," someone else said. "This is what sets Ethereum apart in my mind. Yes, it is open source, but it also has professional and committed visionaries behind it. Thanks for the love from Shanghai, we love you back."

Still, the attacker persisted and kept finding new ways of slowing down the network. Every few hours developers had to huddle in the hotel lobby and in side halls to figure out how to repel the most recent offensive, while talks about scalability, regulation, the Ethereum Virtual Machine, and smart contracts were presented on the conference's stage.

The attacks continued after Devcon ended and kept going for a full month. The developers had to be ready to drop whatever they were doing and jump on their computers at a moment's notice. One morning Martin was taking his daughter to school when a new attack started. He did what he could over the phone and rushed back home to his laptop. In most cases, the hacker was flooding the network with meaningless transactions and slowing everything down. It was a game of Whac-A-Mole where Ethereum developers rushed to patch an issue before the attacker found a new way around it. It wore everyone out. Martin, whose kids were six and eight at the time, thought about quitting if the job meant having to be on call every single minute of the day and night.

"I'll give this a couple of months, but this is not how I wanted my new job to be," he told his wife.

Jeff had been leading Geth, the most used software implementation for Ethereum, during the DAO Wars, the hard fork, and now this, right when his first son was born. The stress was taking its toll on him, too.

"Worst dad award goes to . . . (though in my defense; I was debugging #ethereum)," he tweeted, with a picture of him with one hand on his laptop keyboard while the other one was feeding his tiny baby with a bottle of milk.

The hacker had been hammering on the Geth implementation. Developers called one of the fixes to those attacks "Come at me bro." The attacker really did come at them and started exploiting flaws in Ethereum itself. It cost the hacker very little to create empty accounts, so they created thousands of them and bloated the system. That could only be fixed with another hard fork.

This time the decision wasn't contentious—it had to be done. The fork to reset some of the gas costs, which they called "Tangerine Whistle," was implemented on October 18. This made the types of attacks the network was suffering prohibitively expensive. With that, the so-called Shanghai attacks finally stopped. Another fork, called "Spurious Dragon," was implemented a month later to get rid of all the useless transactions the attacker had dumped on the network.

If the goal was to profit from shorting ether, it's unlikely it was worth it. Martin estimates it cost about 800 ether, or $9,600 at the time, and full-time work to launch between ten and fifteen different types of attacks. The digital currency slumped just 10 cents to $12.59, or less than 1 percent, from when then attacks started in Shanghai until the first fork one month later. Peter's theory is that the persistence in the attacks, even as they likely weren't yielding much profit, signals the hacker's main goal was to destroy Ethereum.

By the end of 2016, Ethereum had withstood two major attacks resulting in three hard forks. The whole experience was an object lesson in blockchain governance. Under the current governance, if a decision on the protocol was being made that the whole of the community doesn't agree with, that group could split and continue running its own network under their own rules. Miners and the market would determine the strength and value of each chain. While most Ethereans agreed to stop The DAO attacker and give the money back to investors, some didn't. They supported Ethereum Classic. In cases where the decisions are straightforward, like after the Shanghai attacks, Ethereum was able to respond quickly and upgrade the network without that having to result in new chains being born.

The attacks also proved that, like Ethereum critics pointed out in the early days, having a Turing-complete computer and the ability to run smart contracts increases flexibility but compromises on security. Adding complexity makes the network more vulnerable to attackers wanting to exploit any flaws in the code.

More broadly, Ethereans learned that they can program computers, but they can't program humans, whose greed, ambition, and ingenuity can be strong enough to find their way around those programs. Code can be made to run in a specific way, but that will always clash with humans, who don't necessarily act predictably. Ethereum was growing up. Developers learned the world can't be crammed into smart contracts, and that smart contracts will only be as smart as the people who wrote them—and those who tried to break them for nefarious or hubristic reasons.

But Ethereum had repelled those attacks, which led many to conclude that it had become stronger than ever. The Ethereum blockchain had been tested repeatedly. Developers behind it were up for the challenge and came out victorious. Not only that, but people were actually building on top of the platform. By the end of 2016,

Ethereum dapps had more than doubled from the previous year to about 250. Those dapps were far from mainstream, though, and only had a few users. Still, the most ambitious blockchain since Bitcoin was starting to look something like the world computer for decentralized applications Vitalik and his fellow believers had envisioned.

PART V

Near-Landing

23

The Burning Wick

The hints that something was stirring in this crossroad of tech and finance were still subtle in late 2016. The number of startups selling their own cryptocurrency for fundraising tripled in November from October, but only to a grand total of nine projects, which raised about $20 million. That's a rounding error in the big leagues. In December, there were nine token sales again, but they raised even less. The biggest indication was in the Bitcoin price chart. The cryptocurrency had a big run-up to near $790 in June and dropped back below $600 in the following month. But it had been steadily climbing ever since and crossed $900 in November. Still, the moves weren't big enough to draw too much attention, and such volatility in bitcoin wasn't news. Ether was still languishing below $10.

Taylor Monahan, a Los Angeles–based film producer turned web developer, was one of the few to realize something was going on. She had bought some ether at the presale, and when Ethereum launched about a year later she went to move the tokens into a secure wallet. The whole process required more than a dozen steps, including opening her computer's coding terminal and typing in a bunch of commands. It wasn't exactly user friendly.

She and her friend Kosala Hemachandra decided to build a digital wallet for the less technically inclined called MyEtherWallet (MEW). It started out as a side project for them and their friends to use; through most of 2015 it had seen no activity. In early 2016 someone on Reddit asked whether the code for the wallet was being maintained, and then every so often others would ask for specific features. They were gradually spending more time on it but still treated it like a side hobby, which didn't make any money.

The real bump-up in users came at the time of The DAO in May 2016, when Taylor was again thinking about the regular, nonprogrammer user. When the white-hat hackers were working on getting people's money back, she kept asking, "Okay, but how are people *actually* going to get their money back?" She learned the developers had designed a smart contract that would let people withdraw their money. And again, she was reading through endless Wiki pages filled with impenetrable instructions, so she decided to make an interface for the smart contract. It was a single button that DAO investors could press to get their money. After that, she started seeing tangible adoption on MyEtherWallet for the first time.

As the second half of 2016 progressed, the number of users on the application gradually increased. They were using the wallet to participate in the growing number of token sales—what came to be known as an Initial Coin Offering, or an ICO. The similarity with the phrase "Initial Public Offering," where relatively established businesses sell shares of a company to investors and list them on stock exchanges, signaled that these ICOs weren't scrappy token sales for a few thousand dollars, maybe a few million if they were lucky, to bootstrap a blockchain startup like before. These ICOs were starting to raise substantial amounts. The DAO proved the appetite was there and that even in the most horrible circumstances nobody lost their money—or went to jail. The Shanghai denial-of-service attacks showed Ethereum was strong enough to survive a month of vicious hackers trying to break the network. So crypto entrepreneurs became bolder.

The whole thing was done over the internet. Startups wrote a white paper, including the technical specification of their project and road map, and put it on a website. Most of the time, that was all these projects had, a website and a white paper. But that was the point of this fundraising mechanism. It opened a new path for early stage, open sourced, decentralized protocols that would usually be shunned by traditional investors to get the necessary funding to build out their projects. They publicized the sale all over Reddit and Twitter, tried to get as much press coverage as possible, and set a date and terms for the sale. They were selling their own digital coins, also known as tokens, in exchange for bitcoin and ether. Because Ethereum's Turing-complete network and ERC20 token standard made building applications and issuing tokens easy, most ICOs were done on Ethereum.

ICOs followed the Ethereum model, where ether was touted as a "utility token," the oil used to run the Ethereum machine, not as an investment contract. These tokens were supposed to be used on the projects' platforms once (and if) they went live, and they could also be traded in the secondary market. That's all token holders could do with them. Unlike shares, tokens don't give buyers any rights over the project that issued them. Much like the name "token" suggests, they're like chips used in an arcade.

Also unlike shares, none of these tokens were registered with regulators. They didn't have to, they argued, because they were utility tokens. At the most, they would pay a law firm to get an opinion letter (like Ethereum's) that said the tokens they were selling were likely not securities.

When the date came, investors—though most projects shied away from calling them that—from all over the world could send over their bitcoin and ether to the specified digital wallets controlled by the ICO-ing startups and get tokens in return. Maybe some people genuinely wanted to buy these coins to use them in the startups' platforms, but they also saw how bitcoin was now worth several hundreds of dollars after once trading under $1 and how ether jumped over $10 when it was listed on exchanges after it was sold at 30 cents in its presale. So when most people bought these little-known tokens they were really trying to strike it rich with the next big thing. Sometimes all they needed was an email address. No minimum assets were required, no investor accreditation, and no proof that funds were squeaky clean.

Was any of this legal? From the first-ever ICO in 2014 with Mastercoin, the crypto community knew there was a risk it might not be. But then Ethereum came up with the utility token definition and first opinion letter, and more projects started doing token sales. So far, while no regulators had come out and said, "ICOs are legal," nobody had said they were illegal, either. And that was good enough for them.

Before the Shanghai attacks, most ICOs were raising less than $1 million. After the attacks—and even while they were happening— they consistently raised more than $1 million. Sales were usually uncapped and lasted a few days. But then First Blood, an online gaming company selling tokens to be used as rewards within its games, capped its September 26 ICO at $5.5 million. The sale was over in five minutes. A company that was less than a year old was able to raise more than $1 million per minute. Ethereum's crowdsale had taken about two months; the sale for Joey Krug's prediction market Augur took about a month; DigixDAO, the project that wanted to tie tokens to gold bars, had its sale in less than a day; and First Blood's took five minutes. They had all raised at least $5 million.

During the second week of November, Taylor was ready to spend some extra time working on MyEtherWallet from her LA home. She knew activity would increase because Golem, a distributed computing protocol, was doing its ICO. It was a well-known project and team, and its sale was due to attract tons of interest.

MyEtherWallet had slowed to a crawl before, once during the DAO crowdsale and once again during the Shanghai attacks. Wanting to prevent this from happening during the Golem ICO, Taylor and Kosala increased the size of their servers and raised the default gas price users paid per transaction to make sure they went through, among other fixes. Taylor went to sleep near 5 a.m. after making sure everything was in place on November 11, the day of the sale.

At 6:30 a.m. her husband, Kevin, who is a music producer but had started to help with MEW, woke her up. Something was wrong with the website. He couldn't get a transaction to send—whenever he clicked the "send" button, nothing happened. When the token sale started half an hour later, the servers didn't crash, but it was taking forever to process requests. The reason was simple: traders had sent 708,490 requests between 7 a.m. and 8 a.m. That's about 200 requests per second from 1,264 unique visitors, but since the crowdsale lasted less than thirty minutes, it's likely most of the requests were crammed in that first half hour. That was way too much for their $100 servers to handle.

People were going crazy trying to send ether to the Golem sale address. In the end it took about 700 transactions to reach the $8.6 million cap, so fewer than 700 people got in. Those who were left out were not happy and took out their rage on Taylor. Since they couldn't send their ether, they sent her increasingly aggressive and misogynistic messages instead.

Stupid MEW, fked the goloem Crowdsale.

You owe me bigtime for fucking up my investment. what fucking wrong with you. dont you know how to code you fucking failure piece of shit.

I'LL RAM MY PIPE SO FAR DOWN YOUR THROAT YOULL WISH YOU HAD NEVER BUILT YOUR PIECE OF SHIT SITE. FUCKING MAKEUP WONT HIDE THIS SHIT WHOER.

Taylor had a knot in her stomach as she went through the messages. She was doing this as a hobby! For free! In little over a year since starting MEW, they had just made $10,000 in ether and Bitcoin donations. She had woken up at 6 a.m. after less than two hours of sleep to make sure a bunch of strangers could fill their bags with crypto. And this is what she gets in return? But she couldn't dwell on that for too long. She collapsed on her bed, exhausted. After six hours of sleep and three slices of pizza, she gathered the courage to check Twitter and Reddit, and was surprised to see the angry mob was (mostly) gone. Ethereans were coming to her aid, and supportive comments were now drowning out the offensive ones. Crypto was proving to be a magnet for the best and worst people.

Before the Golem sale, MEW had supported six ICOs without a glitch. But this time, the hype was just too much. The fear of missing out, or FOMO, had started to spread and like those messages show, it had the ability to obliterate common sense. That was only a taste of what was about to go down in 2017.

24

Accidentally Ether Rich

On January 1, 2017, Bitcoin crossed $1,000 for the first time since December 2013. It was as if the cryptocurrency were announcing: "This will be the year for crypto." It's unclear what exactly was causing the rally. Some of it was actual use. Bitcoin trading volume was picking up in emerging nations with weakening local currencies. One example was Venezuela, where protesters had taken to the streets once more after a push to remove President Nicolas Maduro from power had been squashed in court. Or India, where the rupee was spiraling after a move to stem corruption by pulling large cash notes from circulation backfired. Volume also picked up in Egypt and Nigeria, which devalued their currencies as their economies slumped.

More broadly, emerging nations were struggling after US Federal Reserve chair Janet Yellen raised interest rates at the end of 2016 and signaled more hikes would come in 2017, sending the US dollar index to the highest since 2003. Donald Trump had just been elected president on a platform that promised to close off borders from trade and immigration, which didn't favor developing markets, either. Earlier that year the United Kingdom voted to exit the European Union, another sign that the world was becoming more nationalistic. In a context where walls were coming up and borders were sealing, the appeal for global, digital currencies increased. Media attention blossomed, prompting more trading, not from people who

wanted protection from devaluing currencies or a hedge against xe-
nophobic governments, but from speculators who thought Bitcoin
and most any other digital coin would go higher.

Richard Burton hadn't noticed any of this. Instead, he was starting 2017 in the best way he could imagine, his snowboard pressing
into virgin snow and his arms holding on to a kite pulling him forward and sometimes over the ground. He had gone home to Britain
for the holidays, then spent some time in the French backcountry
slopes kiteboarding, and now he was traversing the Norwegian tundra.

He had just started a fintech company with two cofounders, which
was able to sustain his addiction to kitesurfing, but it had been a
rocky journey for him to get there. After getting a one-year accounting degree, he proceeded to kitesurf wherever the waves called, from
Indonesia to South Africa, with the money he made selling hoodies
online. At twenty-five, one of his friends sat him down for a serious
talk: "Ric, you're a surf bum. You can do better." Richard knew he
was right and applied for a job at Stripe, a payments startup he had
read about. Today Stripe is valued at over $20 billion and has more
than 1,500 employees, but back then, in 2012, it was a two-year-old
company with a thirty-person team.

Richard got the job and knew he had boarded a rocket ship, but
he had trouble following directions and was fired after three months.
He was depressed for a few weeks but bounced back and started a
recruiting company with a friend he met in the dingy hacker house
they shared with fifteen other men in San Francisco. Again, that was
short-lived, and his friend pushed him out of the company. He was so
angry he got into running just to blow off the negativity that was eating him up. On one of those runs, he heard Vitalik. Not like a divine
voice coming down from the sky, but on a podcast.

Richard didn't grasp all of what Vitalik was saying, but it sounded
meaningfully different from any other crypto project he had heard
about before. He saw that Gavin Wood happened to be in town to
give a talk that same week and went to check it out. He was blown
away and asked to contribute. He worked for around three months in

2014 doing interface design and building mock-ups for a presentation Gavin would make on Ethereum's potential. He parted ways when he couldn't make his next credit card payment. He never thought anybody owed him anything, but when Ethereum launched, he was surprised to get a slice of the contributors' share, which added to the ether he bought at the crowdsale. After doing some freelance web design for a while, he had cashed out some of his ether to cofound a fintech called Balance, but he still had a big chunk left when he left for his snowbound vacation.

As he was racing down the slopes, the price of ether had started to go in the opposite direction. About 95 percent of his assets were in the digital currency. That meant every small tick up in the price had a huge impact on him. At some point Richard saw his entire holdings doubled. Then tripled. Ether, which he got at around 30 cents, was trading at under $10 when he started the trip. By the time he got back in April, the price had increased more than five times. A new life had opened up to him. He got the first concrete taste of it one night when the receptionist at the thirty-dollar hostel he was staying at in a Norwegian ski town told him they didn't have more availability on the following days. He thought he'd have to go back to Oslo, but then remembered his Ethereum wallet. Next thing he knew, he was checking in at the five-star hotel down the street. He didn't care—he was now a millionaire.

Meanwhile, in Brooklyn, Joe Lubin's company ConsenSys was still evangelizing and had been doing so through all the drama of the past year—the DAO, the Shanghai attacks, and the growing number of ICOs. The company had been able to recruit more companies to the Ethereum cause. For Andrew Keys, who was leading the effort, the first big get was Microsoft. Like many others, it started with a cold email, in this case to Marley Gray, the director of tech strategy for financial services at Microsoft's Times Square–based technology center. Microsoft had already started accepting bitcoin in its Xbox store so a pitch for a more flexible blockchain wasn't such a foreign concept. That was back in 2015. The partnership meant that clients of Microsoft's cloud-based business service Azure would have access to an enterprise version of Ethereum maintained by ConsenSys. After Microsoft signed on, it became easier for ConsenSys to partner with big corporations.

The goal was that they'd start using Ethereum to build from a faster securities settlement system to a more streamlined back office. The ConsenSys team worked with firms like PwC, which would help connect the company with clients who were open to exploring blockchain technology.

By the end of February 2017 they were ready to announce their progress and gathered all the partnerships they had secured under one roof for what they called the Enterprise Ethereum Alliance. Some of the world's largest, most blue-chip companies joined, including JPMorgan, CME Group, BNY Mellon, Credit Suisse, Banco Santander, BBVA, ING, UBS, BP, Intel, and Microsoft. Though the partnership meant these giants would start testing Ethereum, it wasn't binding and there weren't many concrete goals or actual results. Still, the fact that they agreed to have their names associated with what had been, just a couple of years earlier, a glitchy beta network in an untested technology was a big step. It gave Ethereum a patina of credibility and big, clunky companies the ability to tell shareholders they were innovating in the new, shiny tech buzzword, "blockchain."

The market noticed. At the start of March 2017, ether crossed $20 for the first time from around $11 the previous month. It continued to double every few weeks, surpassing $40 in mid-March and shooting up to $80 at the end of April.

Texture, who was living in Las Vegas at the time, moved to an apartment in Oakland, California, when the price was around $11. As long as the price didn't go below that, he could at least afford to live in California for a year. It wasn't until the Ethereum Enterprise Alliance was announced that he started to believe Ethereum could really succeed. For him, the risk that Ethereum might be regulated out of existence was an ongoing concern, so having some backing from big companies at least gave the project some clout. If the government started coming down on crypto, he surmised, these Fortune 500 companies would enlist their lobbyists to keep regulators at bay.

It wasn't all good news for digital assets. China cracked down on crypto exchanges in January and February, demanding that online trading platforms enforce know-your-customer and anti-money-laundering procedures. This prompted some of the biggest exchanges, like OKCoin and Huobi, to suspend withdrawals. Crypto prices plunged for a couple of days but recovered as analysts were quick to point out that the global nature of crypto means volume will just move elsewhere, and the Chinese could always trade in peer-to-peer platforms, which were harder to regulate. Or, they would say, regulation is a good thing! It means the industry is growing up.

Then in March Bitcoin reached above $1,200 and beat the price of an ounce of gold, prompting a new flurry of headlines saying things like "Bitcoin is more valuable than gold!" The rally was fueled in part on speculation that the long-awaited Bitcoin ETF would be approved. The Winklevoss twins, the same who were locked in a legal fight with Mark Zuckerberg over ownership of Facebook, were determined to become the first to launch a Bitcoin-backed exchange-traded fund. They were deep in the crypto game after backing Charlie Shrem's BitInstant exchange and buying a big chunk of the bitcoins seized by the FBI when they shut down fraudulent Mt. Gox. They had been waiting for their ETF's approval since 2013, when they made their first filing to the SEC.

Bitcoin investors had also been waiting. ETFs are structured like baskets of securities such as stocks, bonds, or commodities, which can be traded over exchanges just like single stocks. ETFs opened up mutual-fund-like instruments to smaller, individual investors. The thinking was that a Bitcoin ETF would open the floodgates for these so-called retail investors, and also for large financial institutions, into the world of crypto and drive the bitcoin price higher.

Bitcoin jumped on the morning of March 10, when the SEC was due to give its verdict, to a new record of almost $1,340. But when the news came that afternoon, the digital currency plunged back below $1,000. The SEC had rejected the proposal because of "concerns about the potential for fraudulent or manipulative acts and practices" in bitcoin trading. The SEC was right to worry about market manipulation. Most crypto trading was (and still is) done in lightly regulated exchanges where practices to inflate volume and trick other traders, such as wash trading and spoofing, are common.

But once again, bitcoin recovered in just a couple of days. There were more Bitcoin ETFs in the pipeline, and it was only a matter of time before the SEC approved at least one of them, or so the thinking was at the time. The wait for the ETF approval fueled the theme that "institutional money is coming" to crypto, which became a constant in 2017.

By the end of May the entire crypto market had grown more than four times, to $80 billion. The fledgling asset class added over $60 billion in just five months. Many of the big names in crypto gathered at the Marriott Marquis in Times Square, New York, for the third-annual Consensus, a conference organized by CoinDesk, one of the longest-standing trade publications covering the burgeoning industry. With over 100 speakers and more than 2,700 attendees, half of which CoinDesk advertised were "C-level," it was the crypto Super Bowl.

The price of bitcoin rallied in anticipation of the event, breaking its previous 2013 record and crossing $2,000. There's something about nice, round numbers that makes journalists and analysts really pay attention and for Bitcoin, the big 2K really did it. Ethereum was making its own round-number headlines, blowing past $100 and $200. Mainstream financial media had dipped their toes into crypto stories before but the price surge, coupled with the recent splatter of blockchain announcements, gave them a reason to really dive in. *Fortune* wrote in a May 21 story, "The digital currency bitcoin is on another remarkable run, soaring nearly 65% in the last month, and smashing the symbolic $2,000 mark for the first time ever this week. Bitcoin has gone on tears in the past, but never quite like this."

I started writing more frequently about crypto for Bloomberg News, too. Readers just couldn't get enough. Almost anything with "Bitcoin" on the headline shot up to the most-read stories of the day in the Bloomberg Terminal and got posted on the front page of Bloomberg.com. The terminal had an index for the Bitcoin price, which it compiles with data from a few of the most regulatory-compliant exchanges, and users were begging for similar data for other coins. There's a band of index prices that continuously scrolls at the bottom of Bloomberg TV, and one day, in 2017, the BTC price started appearing there, too.

On stage at the Consensus conference, IBM announced that it had signed agreements to help Maersk and Walmart leverage block-chain technology to save "tens of billions" of dollars and disrupt the shipping and retail industries. R3, a startup creating a finance-focused blockchain and consortium, announced it had raised $107 million from backers including Bank of America Merrill Lynch, HSBC, and Wells Fargo. Of course, ICOs were announced. One of the most buzzed-about ones was Civic by Vinny Lingham, entrepreneur and *Shark Tank* star in South Africa. He was planning to raise as much as $33 million in an ICO for a blockchain-powered identity system.

The Enterprise Ethereum Alliance said it was almost tripling in size to eighty-six members, just one month after launching with thirty. Samsung, Merck, and Toyota were among the new companies that joined. Almost every industry was represented by its corresponding major company in the EEA. Even the DTCC, which stores and clears US securities, or one of the companies most ripe for block-chain disruption, had joined.

What got the most coverage in mainstream media was Fidelity CEO Abigail Johnson's keynote. She was announcing that Fidelity Investments was rolling out an integration with cryptocurrency exchange Coinbase, but what made the most impact was her enthusiastic endorsement of blockchain technology. The *Wall Street Journal* wrote an article on the keynote titled, "Bitcoin's Unlikely Evangelist: Fidelity CEO Abigail Johnson."

"Some of you might be wondering: Why am I here today?" the *Wall Street Journal* quoted her saying. "I'm here because I love this stuff."

Almost a decade after Satoshi Nakamoto sent his white paper to the cypherpunks' mailing list, blockchain technology and cryptocurrencies were finally being taken seriously by big corporations. Whereas before blockchain events were just Bitcoin events, with maybe a handful of big-name sponsors but mostly techies and startups struggling to fill out a conference space, in 2017 all the biggest players in every industry flooded into standing-room-only panels and keynotes. Most of those original techies turned their noses up at the Consensus crowd. They were mostly white, American men wearing suits, khaki pants or jeans, and blazers, handing out their business cards, trying to get the "inside scoop" of what ICO they should buy, or whether it was too late to snap up some bitcoin. But the attention helped drive BTC to $3,000 and ETH to $400 in June, just two weeks after their previous round numbers of $2,000 and $300.

As bitcoin and ether climbed, crypto investors had more money to spend on other digital assets. It wasn't exactly hard-earned money, which incentivized diving into untested projects and teams. Many felt like they had won the lottery, so they continued gambling. This general sense of euphoria is what helped seventy startups raise $800 million in ICOs by the end June. That was almost three times what had been raised in token sales ever. It was also about twice what blockchain companies raised in traditional venture capital funding. For the first time, startups were raising more money by selling digital tokens than by selling equity in their companies. And the great majority was issuing these tokens on Ethereum.

25

The New IPO

By mid-2017, Taylor was barely treading water with MyEther-Wallet. From January to the end of June, the digital wallet was still in scrappy startup mode, run by Taylor and a team of about five people in what felt like constant chaos. The team had established shifts to watch over MEW twenty-four hours a day, every day, which put them on opposite schedules. Taylor often worked through the night, answering the hundreds of support tickets that were coming in per day, making sure everything was online, and staving off attackers. They didn't store users' funds, but hackers were always trying to take people's money, from trying to break into their servers to creating phishing sites that would trick people into sending over their crypto or keys. At one point there were about one hundred fake MEW websites; she and her team emailed domain and hosting services, trying to get them taken down one by one. She went to bed at 10 a.m., at which point her team took over and made sure nothing went wrong. They'd wake Taylor up if something exploded.

At first, there was about one ICO per week, then it was one every couple of days, and then there could be up to two in the same day. Every other week an ICO seemed to completely dwarf the previous mammoth one. The offerings transitioned from being held to fund projects intended to actually build and deliver decentralized platforms into offerings intended merely to capitalize on the hype.

On May 5 a project called TokenCard raised almost $13 million in ether in thirty minutes to create a Visa debit card powered by smart contacts so that users would be able to pay with crypto wherever Visa was accepted. Like TokenCard, most ICOs launching around that time seemed incredibly ambitious. There was, for instance, SingularDTV, which wanted to be the "decentralized Netflix"; Iconomi, which wanted to be the "Uber for fund management"; and Chronobank, which aimed at "disrupting the HR/recruitment/ finance industries [just like] Upwork represented an evolution in freelancing."

Projects raising millions in minutes had become commonplace, but then came one startup that amped it up to millions in *seconds*. Brave, a web browser founded by Mozilla cofounder and JavaScript creator Brendan Eich, sold $35 million worth of its BAT tokes in thirty seconds on May 31. Traders were going to extremes to try to get in the sale. One investor paid over $6,000 in Ethereum gas fees to make sure their transaction went through. Dominic Steil was one of the crypto enthusiasts eager to get in. He started mining and buying bitcoin in 2013 and his gains as crypto soared allowed him to take time off from his new enterprise blockchain venture, Dapps, and travel with his girlfriend. At the time of the Brave ICO he was in Cinque Terre, on the Italian coast. He had planned his day around the sale and was ready to jump in a cafe when it was about to start. He did just that, but by the time he opened his laptop, the ICO was over. He couldn't believe it. In the end, only 130 people got in.

Galia Benartzi was getting ready to organize the biggest ICO yet. Galia and her brother Guy grew up in Silicon Valley, listening to their father, an engineer who immigrated from Israel, talk about tech and business. After college, they wanted to try their own hand at running a company, and between 2005 and 2011 they, together with other cofounders, built two startups geared toward smartphone games, Mytopia and Particle Code, and sold them both. After that, Galia worked as an entrepreneur in residence at Trinity Ventures, one of the oldest VC firms in Sand Hill Road, and became a venture partner at Peter Thiel's Founders Fund. In 2012 Galia moved to Tel Aviv to be a bridge for Founders Fund and the technology that was coming out of Israel. There she discovered Bitcoin and how developers were starting to think about building different layers and applications on top of it. That journey led her to the works of Bernard Lietaer, an economist who championed alternative currencies before Bitcoin was even invented and advocated for the idea that communities can benefit from creating their own parallel, local currency.

Inspired by cryptocurrencies and Lietaer's ideas, the founding team for her previous ventures, along with internet entrepreneur Eyal Hertzog, came back together to create AppCoin, which Founders Fund and others invested in. They made a (non-blockchain-based) software that would allow anyone to easily make a currency for their community and use it in a marketplace. They ran a pilot with a group of Tel Aviv mothers, and in a year, about twenty thousand users had exchanged approximately $24 million worth of "hearts," the community's virtual currency. The idea is that local currencies can facilitate the exchange of goods and services in a community, without the need for its members to use extra cash, creating abundance and resources that wouldn't have been otherwise available using the traditional currency alone.

But they realized that the group of mothers also operate within other communities, including the national economy. For community coins to succeed, they would have to be exchanged not in one small circle, but wherever users are interacting and have the need to exchange value. The problem is that "hearts" had no liquidity, meaning there weren't enough people buying and selling them, outside of the small circle of mothers, and so their fledgling economy was isolated, as if in a new country that cannot import or export anything from the rest of the world. By the time they got to this conclusion it was 2015 and they would need to shut down the business. In 2016 they saw there was an up-and-coming smart-contract platform called Ethereum, which could allow them to *program* liquidity into alternative currencies, even if there was not a lot of trading volume for them. They saw people were already starting to create their own alternative currencies, so they would create a platform that would give liquidity to any coin, no matter how small. They called this new project Bancor.

Any currency that joins the Bancor network would have to hold a small balance of a reserve currency in its smart contract, and that reserve currency would be used to trade between any other token. There was a lot of debate among the team about whether they should make the reserve currency be ether, or if they should create a specific token with that purpose. They decided to create a platform-specific token called BNT so that, over time, many blockchains, not just Ethereum, could use the Bancor network. Whether it was ether or BNT, they needed a lot of it, and they didn't have it. After analyzing the landscape of options, they decided to do a crowdsale.

But they wanted to improve on previous crowdsales to make it possible for anyone to be able to buy BNT tokens, not just those who were the fastest or were willing to pay the highest gas price. They decided to uncap the sale for the first hour, so that anyone would be able to get BNT tokens in that time. But there would be a hidden maximum amount of ether they would take. If they surpassed it during that hour, the sale would end, and the surplus would be put into a smart contract for BNT holders to take back their ether. If the cap wasn't reached, the sale would continue until it was. They also added a cap on gas fees investors could pay, to avoid traders paying thousands of dollars to skip the line.

The weeks leading up to the token sale were some of the team's most intense. Many were sleeping in the Tel Aviv office and working twenty-hour days as the twelve-person team built the tech, got the regulation in order (they followed the Ethereum model with a Zug-based foundation), communicated their plans and progress, and handled growing interest from people who wanted to work and invest in the project, including from billionaire venture capitalist Tim Draper, who often goes on TV wearing a Bitcoin B-emblazoned tie and ended up buying BNT tokens. Despite interest and even with no clear guidelines from US regulators, the sale was closed to US investors as the team wanted to make sure they were legally compliant.

The day of the sale was not very different from the days leading up to it. Many in the team had slept in the office. They had a couch and a mattress, and the office manager got everyone toothbrushes. Galia and the other founders rallied everyone together as they started settling in at their desks that morning and gave a little pep talk. This sale would help them achieve what they had been working for in the past year—a decentralized automated protocol for the interoperability of all digital assets. They had prepared for this, and they were ready, the founders said.

But Galia couldn't ignore how her stomach was tightening up. All these weeks she had felt like she was hacking through a forest with a machete, with no idea what she would find. There were no blueprints or road maps. So many moving pieces had to line up just exactly right. The smart contract had to accept the ether and give out tokens; the website had to display to the world the real-time information of what was happening; the wallets, office, and all accounts on all channels had to stay secure; all messages needed to be answered accurately and in real time; the power had to stay on; and the Ethereum network had to keep chugging along. There was a flood of interest and money flying into ICOs, and the people at the center of them were just winging it the best they could.

The Bancor team crowded around the couple of tech leads when they pressed the button to launch the sale, and instantly, ether started flowing in. "Please work, please work, please work," Galia said to herself.

And then, almost immediately, everything stopped.

"Guys, transactions aren't going through," someone said, watching on their laptop as buy orders for BNT were coming in and piling up.

"Shit, I think somebody's attacking our website," another team member said.

"Traffic is spiking, it must be a DoS attack," a developer said.

It took some time to realize that, while their website was in fact being attacked, what was really blocking transactions was that their ICO had congested the Ethereum network. There was a backlog of several thousand orders waiting to be confirmed. It meant that the hour they had set as the time to let anyone in the sale was expiring, but almost none of the people who made buy orders had gotten their BNT. They only had a few minutes to decide what to do.

"We could wait until all the orders that came in during the first hour are cleared and then shut down the sale," Galia said.

"But what happens with everyone who put orders in after the hour, while we were waiting for the other transactions to clear, do we just scrap those?"

They had their lawyers in Switzerland on the phone.

"Is extending the sale to deal with this technical hurdle the right thing to do? We promised an hour of accessibility and instead people got an hour of a broken Ethereum. Or would extending the time be different from what we promised?" Galia asked.

Swiss lawyers agreed that what was important was the spirit of the language in the Token Generation contract, as it didn't anticipate what to do in the event that only a small fraction of transactions would pass in the first hour due to external circumstances.

Meanwhile, Galia's phone kept lighting up with messages from everyone in her contact list—investors, longtime mentors, family members, and college friends, all asking how to buy BNT tokens. And the clock on the wall ticked on and on.

They decided to extend the sale to allow all the pending transactions to go through, which would take two and a half hours. They would also have to absorb accusations that they were breaking the terms because they were greedy and wanted more money. When they shut down the ICO, Galia saw there was still about $400 million worth of ether pending. A total of just under 400,000 ether, or about $153 million, came in from eleven thousand buyers. Of that, 80,000 ether went toward an initial reserve pool to provide liquidity for the BNT token in the Bancor network, which was up and running that week, and 120,000 ether went to the buyback contract for participants.

That afternoon, when ether was locked up in their wallet, BNT had gone to everyone who participated, and the Ethereum network was running normally again, the founders gathered their team to thank everyone for their hard work and got back to their desks immediately. Everyone was still reeling from the many things that had gone wrong and not in the best mood to celebrate.

Less than two weeks later, another hyped-up ICO was coming. It was the Status sale. The startup wanted to make a peer-to-peer encrypted messaging service for the Ethereum network where users would be able to chat and send ETH, just as users are able to make payments and transfers on WeChat. Taylor had gone through hell again with Bancor and wanted to make sure nothing broke this time. Once again, she had been up late the night before the June 20 sale, which started at 7 a.m. in Los Angeles. She got a couple of hours of sleep, woke up right before the sale started, and configured MEW so that messages would show up for users to get confirmation they were about to participate in the Status ICO when they sent funds to the correct address, and warning them when they were about to send ether to known scam addresses that pretended to be ICO wallets.

She went back to bed and after lying there unable to sleep, she got in the shower, thinking about a recent Skype conversation. She and other Ethereans had been talking about how huge Status was likely to be. It could even raise $200 million, she said. Vitalik, who was part of the chat group but rarely participated, chimed in this time and said if the market knows the Status sale is overhyped, maybe it would self-correct and fewer people will be willing to participate. Vitalik had never anticipated that decentralized fundraising would take off on Ethereum the way it was, and while encouraged to see increased use, he was also looking at all this mindless speculation with increasing concern. Taylor hoped he was right, though she knew the crypto market was far less rational than Vitalik.

When she got out of the shower, her husband was waiting for her.

"Griff and Jordi want to talk to you," he said.

"Oh no," Taylor said, realizing that no, it wouldn't be fine. "That can't be good."

Griff was the former Slock.it community manager. He and Jordi had worked together in the White Hat Group and they continued working on various blockchain projects together.

Jordi had helped Status on their ICO with the goal to learn from past sales and design a better system, where tokens would be more widely distributed, instead of having them go to a handful of whales in the first few minutes. To make sure SNT tokens were distributed among as many people as possible, the sale was also planned in stages, with a limit to how much ether each address could send to the sale contract in each stage, so that it was harder for one investor to swoop in and buy most of the tokens. The overall amount to be raised was also capped at 300,000 ETH.

The problem was that traders trying to buy large amounts got around the investment ceiling by sending orders in many smaller separate transactions, clogging up the Ethereum network. The congested network would prevent other transactions from going through and people would respond by resending them over and over, causing even greater congestion.

Taylor got on the Skype call, her wet hair dripping.

"The sale is technically over," Jordi said. "Based on the number of pending transactions, it's going to take nine hours for all of these transactions to go through."

"So people are going to keep sending ETH thinking they'll get in the ICO, just to see their transactions eventually fail?" she said.

"Yeah . . . this was such a bad idea!" Jordi groaned.

"No! You were trying to accomplish a goal and you accomplished that goal; you wanted to help improve the distribution of the sale and you probably did," she said. "But now, what do we do?"

Taylor's solution was to have a message pop up on MEW saying that the Status ICO was likely over based on the pending number of transactions. Average Ethereum transaction fees had spiked to a record of over $1 and block confirmation times also climbed. Big exchanges like Coinbase and Bitfinex put ether transactions on hold until the network went back to normal.

"We are suspending all ETH withdrawal until the network backlog subsides and we are able to reliably post transactions to [the] blockchain," Bitfinex tweeted.

Status reached its fundraising goal after three hours, selling almost $100 million of SNT tokens. More people than at previous sales, or around fifteen thousand, were able to participate. And while it was over in three hours, it took nearly two days before all the pending transactions were cleared and the network was back to normal again. Still, many were left out, and Taylor again took a lot of the blame—through a barrage of angry tweets and emails—for the sale not going smoothly.

"I'm sick of the sleepless nights so you can throw $$ at someone & bitch at us when the blocks are full of FOMO," she tweeted back at the mob.

In forums, Status was also blamed for being overly greedy. Did they really need $100 million to develop a chat app? Hadn't Ethereum raised just a fraction of that? WeChat itself only raised $3.5 million in its seed round. The word "greed" was coming up more and more often whenever ICOs were being discussed.

Jackson Palmer, the founder of the digital currency Dogecoin, posted a YouTube video around the time of the Status sale saying, "The real reason the [ether] price has been going up something like a hundred dollars per week for the past month is really just greed: Greed from developers, greed from investors [and] greed from everybody in this speculative market." The coin he created is a joke based on an internet meme, but he was one of the few crypto personalities strongly voicing rationality.

There was plenty of blame and recriminations to go around for

ICOs breaking down—investors and developers were too greedy, that was one claim. It was also true that a lot of the infrastructure needed to run these increasingly high-velocity ICOs just wasn't ready for prime time. But in the end, something more troubling was happening. Ethereum wasn't able to handle traffic from its first killer app: fundraising.

26

The Friendly Ghost

On June 2, 2017, as blockchain startups raised millions of dollars in minutes, bitcoin was topping $2,000, and ether had just blown through $200, Vitalik was walking into a closed-door meeting at a stadium-sized glass-and-steel conference center in St. Petersburg, Russia. He was about to speak with one of the most powerful men on earth. Vladimir Putin had just sat with a group of CEOs running multibillion-dollar companies, and now he would grace the creator of a $20 billion blockchain with his presence. The meeting was only a couple of minutes long, and not recorded. The Russian government's press department said, "Mr. Buterin described the opportunities for using the technologies he developed in Russia. The President supported the idea of establishing ties with possible Russian partners." Vitalik had ditched his usual uniform (a cartoon-emblazoned T-shirt) for a button-down shirt, but still no tie. He later reported that he'd told Putin that "blockchains are cool."

Like so many Fortune 500 companies, the world's most powerful governments were also looking at blockchain technology. Russian officials had a hot and cold relationship with cryptos, at times calling them a Ponzi scheme, at times backing blockchain initiatives. After the meeting with Vitalik, a constant stream of news reports suggested that Russia was turning more pro-crypto. A consortium of the country's biggest banks developed Masterchain, a distributed ledger using a modified Ethereum protocol; some headlines suggested the country wanted to create its own national digital currency; and most outrageous of all: when the country's Burger King chains started offering a loyalty points token called "Whoppercoin."

Authoritarian governments don't spark much love from the libertarian-leaning crypto community, and many were quick to criticize Vitalik for his meeting with Putin. Vitalik replied he'd had "generally friendly discussions" with government officials including from the "US, Canada, UK, EU, Switzerland, Russia, Singapore, China and Taiwan." He cheekily added that he "fully intend[s] to refuse any requests to facilitate dictating, killing, or oppressing people."

Vitalik understood that for Ethereum to become a world computer, he would have to work hard toward building a broad and supportive community; that effort would be as important as developing the tech. He constantly traveled to conferences, community meetups, hackathons, and business meetings with CEOs and government officials, wherever they were in the world. He was on so many panels and giving so many presentations that his initial awkwardness in front of an audience started fading. He loosened up his rigid, technical speech, smoothed out jerky hand movements, and let his nerdy sense of humor shine through. Standing in front of packed rooms, speaking about the revolutionary blockchain he had brought to life, he had come a long way from the painfully shy kid who could hardly speak up in class. His parents would sometimes go to the conferences where he spoke and watch from the front row, proud of his progress.

By mid-2017, other than St. Petersburg, he had also been to Shanghai, Paris, Vienna, Singapore, Malta, Taipei, and Auckland. That year he made as many as four or five international trips per month, says Ming, who often traveled with him to participate in meetings. It's no wonder he changed the bio on his personal website to say his residence is "Cathay Pacific Airlines." Other facts he lists there are "political affiliation: Intellectual hipster meta-contrarian," "drinks/smokes/drugs: green tea," and "religion: crypto."

On those trips he carries no more than a duffel bag, with two pairs of pants and a few T-shirts, and would never, ever check a bag. Unlike many of those who had become rich thanks to his invention, he flew in coach and stayed in cheap hotels. He made it a game with Ming to find the cheapest room possible. The most extreme case was a $19 per night hotel in Mexico, where the windows on the rooms opened into a public toilet. It was so dirty they both got sick. After that, Ming started drawing a line on how cheap they would go. He had always been frugal, and having come so close to running out of Ethereum funds made him even more careful. He detested wastefulness. Paying hundreds more for a room he would only use to sleep and shower in seemed unnecessarily wasteful.

He was also focused on research to reduce what he saw as another kind of waste: the amount of energy spent in keeping proof-of-work blockchains like Bitcoin and Ethereum secure. There have been different estimates to quantify exactly how much energy the Bitcoin network consumes, but one often-cited report, a 2018 paper by PwC senior consultant Alex de Vries, compared Bitcoin's energy consumption to that of Austria and Ireland.

It's also been debated how clean that energy is. China, which gets about 60 percent of its energy from coal, accounts for about half of the power used to mine Bitcoin, according to a 2017 University of Cambridge report. Bitcoin company Coinshares disputed that with a study that showed most Chinese Bitcoin mines were in Sichuan and use hydropower.

Even before Ethereum was launched in 2015, Vitalik thought it was worth finding a way to achieve the same level of security without spending as much energy. Remember, proof-of-work is one kind of consensus algorithm, and consensus algorithms are how distributed systems decide, without the need of third parties, which blocks of data should be included in the chain. There was an alternative way a handful of small chains had experimented with called proof of stake (PoS), where miners vote on which blocks to include and receive rewards in proportion to the coins they hold, not according to the energy they spend. In PoS, miners are called validators. Besides being more environmentally friendly, it also guarantees that the network won't become concentrated around the few players with better mining hardware, though it still concentrates around those with the most economic power.

"Proof of stake is the future," he would repeatedly tell Vlad Zamfir in early 2014. Vlad is a bespectacled, long-haired blockchain researcher. When he started digging into Bitcoin in 2013 he saw it as a battle waging between underground developers and central bankers for a better financial system. In 2014 he grew more interested in the promise of a general-purpose smart contract blockchain with Ethereum. He met Vitalik at a hackathon in Toronto, and by April Charles Hoskinson had offered him a contract job with the foundation. As a former Bitcoiner, he was still in love with proof-of-work and wasn't convinced by Vitalik's enthusiastic claims about a more ecological alternative.

Vitalik had told him about his solution to the "nothing at stake" problem, a common issue in proof-of-stake chains, where in the event of a fork, miners are incentivized to mine on both chains so that they get rewards no matter which wins. PoS had been deemed too insecure for this reason. To solve it, Vitalik came up with "Slasher," an algorithm that guarantees miners would lose their block rewards if they're mining on different chains at the same time. Vlad was thinking about this at an Ethereum meetup in London. He spent the whole time at the after party in Amir Taaki's squat discussing Slasher with another hacker, until he thought about taking the concept further. Miners should stake crypto deposits. If they play nice and mine only one chain, they make a small return on the deposit. If they don't, they lose their entire deposit. This would provide stronger incentives and make the chain more secure. By the morning of September 12, 2014, Vlad was telling anyone who would listen that Ethereum should move to proof of stake. Based on the concepts of Slasher and miner deposits, Vlad and Vitalik started collaborating to make that happen.

By mid-2017 their version of proof of stake was called Casper, and their research had diverged into two different approaches. Vlad was working on Casper Correct by Construction, or Casper CBC, while Vitalik was working on Casper the Friendly Finality Gadget, or Casper FFG. The many steps it took them to get there and the difference between the two are all too technical to get into in much detail here, but at the time of writing, Vitalik's Casper FFG was the proof-of-stake version to be included in the Ethereum road map first, while Vlad's would be added at a later stage.

Vitalik was also researching how Ethereum would be able to process more transactions per second, or in other words, how Ethereum would be able to scale. There are different mechanisms that blockchain developers have concocted to solve this issue. Sharding, plasma, zero-knowledge proofs, and state channels are so far the best-known ones. Of those, sharding is the only one that's meant to be built into the Ethereum blockchain itself, or what's known as a "Layer 1 solution," while the others are "Layer 2 solutions," which are built on top of the main chain and don't require changes to the base-level protocol. At a very basic level, they all have some complex way of alleviating the load on blockchain nodes so that each transaction doesn't have to be propagated and validated by the entire network, often making some compromise on decentralization and/ or security.

They're supposed to make Ethereum orders of magnitude more efficient and able to truly support mass-market applications. Sharding would be implemented together with proof of stake in Serenity, the final major update on Ethereum's road map, which in 2017 still didn't have an estimated launch date. It's hard to understate the complexity of this upgrade. This proof-of-stake chain with greater capacity to scale was planned to be an entirely new blockchain, known as Ethereum 2.0, separate from the old proof-of-work chain. There would be multiple steps involved for ether and dapps in the old chain to migrate to the new chain. But before that happened, the current chain would also require its own upgrades to help it continue supporting the growing activity until Ethereum 2.0 launches. The revamped version of the current chain was known as Ethereum 1.x. The new proof-of-stake chain was the big goal that lay ahead for Ethereum, but for the next couple of years at least, the old chain would have to support all the dapps that continued to get built.

In the meantime, Layer 2 solutions can help developers build more scalable applications, but even they were in the early stages of development in 2017, and ICOs were still clogging up the network. Still, that didn't stop startups from holding more and more of these crowdsales, or investors from buying up their tokens.

Some argued it was a good problem to have. Ethereum was attracting thousands of entrepreneurs who wanted to crowdfund their projects and investors who wanted exposure to cutting-edge tech. On the flip side, it was also attracting opportunists and scammers who wanted to take advantage of the hype to get rich quick. Others thought the constant network congestions just highlighted that Ethereum was far from a true world computer. It couldn't even handle ICOs.

"Isn't it a huge issue that recent ICOs are basically a DDoS on the entire Ethereum network?" Ladislav Stejskal, who was building a blockchain company, wrote in a June 17 post on Reddit.

> Basically, the recent Bancor and BAT ICOs made the entire blockchain unusable for 3 hours unless you paid extremely high fees. This is just unacceptable.
>
> [...]
>
> This is a huge issue to me. Seriously. We need scaling features yesterday!

But those features were still missing, and the market was just starting to heat up.

27

The Boom

Satoshi Nakamoto has remained anonymous, so there's no one to idolize for the birth of Bitcoin. But the Ethereum creator is the complete opposite. Not only is his identity known, but he is also a very public figure, publishing Ethereum research, speaking at conferences, posting on Reddit, and responding with increasing sassiness to trolls on Twitter. The surge on the ether price, the ICO mania, and Vitalik's globetrotting had elevated him to the status of a crypto rock star. Adoring fans hung on his every word as he talked about blockchain technology onstage and waited for him in longer and longer lines when he was done, just so they could take a selfie with him. Vitalik complied, and dozens of pictures of him standing stiffly in the middle of a group with a smile on his face, conference badges hanging from everyone's necks, began to populate the internet. Some were just fans, but others used the snapshot to intimate that the Ethereum cofounder was supporting their ICO. Those claims weren't always far-fetched, as Vitalik was indeed sometimes also acting as an official advisor to a handful of crypto startups.

Young entrepreneurs desperate to make it in the crypto world went all the way to the Ethereum office in Switzerland to make their case. Ming would open the door and find travelers, who were there unannounced, asking for advice, support, a tour of the office, or a job at the foundation. Most of the time Ming would apologize and turn them away. Sometimes she just couldn't face disappointing yet another hopeful programmer who had waited for her all day, and she would just leave through the building's back door.

She worried that Vitalik was having trouble saying no to the endless number of people who wanted something from him. To her it seemed like, because his intentions were generally good, he didn't always see that was not the case with everyone else. She felt it was her duty to protect Vitalik, especially when he was being pressured and it was unclear when people were genuine or looking to take advantage of him. To help protect him and the foundation, she joined him on meetings and looked over his agenda.

Vitalik was tired of getting constantly begged to advise and invest in ICOs, too. On June 13, the day after Bancor raised $153 million, he tweeted that he would no longer be an advisor for future ICO projects with the exceptions of OmiseGo and Kyber Network, which he was already committed to. He would continue to privately give advice and people would be free to privately say he's doing so, "but no plastering my face up on websites." He said he was never paid for most projects that listed him as an advisor and that the best way for him to help is to focus on proof of stake, and scaling solutions.

People bought ether to invest in ICOs, which drove the price higher still, and as prices soared, more people wanted to do ICOs. It was a feverish cycle. Still, Ethereum easily left all the smaller cryptos behind and by June it represented one-fourth of the entire cryptocurrency market. Meanwhile, Bitcoin's market capitalization fell below 45 percent of the total market for the first time ever. Ethereum's quickly growing market cap sparked speculation it would soon overtake Bitcoin's, a phenomenon that was dubbed "the flippening." There was a website dedicated to tracking Ethereum's advance, and news articles popped up fueling the expectation. "Move Over, Bitcoin. Ether Is the Digital Currency of the Moment," headlined the *New York Times*. Bitcoin's market dominance had eroded from almost 90 percent at the start of the year, a reflection of how much smaller coins were surging.

Total cryptocurrency market cap surpassed $100 billion on the first week of June, from $47 billion a month earlier and $18 billion at the start of the year. That means the crypto market doubled in thirty days and soared more than 400 percent in a little over five months. In 2017, there were almost 1,000 different coins listed on CoinMarket-Cap, which ranked cryptocurrencies based on their market capitalization, with 137 of them worth more than $10 billion. Nasdaq-listed companies like Dropbox, Norwegian Cruise Line, and Hasbro had roughly the same market caps as zombie tokens called things like FedoraCoin, PotCoin, SmileyCoin, Foldingcoin, Pepe Cash, and Einsteinium, which exchanged hands on shady crypto trading platforms.

There was Jesus Coin, which promised record transaction times between token holders and God's son. There was TrumpCoin, Putin-Coin, Dentacoin ("the blockchain solution for the global dental industry"), and the scathingly honest "Useless Ethereum Token," which promoted its ICO as "the world's first 100% honest Ethereum ICO," saying it "transparently offers investors no value." Its logo was a hand raising its middle finger and the website said, "seriously, don't buy these tokens." Still, people handed over almost $75,000 in its ICO. At the height of the dot-com bubble in the late 1990s, Pets.com became the poster child of irrational hype. In the middle of the ICO mania, Pets.com would have been one of the most conservative, well-grounded business ideas.

And it wasn't just the niche crypto enthusiasts buying these coins. Celebrities started promoting them, usually in exchange for pay, encouraging their fans to buy obscure digital tokens. These posts may have been the first time their millions of followers heard of an ICO. Floyd Mayweather, an unbeaten boxer who often uses social media to flash the millions he's made in the ring, told his more than thirteen million followers on Facebook that they should buy "Centra token." Soon after, music producer DJ Khaled posted on Instagram a picture of himself sitting on a white armchair, a Jean-Michel Basquiat portrait on the background. He's facing the camera, holding a bottle of Ciroc vodka in one hand, a silver credit card in the other. The caption said, "I just received my titanium centra debit card. . . . This is a Game changer here. Get your CTR tokens now!" Heiress and socialite Paris Hilton tweeted that she was "looking forward to participating in the new" LydianCoin ICO, and actor Jamie Foxx followed a similar script, tweeting, "Looking forward to participating in the new @cobinhood Token! ZERO fee trading!"

As cryptocurrencies soared, headlines about early buyers who were now millionaires multiplied. "A Swedish Guy Bet His Life Savings on Bitcoin—and His Net Worth Has Exploded by More Than 13,000%," and "Meet 'The Wolf of Crypto Street,' an Ohio Teenager Who Used His Entire Savings to Become a Cryptocurrency Millionaire," wrote *Business Insider*, while *Forbes* wrote, "Meet the Man Traveling the World on $25 Million of Bitcoin Profits." Stories about those who were doing the same amid the current hype inevitably followed. CNBC reported on a Dutch family of five who sold "pretty much everything they own—from their 2,500-square-foot house, to their shoes," to buy bitcoin. *Vice* interviewed a group of computer science students in Spain who used all their meager savings to buy ether. An anonymous Reddit user said he took out a loan of more than $300,000, using his house as collateral, to buy bitcoin.

A YouTube video appeared, featuring a twentysomething self-described entrepreneur recounting how he'd bought a white Lamborghini Huracán with 45 bitcoins, which he got for an initial investment of $115 in 2011; it quickly racked up over a million views. Stories about overnight millionaires cashing out their digital coins to buy sport cars started popping up everywhere, and Lamborghinis, or "Lambos," became the ultimate status symbol for the new crypto rich. It evolved into an internet meme. Tech-savvy millennials founding crypto startups and investing in their tokens lived on the internet, which meant that this financial bubble happened online maybe more so than any other speculative mania before it.

As the market exploded, so did the memes and hashtags. "Hodl" was a classic one, stemming from a maybe drunk BitcoinTalk user who misspelled "hold" in a post where he frantically argued for keeping his bitcoin amid a crash. #Tothemoon, #whenmoon, and #when-lambo were other favorite ones.

It didn't matter that only a tiny sliver of trading was being done by people who were actually using these coins for their original use case (peer-to-peer cash in the case of bitcoin, fuel for a world computer in the case of ether). It also didn't matter that digital coins with no live platform on which to be used—essentially, just lines of code—were now worth more than actual companies with earnings and assets.

This behavior is actually "largely rational and intelligent," economist and Nobel Prize winner Robert J. Shiller wrote in his book *Irrational Exuberance*. "Experiments demonstrate that people are ready to believe the majority view or to believe authorities even when they plainly contradict matter-of-fact judgment," Shiller wrote. But that conduct can easily turn irrational when the only reason why people are crowding in the same direction is that they see more people have done the same and, in the case of markets, there's a failure to disseminate information about the fundamental value of an asset. As mentioned before, the internet has summarized this behavior as FOMO, and that's exactly what was going on in crypto in 2017.

Warnings that crypto was in a bubble started appearing everywhere. Entrepreneur Mark Cuban tweeted in response to a request to talk about Bitcoin in a podcast, "I think it's in a bubble. I just don't know when or how much it corrects." Someone noted in the thread that bitcoin dropped 5 percent after his comment, to which he replied, "So testy. Lol. You know it's a bubble when a random twitter thread bounces the price." Richard Turnill, formerly chief investment strategist at BlackRock, the world's largest asset manager, said in an interview, "I look at the charts, and to me that looks pretty scary." Stock market analyst Elliott Prechter said in his newsletter, "The price activity and manic sentiment that led to present prices have dwarfed even the Tulip mania of nearly 400 years ago," and that most altcoins are no more than "high-tech, pump-and-dump schemes." Howard Marks, billionaire investor and Oaktree Capital cofounder, wrote in a letter to investors that "digital currencies are nothing but an unfounded fad (or perhaps even a pyramid scheme)." For one headline writer at *The Economist* the question wasn't whether crypto was in a bubble, the question was, "What If the Bitcoin Bubble Bursts?"

Other analysts were more bullish. Cryptocurrencies were surging because they were erupting into the mainstream, and their still-low penetration in investment portfolios or merchant acceptance was actually a good thing because it pointed to a higher upside. Fundstrat was the first Wall Street stock research firm to publish a Bitcoin price target, and its analyst, Tom Lee, quickly became one of the biggest Bitcoin bulls when he predicted BTC could soar to as high as $55,000 by 2022. Bigger Wall Street firms, though more cautious, were also publishing positive reports. Bank of America Merrill Lynch said digital assets score well when it comes to diversification, as their correlation with other assets is near zero. A Morgan Stanley equity strategist said Bitcoin compares to gold in that both offer similar benefits as a store of value, and a Goldman Sachs analysts said the space is getting big enough at over $100 billion in market capitalization that it "warrants watching." And if traditional investment banks were publishing upbeat crypto reports amid the bubble, enthusiasts were proclaiming the recent rally was just the beginning and that Bitcoin would continue climbing to breathtaking heights. Crypto funds forecasted that Bitcoin would surge to anywhere between $20,000 and $100,000 in 2018.

Other observers argued that cryptocurrencies shouldn't be analyzed like stocks or other securities. They were a whole new beast, which explained the high valuations. "Maybe these currencies are actually worth these high prices, and maybe even worth many times more," a column on TechCrunch said. "But the problem is we have no way to figure out their value. Cryptocurrencies aren't public companies with earnings and expenses and EPS." The most extreme case was John McAfee, mostly known for creating the antivirus software that carries his name, and, since 2017, for relentlessly shilling ICOs. He said, "Those of you in the old school who believe this is a bubble simply have not understood the new mathematics of the Blockchain, or you did not care enough to try. Bubbles are mathematically impossible in this new paradigm. So are corrections and all else."

That wasn't a new story line. The same arguments popped up in the late 1990s, before the dot-com bubble popped, as stock analysts rationalized sky-high valuations by declaring that internet companies can't be compared with "regular" companies. Things like revenue don't matter like they used to and increased productivity thanks to technological developments reduced the risk of a recession. Then Fed chairman Alan Greenspan told the Senate Banking Committee that recent economic performance had been so "exceptional" that it might "carry productivity trends nationally and globally to a new higher track." Technological developments were bringing forth a new system that couldn't be measured by the standards of the old one. This idea came to be known as the "New Economy" in the 1990s. Similar arguments were made in the Roaring Twenties with the "New Economics," John Cassidy wrote in *Dot.Con*, a book about the dot-com bubble. And now we had the same kind of hyperbolic lingo with crypto.

It wasn't just crypto heating up. The entire stock market was reaching new highs. The S&P 500 climbed to a new record in July 2017, as optimism about technology stocks pushed the S&P's tech index over its dot-com-boom-fueled record in 2000 for the first time. Easy monetary policy spread across the globe, as central banks continued to prop up limping economies, pushing all asset classes, but especially riskier securities, higher. It's been proven time and time again that there is no correlation between cryptocurrencies and other assets, including stocks, gold, and bonds. That means that it doesn't matter whether traditional assets are moving up or down, crypto will dance to its own tune. Still, as investors flush with cash pushed assets higher, it's hard to believe that optimism didn't spill over to crypto.

The gap between Bitcoin and Ethereum measured by market cap continued to close until Ethereum was 32 percent of the market on June 18, a stone's throw away from Bitcoin's 38 percent. The two-year-old coin had become almost as valuable as the grandfather of crypto.

But ether had recently breached $400 for the first time and was struggling to advance much further. Then, five days later, on June 22, a multimillion-dollar sell ordered triggered so-called stop-loss orders, or instructions to automatically sell when the price falls below a certain point, and that cascaded into even more stop losses. The domino effect caused a flash crash that pulled ether from $320 to 10 cents in seconds. The price recovered just as quickly but started plunging again two days later as the market remained jittery and rumors surfaced online that Vitalik had been involved in a deadly accident.

"Vitalik Buterin confirmed dead. Insiders unloading ETH. Fatal car crash," someone posted on 4chan, an anonymous online forum known for enabling harassment and pranks.

> And now we have our answer. He was the glue. It will be difficult for ETH to recover and the entire crypto sphere is in big trouble.

The price dropped 22 percent to as low as $253 on June 25, from a high of $325 the day before the post. But Vitalik was just holed up in some far-flung part of the world working on Ethereum scaling. When he saw what was going on, he tweeted a picture of himself holding a piece of paper with a garble of numbers and letters. It was Ethereum's latest block, or a crypto equivalent of taking a picture with the day's newspaper. The tweet read, "Another day, another blockchain use case."

The price dropped to as low as $204 in the next two days and rebounded from there. But the prank (or attempted market manipulation, more likely) made it painfully clear just how much Ethereum, for all its ambitions of decentralization, still relied on one man, its twenty-three-year-old creator.

The crypto space was soon dealt a new blow. This time it was no rumor in 4chan, but a statement by the SEC. Almost one year after The DAO debacle, regulators had investigated the sale and concluded that DAO tokens were securities. That meant that The DAO, Slock.it, Slock.it's cofounders, and intermediaries in the sale "may have violated the federal securities laws," the commission said in a July 25 statement.

After years of speculation, the US securities regulator finally had an answer for crypto enthusiasts, and it wasn't the one they were hoping for: yes, digital tokens could be considered investment contracts. That had huge repercussions for the space. It meant all these startups that had been selling digital coins to anyone with an email might have been breaking US securities laws. Investors who bought and sold those tokens might be under fire, too, and so were all the crypto trading platforms. These websites called themselves "exchanges" but weren't actually registered as such, and if digital tokens really were securities, they didn't have the license to be trading them in the United States.

The SEC said it didn't matter if the sale was taking place with cryptocurrencies and not dollars. It also didn't care what technology was underpinning it, or if there was computer code automating certain functions. Digital tokens sold might still be securities, and must be registered with the commission or qualify for an exemption. But how would issuers know if they're selling securities? Regulators didn't provide a clear guideline to answer that, just that "it will depend on the facts and circumstances, including the economic realities of the transaction." On the bright side for those involved, while The DAO and Slock.it members likely broke securities laws, the SEC let them off with a warning and decided not to pursue an enforcement action.

A flurry of stories, thought pieces, tweets, and TV hits analyzing the latest bombshell followed. What did this mean? Were ICOs dead? Was crypto over? On July 26, the day after the SEC issued its report, there were not one but *three* ICOs and five more the rest of the month. In August sales did slow to $134 million from $574 million in July, signaling that perhaps crypto founders and investors were heeding the US regulators' warnings. But that didn't last long. After an initial shock from the SEC's slap on the wrist, crypto enthusiasts were reenergized. This is what they had been fearing and now that it had happened, it wasn't too bad. With all the blatant scams out there, the SEC had only focused on The DAO, one year after the fact, and even if they did conclude DAO tokens were securities, there were no consequences for the issuers or investors. ICOs were back with a bang in September, raising $705 million, a monthly record.

Prices had started to recover even sooner. There was a pullback in June and July, but starting in August the market started to shoot up again. Bitcoin crossed $3,000 on August 5 for the first time, and eight days later it surged past $4,000. Ether recovered all the ground it had lost and climbed back to just below $400. SEC news seemed like ancient history.

As prices soared, Richard Burton, the kitesurfing entrepreneur, was heading to the Caribbean. After getting back to San Francisco earlier in 2017, he decided to look into why his ether holdings and the entire cryptocurrency market were going up. He found there was so much interest, optimism, and activity in the space, with developers from all over the world building new applications and protocols, and big companies testing blockchains, that he was eager to jump back in the crypto world. At the same time, banks pulled the data feeds Richard had been using in his fintech company Balance, so that the app became largely unusable. As he was getting deeper into decentralized, open sourced systems, he experienced firsthand how centralized corporations could unilaterally and unexpectedly change the rules of the game. The move prompted him and his cofounders to rebuild Balance as a cryptocurrency wallet.

His cofounder was already involved in crypto through Protocol Labs, the software company developing decentralized data storage networks IPFS and Filecoin. IPFS, short for InterPlanetary File System, is a protocol that enables peer-to-peer file sharing and storage, and Filecoin uses the IPFS protocol to build a network with a built-in token to incentivize users. Like so many crypto projects in 2017, Filecoin was doing an ICO. In the lead-up to the sale, Protocol Lab employees, advisors, and potential investors were all put up in a beachside resort for a company retreat on the island of Curacao. Richard, whose ether stash now made him a candidate to participate in the coveted token sale, scored an invite through his cofounder.

At first Richard was blown away by IPFS and Filecoin cofounder Juan Benet's vision. Juan described how, even as data creation and sharing had exponentially grown, only a few entities oversaw its storage, creating dangerous single points of failure. A system that helped to decentralize data storage would not only eliminate that risk, but it also had the potential to generate extra income for those providing the hard drive space. He painted data storage not as some boring back-office service but as a social equalizer, where the poor in third-world countries could make a living with cryptocurrencies earned by lending out their computer space to anyone in the world.

But a few days into the Curacao retreat, it started to get harder for Richard to reconcile that vision with the one he had right in front of him: The Filecoin team was whooshing by across the turquoise Caribbean ocean on jet-skis. The group was flown down to the paradisiac island and put up in luxurious rooms to spend a week cavorting at the beach, piling on food from the buffet and drinking colorful cocktails by the pool. Crypto hedge funds and venture capitalists' chatter indicated Filecoin would have no problem raising tens of millions of dollars. They were shaping up to be the biggest ICO ever, and they were spending accordingly. But by the end of the week, Richard's stomach could hardly stand the mix of tempura sushi, rum, and blockchain talk anymore.

Protocol Labs was doing an initial private sale before their ICO, where advisors like Richard had the chance to buy coins at a steep discount of $0.75 compared with tokens that would start at $1 and could go up to around $6 at the sale. The ICO would be restricted to accredited investors (those with over $200,000 in income or a net worth of over $1 million), a sign that at least some crypto startups were getting worried about breaking securities laws. They were doing the sale through CoinList, a new platform focusing on SEC-compliant ICOs. In an additional cautionary measure, Protocol Labs wasn't distributing Filecoin tokens at the time of the sale; rather, they'd sell an agreement to buy the coins once the network launched. The contract, called a Simple Agreement for Future Tokens or SAFT, was gaining popularity as lawyers advised founders it was a good way to reduce regulatory risk.

While it was understandable that Filecoin wanted to be cautious about its sale, with regulators tightening their grip, many in the crypto community felt betrayed. This was one of the most promising projects, and it would be inaccessible to most people. The point of ICOs was to democratize investment. Instead, Filecoin was going back to the same practices as before, with preferential deals for those close to the project and a sale where only the rich could participate.

In addition, some criticized them for taking an excessive portion of the coins. Protocol Labs and the Filecoin Foundation were to keep about 70 percent of the tokens created on the first block of the network. Those stakes would shrink as miners started earning coins as rewards and both the foundation and Protocol Labs had to wait six years before selling their tokens, but it still struck some as greedy.

Richard thought the terms of the sale and the excessive spending were bad signs. To him, Filecoin had sold out their community. Almost none of the developers who had built IPFS would be able to participate in the sale. At the end of the trip he told Juan he wouldn't put money in the project.

The following month, Palo Alto–based Protocol Labs got $52 million from major venture capital firms including Andreessen Horowitz, Union Square Ventures, and Sequoia Capital in its private sale, and in September it got an additional $205 million in the public sale for accredited investors. The combined $257 million sale of tokens was the biggest ever, breaking Tezos's record of $232 million raised in July to build a smart-contracts platform to compete with Ethereum. At the time of writing, the Filecoin network still hadn't launched and only Filecoin futures (a derivative used to bet on the price of the tokens once they're listed) were trading at around $4 from a high of $29 in January 2018. IPFS was already running at the time of the Filecoin ICO.

As ICOs continued to pull in millions of dollars, cryptocurrencies kept climbing, and the whole world had turned to look, hardly a word about it was uttered by Ethereum developers. Throughout the previous "year of the DAO," Ming had continually enforced the language policy she wrote to legally protect the foundation, and in the "year of the ICO" she continued to ask foundation contractors and employees to refrain from talk about crypto prices. She wanted to distance the EF as much as possible from scammy-looking ICOs and money-hungry crypto bros—though she would never use that language herself. So as crypto prices became the default watercooler topic at offices everywhere, the people building the nuts and bolts of the second-largest coin, and the one responsible for much of the hype, weren't talking about it. At least not at work.

Instead they were getting ready to roll out Ethereum's third post-launch stage, called Metropolis—the first two were Frontier and Homestead. Metropolis would be composed of two separate updates via hard forks. The first one was called Byzantium, set for October 16, and the second one, Constantinople, would be implemented at a later date. Byzantium would pave the way for proof of stake by reducing miners' block rewards to gradually wean them off proof-of-work. There were also plans to increase mining difficulty to incentivize miners to switch to proof of stake, the so-called difficulty bomb.

The Byzantium fork also included the ability for Ethereum to use a privacy-enhancing function called zero-knowledge proofs, which allow users to prove they meet specific requirements, without revealing more information about themselves. For example, it could potentially allow someone applying for a mortgage to prove, without using a third party, that they meet the lender's requirements without disclosing anything else about their account of personal information.

They were all small steps forward and nice changes to have in the network, but nothing to meaningfully help Ethereum scale up. Still, it was an uncontentious update that went through with no major issues. Vitalik celebrated with a picture of him and two friends raising their forks together, like nineties cartoon superheroes would clash their swords. They were in Waterloo, Vitalik's old college town, for the first official Ethereum hackathon, which is an event usually held over a weekend where small teams of developers huddle together to build a project over a couple of days in exchange for funding.

The Byzantium fork wasn't the only thing that would change the course of Ethereum going on at the Waterloo hackathon, though none of the developers present would have guessed it. Benny Giang was busy plastering the bathrooms with cat posters and handing out Pokémon playing cards with cat stickers on them. He had also tied feline-shaped balloons onto his workstation. He was part of the team at a Vancouver-based software incubator called Axiom Zen. They focused on bringing cutting-edge tech to the masses. Benny had been one of the first people to test out Google Glass smart glasses, and virtual reality headsets, and when cryptocurrencies became the thing everyone was talking about but not really using, they decided to give it a shot.

Roham Gharegozlou, Axiom Zen founder, brought their team together and had them come up with a list of twenty or so blockchain ideas on a whiteboard. From there, the tech people went off to think about the best ideas and the designers did the same. At the end of the day they regrouped. The tech people were excited about creating personalized tokens, that is, tokens that weren't meant to serve as cryptocurrency, but rather as things to collect. The designers had come to one important conclusion: whatever they did, it had to involve cats. Cats ruled the internet for a reason: they were so cute and funny, they just couldn't help but make anything go viral.

The logical step from there was that they'd make collectible cats. They would call them CryptoKitties, and the first version would be built at the Ethereum hackathon in Waterloo. Behind what seemed like a frivolous game was serious blockchain innovation. Rather than just link an image to a regular ERC20 token, the same standard that was used for ICOs, Roham and his team decided to create an entirely new Ethereum token standard, made specifically to represent individual "things," not currencies. They would be a whole new category of coins. Roham and his team discussed what the right word for them would be and settled on "non-fungible tokens," meaning each was unique, not interchangeable like ether, bitcoin, or ERC20 tokens sold in ICOs. Beyond collectible digital cats, the broader vision was that tokens under this new standard, called ERC721, could be linked to scarce, high-value items like artwork and luxury goods; other collectibles, like baseball cards; and items used and traded inside video games, like virtual weapons.

Benny was there to spread the word and by the end of the three days, the Ethereum hackers were almost as interested in buying and selling CryptoKitties as they were in working on their projects. It would be a sign of what was to come.

28

Futures and Cats

As the end of 2017 approached, crypto was about to get what looked like the best news so far, at least from an investment perspective. On October 31, CME Group, which ran the world's largest exchange, announced its plans to offer bitcoin futures by the end of the year. In August, Cboe, the largest US options exchange, said it was planning to list bitcoin futures in 2018 but moved the launch date to 2017 after CME's announcement. That meant Wall Street traders would be able to get exposure to bitcoin just as easily as they could trade derivatives tied to the price of gold or oil. They wouldn't actually own any digital currency, because the contracts were cash based, not physically delivered, but most in the crypto sphere saw this as a huge step forward. The two leading US derivatives trading houses wanted to give investors access to bitcoin. Their Wall Street clients must have been begging for it! It's true that these instruments wouldn't increase demand for the digital currency itself, but bulls saw them as the gateway drug for the real thing.

It was only a matter of time before Ethereum contracts came, and if there were cryptocurrency-based derivatives regulated by the Commodity Futures Trading Commission (CFTC), that meant ETFs were just around the corner. After all, a lack of a regulated market was one of the reasons the SEC gave for not approving a bitcoin ETF, so once that was sorted out . . . "institutional investors are coming!"

There would be a flood of money coming into crypto soon and prices would continue to skyrocket, enthusiasts reasoned. "Bitcoin isn't the bubble, it's the pin," was one of the mantras they repeated.

Vitalik wasn't particularly excited about any of this news. He thought there was too much emphasis on ETFs, and not enough on making it easier for people to buy small amounts of cryptocurrency at corner stores. "The former is better for pumping price, but the latter is much better for actual adoption," he tweeted.

But investors were thrilled. The cherry on top for the institutional interest narrative came in late December when Bloomberg News, citing unidentified sources, reported that Goldman Sachs was getting ready to set up a trading desk to make markets in digital currencies by the first half of 2018.

While the actual level of institutional investor interest remained to be seen, it was clear cryptocurrency buyers had evolved from the anarchist cypherpunks and hackers buying crypto to protest against the financial establishment. Cryptocurrencies were now increasingly viewed as a separate asset class, and dedicated funds started popping up accordingly. The number of digital-currency-focused hedge funds and venture funds exploded in 2017. More than two hundred funds were created that year; that's more than four times the number of funds launched in the previous year. They offered everything from market-weighted investment on the top ten cryptos to more sophisticated algorithmic trading.

Meanwhile, Ming was in Mexico leading the organization for what would be Ethereum's biggest event yet, Devcon3. More than two thousand people would fill 75,000 square feet of space in three floors and on two stages at a Cancun conference center. She was working almost literally around the clock with conference vendors on the design, the layout, the panel topics, who would speak, and who would sponsor. It was when the entire Ethereum community came together and so everything had to be perfect.

While Ming was mostly in Mexico, Europe, and the United States, Vitalik was spending more time in Asia. Much of Ethereum's early history was in North America and Europe, so Vitalik was focused on China and starting to support emerging Ethereum communities in the eastern part of the world. He had established Singapore-based entity Ethereum Asia Pacific Ltd., which would focus chiefly on research, and by the end of 2016 he'd bring on other researchers and spend more time diving deep into scaling and proof of stake. The crypto startups he was close with were also based in the region, with OmiseGo in Thailand and Kyber Network in Singapore.

Ming started to notice Vitalik didn't come to her for advice as often, and others had greater influence on him. Soon she wasn't involved in the day-to-day detail of his agenda or the issues he was dealing with. The stress from the cooling work relationship with Vitalik added to the strain she was already feeling from the job. Her health had deteriorated so much that she decided to leave the foundation after Devcon, and worked with Vitalik to coordinate her transition in December until the end of January. Ming felt she had accomplished her goals at Ethereum and was at peace with the decision, but it was important for her to leave with a proper executive director handover, where she could provide the incoming ED with the knowledge about the foundation she had gained.

The ether price, the money raised in ICOs, the number of transactions per second, really almost any variable, pointed to an exponential growth in Ethereum. But as Ethereans walked into Devcon3, all those charts in a screen dissolved and gave way to what was really at the core of the network: a sprawling community. The entire space was packed with a sea of Ethereum coders in colorful T-shirts, unicorn headbands, and even a presenter wearing a dinosaur costume onstage. Seeing the massive turnout meant so much more than looking at a price chart. Ether might very well drop from around $300, where it was trading at the start of the conference on November 1. The market was subject to fickle traders. But what mattered was that all those people buzzing around were there to keep building on Ethereum.

Vitalik, sporting a green T-shirt with a Doge on it—the Shiba

Inu dog meme—could be seen chatting with small groups in a quieter section of the venue. Griff Green went around giving what by that time were his famous hugs. Fabian Vogelsteller, of the ERC20 standard, was also there talking about how to improve the fundraising mechanism. Those like Alex Van de Sande, Vlad Zamfir, Martin Becze, and Peter Szilagyi who had been part of Ethereum from the very early days were there, too, but so were several hundreds more who had just joined. The atmosphere was electric as technical panels filled up rooms down to the last chair, making it hard to freely circulate around the halls as groups congregated to chat about what they had been hearing and to catch up on their projects. The crowd went from the conference center during the day to rowdy bars in Cancun's hotel zone at night. In four years, Devcon had grown from about thirty people who fit in a room in Berlin to a four-day event with catered food, multiple stages, and over two thousand people.

Many of the earliest Ethereum team members, the initial eight who wore the cofounder label, were also there. But they weren't working on the Ethereum protocol. They had moved on to focus on their own, mostly crypto-related projects. Joe Lubin had ConsenSys, Gavin Wood had Parity, and Jeff Wilcke had handed the reins of Geth over to Peter Szilagyi so that he could spend more time with his family and recover from his burnout. Charles Hoskinson was developing his own blockchain called Cardano, while Anthony Di Iorio was focusing on his Jaxx digital wallet, and Mihai Alisie was now working on a decentralized social network called Akasha. Amir Chetrit was still happy to keep a low profile, and hardly anyone recognized him as an Ethereum cofounder as he mingled on the conference sidelines. He was quietly supporting different blockchain projects. Really, the only one left working on Ethereum itself of the original team drawing up pie charts in Miami was Vitalik.

Bitcoin had broken $1,000 at the start of the year, symbolically proclaiming 2017 was the year of crypto. Now it needed to end the year in an equally spectacular manner. Fueled by the ICO frenzy, bitcoin futures news, ETFs, and institutional investor speculation, the whole sector started to shoot up in late November even faster than during the rest of the year, with ether soaring through $400 and bitcoin shooting past $8,000.

Texture couldn't believe what was happening. He kept checking his digital wallet to make sure it was true. One day he was doing fine, thinking he might have enough money to make it another year in California, and over the span of a few weeks he knew he wouldn't have to worry about where to live for the rest of his life. The analogy has been used before, but it was true for so many people holding crypto at the end of 2017: he felt like he had won the lottery. When he moved into his Oakland apartment with his girlfriend and their daughter earlier that year, one of their pastimes was to drive around nice neighborhoods or go to open houses. They didn't have the money for any of the places they saw, but Texture thought it would be good inspiration for his daughter and his daughter's sister, who later came to live with them, and also it was just fun to dream. They had even created a vision board for what their perfect house should look like.

One day he said, "Hey, do you know some houses have elevators in them? Do you want to go check one out?" They looked up on Zillow if there were any houses with elevators for sale in Oakland and found just one. It didn't have an open house, so they called up the real estate agent to go see it. When they walked in, everyone's face lit up. It didn't only have an elevator, it had a pool overlooking the San Francisco skyline. A hot tub, a dry sauna, a hot sauna, and enough rooms for everyone's whims and hobbies. Every house they had looked at before was missing something, or wasn't quite right. This Tuscan-style mansion was the exact house they had pictured in the vision board.

As the girls went up and down the stairs and elevator, he started to feel bad. "We need to be straight with this real estate lady," he told his partner. "She thinks we're going to buy the house and we're 100 percent not buying the house." It wasn't so much about the money anymore, but Texture thought a house that big would be hard and stressful to maintain. When they went back home and everyone couldn't stop talking about the big house, he started having second thoughts. In the next couple of days he decided he'd regret it if he didn't buy it. He had been to enough properties to know something this perfect was hard to find. They moved in in December, right as crypto was shooting up. "If your dreams are big enough, you can live in them," he posted on Instagram, looking reflexively at the expansive view from his balcony.

It was similar for Jeff Scott Ward from ConsenSys. As ether kept climbing, he was looking at a glass skyscraper that was being built down the street from his Brooklyn apartment, by the water. Every time ether touched a new record, he saw from his living room window that a few floors were added to the tower. Owning a place there would have been unthinkable just a year earlier, but as the market kept going up, an idea started to sneak into Jeff's head: "When that skyscraper is finished, I'm buying the penthouse." At the end of December, when ether was soaring above $700 one day and $800 the next, the building was nearing completion, and he was finally able to buy the penthouse in March. As he took in his fortieth-floor views of Manhattan, he felt grateful to have been able to escape his generation's economic ruin. It had been thanks to grit, true belief, and Ethereum.

Meanwhile, though ConsenSys had stayed in Bushwick, it had quickly grown out of the coworking space where it started, expanding aggressively with several hundreds of new hires and offices in about ten different cities from San Francisco to Paris and Singapore.

Gavin Wood was also riding this wave. His company, Parity Technologies, continued to develop one of the most used Ethereum clients. There had been a hack in July while much of the team was at a company retreat in Ibiza, and the attacker was able to steal about $30 million from Parity-developed smart contracts, which they quickly fixed. Three months later the hack was old news and the Web 3 Foundation, of which Gavin is founder and director, was able to raise about $130 million in an ICO to develop Polkadot, a new blockchain aimed at connecting all the other blockchains, to fulfill Gavin's dream of a decentralized web.

But in November, their stellar year would be interrupted again. They were alerted that something was wrong when someone going by the internet name of "devops199" posted on GitHub that there was a vulnerability in Parity's multisig wallets, the same ones involved in the July hack. Multisig wallets are a type of smart contract that allows more than one person to control the wallet; they are frequently used by startups to hold their ICO funds. Devops199 had bad news for the owners of more than five hundred wallets, holding about 500,000 ether, or about $150 million at the time. "Anyone can kill your contract," the anonymous hacker wrote. But much worse is what he or she said shortly after: "I accidentally killed it."

The hacker had erased, seemingly by accident, the contract's code library, where the smart contract goes for instructions when it needs to execute any actions. That meant that there was no way to interact with multisig wallets developed by Parity. The funds were essentially frozen—not even the hacker could get to them—and a large chunk of those funds, or more than $90 million, was from Polkadot's own ICO. That means Parity had just lost millions because of a vulnerability in its own code. It was the biggest hurdle Gavin's young company had faced, and it was caused by a flaw in the code, something he prided himself on doing better than most.

Jutta Steiner, Parity's cofounder, was the public face in dealing with the blowback, talking with the affected teams, and deciding how to respond. They decided to shut down multisig wallets, commissioned an audit, and pushed to change Ethereum's code to allow for fund recovery, which would require a hard fork. That smelled a lot like a second DAO, so the community treaded very carefully around that topic. Also, with so many other, happier things going on, fund recovery failed to get much traction. One of those happy things was digital cats.

When Benny Giang and the others got back from the hackathon

in Waterloo and described people's reaction to CryptoKitties, Roham decided to increase the team to twelve people from about five people working full-time on the project. It had been intense work leading up to the launch on November 28, as developers were under the pressure that, once a smart contract is deployed, it can't be changed and would be carrying people's money. The day of the launch went smoothly. The developers who had tested the app in EthWaterloo were the main users. They were buying, selling, and also breeding the cats, which carry a unique number and a 256-bit, distinct "genome" with different attributes (or cattributes, as they called them) that were passed down to kittens. The gaming aspect increased use and cats started to multiply, so that cats from the original batch gained in value. When these early cats started going for thousands of dollars, people started paying attention. With the hype around crypto already at a fever pitch, news of the invention of crypto-based cats quickly drove thousands of new users to the game.

By early December, CryptoKitties accounted for about 15 percent of total Ethereum transactions and had clogged the Ethereum network, slowing confirmation times to several hours and driving up fees. As some cats sold for over $100,000, Roham started getting irate calls from Ethereans who were angry that he was causing congestion on the network. But he didn't feel too bad. So maybe he'd be keeping somebody from participating in a useless ICO. At least he was demonstrating a valuable use case for something other than raising money on unrealistic promises. Still, he tried to make things better by raising the breeding fees and other tweaks that helped slow use.

In the first week of December, BTC shot through $13,000, $14,000, $15,000, and $16,000 in less than a day. Bitcoin futures would begin trading that weekend, and the market started spinning out of control. While crossing $1,000 was a big milestone in the early days, the biggest digital asset was now adding $1,000 in value as easily as scooping ice cream on a cone. Many suspected the bitcoin price was probably just as unstable as several ice-cream scoops balancing on top of each other, but they were still trying to get a taste before it all splattered to the ground.

Traditional markets were also climbing higher. As 2017 ended, the three main US stock indexes—the S&P 500, the Dow Jones Industrial Average, and the Nasdaq—continued to make new records, some days even all at the same time. The Dow had been making big, flashy round numbers again and again, and crossing 22,000 and 23,000 between August and October and closing at new highs seventy-one times that year. Global stocks, measured by the MSCI All-Country World Index, gained every single month of 2017, the first time that had happened in data going back to 1988. Driving the rally in the United States were company results beating analyst expectations, optimism around tech, the expectation that tax reform in the States would spur spending, and speculation that higher government spending would prop up the economy. The overarching theme continued to be easy money in the form of low global interest rates.

It was Sunday, December 10, in the afternoon and I was walking into Bloomberg's New York headquarters on Fifty-Ninth Street and Lexington Avenue. Rows and rows of long tables decked with Bloomberg Terminals side by side in the open-plan newsroom were empty. I went to say hello to the editor who would be covering the news with me. He told me to get some traders on the phone ahead of the big event. Cboe would start offering Bitcoin futures at 6 p.m. It would mark the first time a major US exchange offered a Bitcoin derivative.

I had the screen for Cboe's Bitcoin futures, ticker XBTF, in front of me. Like everything in the Bloomberg Terminal, which has a black background and orange letters in a fax-machine-like font, it looked very technical and ugly. But as the minutes ticked closer to 6 p.m., I wouldn't have been more excited binge-watching a show on Netflix. When the clock hit exactly 6:00, the empty columns for the Bid, Ask, and Last Price filled up. The first trades for the January- and March-expiring contracts appeared, and I had witnessed history being made.

One week later, even bigger player CME was launching its own contracts. Bitcoin had continued to climb after the Cboe futures launch, crossing $17,000, and on Saturday it breached $18,000 and $19,000. It was a dizzying rally, with bitcoin up 1,800 percent in just one year. For those who had bought crypto early on, the numbers were hard to comprehend. "It was a mind fuck," Texture said. Sunday, a couple of hours before futures started trading on CME, the biggest cryptocurrency crossed just marginally above $20,000 on some exchanges. Ether jumped to just below $800.

Far from celebrating, Vitalik was preparing to make a difficult call: he told Ming over Skype that she wouldn't be involved in the handover. Ming had led the foundation through challenging times, and now a different style of leadership was needed, one that was more suited to the peaceful times ahead, he said.

To Ming, it was a shock they would skip the "knowledge transfer" they had discussed. For almost three years she had dedicated her entire life to Ethereum, losing sleep, neglecting friends and family, wearing herself out with the constant travel, and juggling a million different delicate issues and difficult personalities. She thought she was in the best position to help whoever was replacing her start their role in the best way, but now she wouldn't even meet the new team.

"They want a clean slate," Vitalik explained. Ming assumed Vitalik was talking about the new leadership at the foundation, though she wasn't sure exactly who "they" were. He was still wearing the purple and pink watch with a Cheshire cat grinning beneath its ticking hands that Ming had given him. It was a reminder of one of the many nicknames she had for him: Vitali-cat. But no number of nicknames mattered. As soon as he believed others would better serve the project, Ming had to be out. Once more Vitalik had shown that his loyalty lay with Ethereum.

It had arguably been the best year yet for the second-biggest blockchain. It had become the dominant platform for startups to fundraise through crypto, disrupting the traditional venture capital model with more than $5 billion raised in ICOs. Partly as a result of that, ether was soaring and applications being built on Ethereum mushroomed, with several hundreds of developers in the space, even eclipsing programmers working on Bitcoin. Big corporations, non-profits, and government entities were all testing the network.

"Transaction volume more than doubled, number of new accounts created per day passed 100,000, and the number of nodes increased," said an upbeat fourth-quarter roundup posted by the Ethereum Foundation on January 2, 2018. "We are entering a new phase in the industry's growth: the phase where we are finally going from experiments and tests to real, live applications."

Vitalik posted news on Ethereum's scaling efforts on the same day. "With the Ethereum blockchain reaching 1 million transactions per day, and both Ethereum and other blockchain projects frequently reaching their full transaction capacity, the need for scaling progress is becoming more and more clear and urgent," he wrote. To that end, the foundation was going to fund outside researchers to work on scaling solutions. Grants of $50,000 to $1,000,000 would be awarded for research on Layer 1 and Layer 2 solutions, the post said. Aya Miyaguchi, who previously led cryptocurrency exchange Kraken's operations in Japan and had replaced Ming as ED, was leading the effort. After ether's massive rally, the EF was in the position to financially support the broader Ethereum community, and organized enough to do so, for the first time.

Separately, a testnet for Casper FFG launched on Ethereum's python language implementation, or pyethereum. Karl Floersch, a pyethereum developer, tweeted the news together with unicorn and rainbow emojis on December 31. It was still several steps away from launch, but the testnet represented concrete progress in one of Ethereum's most ambitious undertakings, the switch to proof of stake.

News outlets alternated their coverage between the foundation's grants, the fourth quarter roundup, and the proof of stake testnet to explain what happened next, though as happens with most market moves, it's impossible to tell exactly what the trigger was. The fact is that ether, which had ended 2017 at around $750, shot up over $900 on January 2 and continued to skyrocket, crossing $1,000 two days later, and touching a record of more than $1,400 on January 12. The digital currency soared more than 70 percent in almost two weeks. One year earlier it had been trading at just below $10. Now its value had ballooned more than 130 times. Anyone who had held on to the ETH they got at the sale for 30 cents had increased their investment by more than 4,000 times. It would have taken an investment of just $250 to become a millionaire less than four years later. Vitalik's public ether wallet showed he had about 375,000 ether, or more than $500 million, at the peak.

Ethereum was now worth over $100 billion. Traders were piling into the market so quickly, they momentarily crashed some of the biggest cryptocurrency exchanges, like Coinbase, where ETH buy and sell orders were disabled for two hours. A CNBC chyron screamed "THE AGE OF ETHEREUM" in all caps as the news anchor pointed to the parabolic ether charts over his head.

But skyrocketing prices continued to make Vitalik and other long-time crypto enthusiasts uneasy. Amir Taaki, who was writing code for Bitcoin when it was worth less than $10, was one of them.

"Bitcoin is turning into a failed project. The seeds of its destruction [are] among the debris of a community blinded by numerical price increases," he tweeted on December 26.

Vitalik responded, "*All* crypto communities, ethereum included, should heed these words of warning. Need to differentiate between getting hundreds of billions of dollars of digital paper wealth sloshing around and actually achieving something meaningful for society."

To him, the spectacular price increases and the millions sitting in his digital wallet were worthless if they were just based on speculation and not actual use.

"If all that we accomplish is lambo memes and immature puns about 'sharting,' then I WILL leave," he wrote. "Though I still have a lot of hope that the community can steer in the right direction."

PART VI

Back to Earth

29

The Crash

Vitalik hoped the crypto community would steer away from the hype, but there soon wouldn't be another choice. A small tear in this gigantic hot air balloon that was the crypto market in 2017 had already started to open in November, when Palo Alto–based marketer Chelsea Lam got an email from the Securities and Exchange Commission.

Her story began at the end of 2015, when she decided to follow the dream of so many millennials in the Bay Area and started her own company. She wanted to make a reviews app that focused on food, like Yelp, but without all the comments about the atmosphere or parking space. It would be just about the food. Every review would require a picture of the actual dish, and that would also help weed out fake posts. She had a little under two years of marketing experience at software company VMware and Google, and she brought on two cofounders, an engineer and a computer scientist, to start Munchee. By mid-2017 they had launched the Munchee app for Apple devices and started seeing some traction. Then, inevitably, they learned about ICOs. They decided Munchee should be "on the blockchain" and have an Ethereum-based digital token to use within an ecosystem of diners and restaurants. In early October 2017 they announced a plan to raise $15 million in a token sale.

The idea was innocent enough: restaurants would pay diners for reviews with a token, diners would be able to use tokens to buy food at partner restaurants, and restaurants would also be able to use those tokens to pay for ads on the app. Of course they had read about the SEC's DAO investigation, which concluded that digital tokens could be considered securities. But they thought they'd be safe because their tokens would be sold to be used on the Munchee app, not as an investment. They even said so in their white paper: "As currently designed, the sale of MUN utility tokens does not pose a significant risk of implicating federal securities laws."

Things went awry when the team started to focus more and more on getting buyers for the ICO, regardless of whether they'd actually use the app. Munchee was made for the US market, but they promoted Munchee tokens everywhere. Chelsea talked it up at an Ethereum meetup in Singapore, and they were even offering tokens in exchange for promotional reviews on YouTube channels targeted to traders. One of these YouTubers said in a video, "Munchee is a crazy ICO. If you don't know what an ICO is, it is called an initial coin offering. Pretty much, if you get into it early enough, you'll probably most likely get a return on it," and somehow speculated that a $1,000 investment could create a $94,000 return. "7 Reasons You Need to Join the Munchee Token Generation Event" was the headline on an October 30 blog post by Munchee. Reason 4 was "as more users get on the platform, the more valuable your MUN tokens will become."

Money started flowing in as soon as the sale started and one day later, on November 1, the SEC's email came in. It's the last thing an ICO team wants to see in their inbox, and Chelsea and the rest were scared enough to shut the entire thing down and give back the $60,000 they raised from around forty people who had participated so far. On December 11 the SEC issued a cease-and-desist order for Munchee and a press release saying its "conduct constituted unregistered securities offers and sales." The SEC had determined Munchee tokens were securities. The key was in the then seven-decades-old Howey Test, which says that buyers are entering into investment contracts when they expect to profit from "entrepreneurial and managerial efforts of others." It was clear to SEC officials that Munchee was selling MUN tokens to investors who hoped to get a return on their purchase, and those returns depended directly on the Munchee management team.

Munchee was the second ICO case the SEC processed after the DAO statement. The first case came two months earlier in September, when the US regulator charged Maksim Zaslavskiy and his companies REcoin Group Foundation and Diamond Reserve Club with defrauding investors. Everything about Zaslavskiy's "business" was a lie, according to the SEC. There were no tokens, much less the real estate and diamonds investments that were supposed to be backing them. But Munchee was different. It was the first ICO case that signaled even companies not involved in actual scams could be under fire for selling digital assets.

As with other bad news during 2017, the market and crypto enthusiasts brushed it off. The SEC's press release came the day after Bitcoin futures launched on Cboe, and traders were still riding that high. But when Bitcoin touched its December 26 record of almost $20,000, it immediately started to tumble. There was no single piece of news that caused it. It had simply reached its tipping point. The day after the record, the largest cryptocurrency had dropped back to the $18,000s. Just one day later, it went to the $17,000s, and dropped to the $16,000s the next day. It hovered between around $13,600 and $17,000 for the next few days, and when January 2018 came, it continued dropping.

Ether was still soaring "to the moon" in January, but as soon as it reached over $1,400 the same thing happened. It had gone too far and the drop back down was precipitous. It went to as low as $765 just four days after the record.

The plunging market at the beginning of 2018 was a sign of what was to come, just like the splashy gains at the beginning of 2017. Like predators pouncing at the smell of blood, crypto's "enemies" started coming down hard on the nascent industry. South Korean police and tax authorities raided two of the largest cryptocurrency exchanges, and the country's regulators said they were planning greater oversight on trading platforms. China, which had already banned cryptocurrency exchanges in 2017, said it would escalate its crackdown as alternative trading venues continued to pop up. In India, the finance minister said the government would take measures to eliminate the use of cryptocurrencies in the payments system because they are not legal tender. A record $500 million heist at Japanese exchange Coincheck further spooked the market. Facebook banned cryptocurrency ads and US banks cut off credit card purchases of cryptocurrencies. And that was only January.

At the end of the month, US regulators made it clear that the couple of ICO cases it had gone after in 2017 had been just the beginning. On January 26, Jared Rice, a serial hustler whose latest attempt at getting rich was to do an ICO, woke up to FBI agents bursting into his East Dallas home. Rice wasn't only selling unregistered securities, he was also running a fraudulent business. He lied about buying a bank with "hundreds of banking partnerships" and deposits insured by US government agency FDIC. The truth was that they had no banking license. He said AriseBank clients would be able to spend "over 700 cryptocurrencies" with Visa debit and credit cards, when in reality he had no partnership with Visa.

He omitted the material fact that he was on probation for charges of felony and tampering with government records. They even lied about raising $600 million in their ongoing ICO. They actually raised less than $5 million, which court documents later showed they spent on hotel rooms, Uber rides, and clothes. They had also promised former heavyweight boxing champion Evander Holyfield AriseCoins in exchange for tweets promoting the ICO, even as the SEC had issued a statement saying it frowned upon celebrity endorsements. Later in 2018, the SEC got a court order to make Rice and cofounder Stanley Ford pay almost $2.7 million and banned them from leading public companies or participating in other digital securities offerings.

While Vitalik was glad people were using Ethereum, and he liked the idea of decentralized fundraising, he was disgusted that ICOs had also become a convenient vehicle for scammers. It was clear that initial coin offerings in their current form were broken. He wanted to better align the incentives of ICO investors with the teams issuing the coins. In January 2018, he came up with an improved model. In the original model, with startups getting millions up front, there was not much preventing ICO teams from running off with the money and never delivering a product, or simply dragging out development. Vitalik proposed to combine ICOs with decentralized autonomous organizations, or DAOs. The so-called DAICO would have a voting mechanism so that token holders could control the release of funds to the development team. Voters would release funds as milestones were met, and if they were unhappy, they could just shut down the DAICO and get their money back. Some teams tried this out, but the damage was done.

Many of the scams that mushroomed in 2017 started getting uncovered. Plexcoin was one of the many obvious Ponzi schemes, with promoters guaranteeing 1,300 percent monthly returns. The SEC shut them down in January. The two creators of CentraTech, the company behind the ICO promoted by Floyd Mayweather and DJ Khaled, were arrested for securities fraud. A Vietnamese company called Modern Tech, which had raised $660 million in two ICOs, simply disappeared with the money. Probably the most notorious scam was Bitconnect, another Ponzi scheme, infamous for a cultlike gathering where spokesman Carlos Matos half-danced, half-jumped around onstage as he told the cheering crowd how he was putting his money in the scheme even as his wife and friends told him it was a scam. At the end of his talk he derangedly screamed at the top of his lungs that he loves "Bit-Co-Neeeeect!" The company did an ICO and its coin was one of the best performing of 2017, reaching a market cap of $2.6 billion. At the start of 2018, the founders ran off with investors' money.

As many Ethereum-based tokens were abandoned or proven to be scams, others were showing actual use. One was MakerDAO's stablecoin Dai. When founder Rune Christensen decided to blow off crypto and do some soul-searching in Southeast Asia after The DAO hack, he had trusted the community would be able to push MakerDAO forward, but by the end of 2016 the project was stuck. The group of people working on it hadn't been able to decide at what price they should be selling the project's token MKR—it can be confusing, but the Maker platform has two tokens: Dai, which is the stablecoin, and MKR, which is used to pay stability fees (similar to interest) on Dai loans and vote on governance decisions.

Seeing this standstill, Rune decided to come back. He realized decentralization can only go so far. While MakerDAO was still in the early development phase, the project needed leadership and direction to keep moving forward. Leadership was critical if they wanted to launch the decentralized protocol and get to a state where it could function successfully in a fully decentralized manner. Early on, the team had opted to sell MKR tokens in periodic private sales to people actively involved in the community, rather than do a traditional ICO. When he came back from his voluntary exile, Rune argued in favor of selling MKR tokens at whatever price buyers were willing to pay, even if that meant pushing the price lower and lower. It worked and soon the project built enough traction that it was able to sell $12 million of MKR tokens in a funding round led by Silicon Valley–based venture capital firm Andreessen Horowitz and renowned crypto fund Polychain Capital. With that, the project was able to move forward, and in December 2017 they launched the first version of Dai.

Mariano Conti, an Argentine programmer, had joined Maker a few weeks after The DAO hack. Before that, he was designing websites for foreign clients, which is what got him into crypto. He would lose almost half of his earnings when clients paid him in dollars.

Argentina had currency controls at the time, which meant the money he received through international bank transfers was converted to pesos at the official dollar rate, which was around 30 to 50 percent lower than the black-market rate. That meant that if he went to the black market to buy dollars (the only way he could get his hands on actual USD), he'd be able to buy only about half of what he actually made. If he kept the money in pesos, annual inflation of as high as 40 percent would eat up his savings. So he started asking clients to pay him in bitcoin. He would cash out some of it into pesos for rent and other expenses at the start of the month and save the rest in the digital currency. In 2015, he heard about Ethereum for the first time and loved the idea of a more flexible Bitcoin, so he asked to get paid in ether instead.

The following year, his boss asked Mariano to work part-time with him on a new Ethereum-based project called MakerDAO. He liked bitcoin and ether better than his own currency, but the drawback of cryptocurrencies was that they're highly volatile. A cryptocurrency that's pegged to the dollar, like MakerDAO's Dai, keeps all the features of bitcoin and ether he liked (easy to transfer across borders, hard for governments to control), but was better at storing wealth. Unlike popular, fiat-backed stablecoin Tether, it also allowed holders to verify the funds backing it, and the community decided all monetary policy decisions in public votes. Dai was stable, transparent, decentralized, and programmable. He was sold and joined the Maker team full-time.

In February 2018, Mariano decided to use the MakerDAO platform to buy a car. The system allows users to put their ether in a smart contract and borrow Dai in exchange. This was right after ether had shot to an all-time high of over $1,400 and was trading at around $800. Mariano thought ether would continue climbing in the long term, so he didn't want to cash out to buy the 2015 Ford Focus he had his eye on. It wasn't a Lambo, but it would do, he joked with his longtime girlfriend. He put his ether in a smart contract, got the Dai loan, and traded Dai for Argentine pesos, which he used to buy the car. In three months, he paid back his loan plus 0.5 percent annual interest, and got his ether back. That was one of the first real-world purchases somebody made using Maker's so-called Collateralized Debt Positions, or CDPs, also known as Vaults.

But the progress being made by Maker and others in 2018 was lost amid a deluge of bad news. In April, reports that US regulators were investigating Bitfinex, one of the world's biggest cryptocurrency exchanges, and Tether, which issues a widely used stablecoin, would destabilize prices further. The US Commodity Futures Trading Commission on December 6 had sent subpoenas to the companies, which are operated by the same group of people, Bloomberg News reported. Tether claims each Tether coin, or USDT, is backed by one US dollar, and that's how it can maintain its 1 USDT equals $1 peg. But the company continuously failed to produce trustworthy evidence (like audited reports of its bank accounts) proving that its dollar reserves equal the amount of outstanding USDT. News stories didn't say what the CFTC was investigating, but the fact that there was an investigation taking place gave critics more credibility. An increasing number of skeptics started doubting Tethers were fully backed by dollars, and some said that the stablecoin was being used to manipulate cryptocurrency prices.

The following year, Tether admitted that USDT was not fully backed by US dollars and that in fact, only about three-fourths of the stablecoin was backed by fiat equivalents, including cash and short-term securities. Still, the company has denied claims about it using USDT to manipulate crypto markets.

Tether issuance started gradually rising in April 2017 and dramatically shot up in November, coinciding with the height of the boom and often accelerating when prices dropped. To some, the data showed Tether was being printed out of thin air and used to buy bitcoin to artificially pump up the price. About 80 percent of crypto trading is conducted through Tether, according to CryptoCompare. It does have a legitimate use case. Investors who want to minimize volatility but don't want to cash out into fiat will buy Tether and use it to cycle in and out of other cryptos. One potential explanation for its issuance patterns would be that a growing number of people were genuinely buying USDT to trade at those times. But if critics are right, much of the incredible rally, which made bulls think crypto had finally arrived into the mainstream, was nothing but a lie. It was a scary thought and it added to market jitters.

By mid-June, bitcoin had plunged below $7,000 for the first time since November, and ether dropped below $600, both halving their value from the recent record highs. The rest of the market was tumbling, too. Adding to suspicion that Tether might have been pumping the market, a growing number of reports on cryptocurrency exchanges' inflated volume started surfacing. Research firm Blockchain Transparency Institute said in an August report that almost 70 percent of the top 130 platforms listed in CoinMarketCap was likely engaging in wash trading, overstating their volume by at least three times. Crypto investor Sylvain Ribes said his research showed some exchanges were overstating their volumes by as much as 95 percent.

Crypto started to look like nothing more than magic internet money, traded on sketchy websites faking their volume, with a stablecoin that may or may not be fully backed by actual dollars as it claimed. On top of that, tokens sold in ICOs were probably unregistered securities in the United States and the teams behind them could potentially end up in jail. After coming down on Munchee and AriseBank, the SEC started sending out subpoenas to ICO teams like they were Christmas cards.

But surely real, nonspeculative use cases should be able to prop up digital assets, some may have asked. And they would have had trouble finding these users. About 90 percent of cryptocurrency trading in 2017 was for speculation, Lilita Infante, a member of the FBI's Cyber Investigative Task Force, told me for a Bloomberg News interview. Very few people were making payments and sending cross-border transfers with Bitcoin, and even fewer were using tokens on decentralized applications built on Ethereum. The decentralized ledger technology used by Bitcoin and Ethereum could only process a few transactions per second, and even if it could do more, applications and wallets were still too clunky to attract mainstream adoption. As prices fell, it became clear the main driver for digital asset prices in the previous year was the belief they would go higher. Cryptocurrencies had been mispriced as investors bought up coins before actual users could catch up to the promise of groundbreaking technology.

And so much for institutional respectability. At least nine firms waiting for approval to list Bitcoin ETFs pulled their filings in January at the request of the SEC. Regulators sent a letter to trade groups pushing for the investing vehicle, where they questioned how Bitcoin's volatility and lack of liquidity would fit with funds that have to calculate a fair market price for their portfolio at the end of every trading day and allow investors to easily cash out their shares. The SEC won't believe it's "appropriate" to register cryptocurrency exchange-traded funds until those questions are answered, the letter said. The fabled Goldman Sachs crypto trading desk touted by anonymously sourced reports was scrapped, according to other anonymous reports. The investing giant was getting cold feet on its big blockchain jump as regulators tightened their grip, a *Business Insider* article said. Volume on bitcoin futures in Cboe and CME was pitiful.

In mid-May, when New York blockchain week came around with its flagship Consensus conference and dozens of other events, the crowds were still there but the vodka–Red Bull drenched parties at strip clubs, vapid enterprise blockchain announcements, and rented Lambos smelled of desperation. After a small increase in crypto prices, or what hopeful enthusiasts call the "Consensus bump," digital coins continued their slide in the second half of the year.

Blockchain startups who raised money in ICOs during the boom were in a difficult position. Many of the twentysomething-year-old tech geeks with no experience in treasury management had kept most of their funds in ether instead of cashing some out into a more stable asset, thinking the cryptocurrency would continue rising, or at least wouldn't plunge so steeply. Now they had to decide whether they could ride the bear market and hope the price recovered, or cash out at a significantly lower price than when they had raised. The majority had no choice but to sell, and that put additional pressure on ether. Withdrawals accelerated in July, when ETH slumped below $500, and continued through the rest of the year as the cryptocurrency slid further. By the end of 2018 about 25 percent of ETH holdings had been withdrawn from a hundred startups' wallets, according to data by research firm Diar. ICOs had been the rocket fuel pushing ether into the stratosphere, and now they were forcing it back to earth.

ICOs had continued to soar at the start of the year, making new records in January and February with $1.8 billion and $2.4 billion raised, respectively, but then sales gradually started to decline. US regulators still hadn't clarified exactly when a digital token sale constituted an unregistered securities offering, just that depending on the circumstances, they all may be. Crypto startups had to be rattled when they heard SEC chairman Jay Clayton say in a Senate hearing in February, "I believe every ICO I've seen is a security," and they increasingly started switching to traditional venture capital fundraising.

With ICOs no longer a very viable source of funding, and many investors shying away from cryptocurrency startups, many teams were finding it difficult to bootstrap their projects. This included programmers working on Ethereum itself. The Ethereum Foundation has fewer than fifty contractors it pays below-market rates to develop the technology, research different solutions to make the network stronger and more scalable, and do administrative work. The rest of the thousands of developers working on Ethereum are doing so in independent companies, responsible for guaranteeing their own funding.

One of the main roles of the foundation is to financially support this ecosystem through grants, but since the grants program started, there has been little transparency on how funds are allocated. It's unclear what the application criteria and steps are, who is making the decisions, and exactly which projects have been funded and by how much. For a network and community built on blockchain, a technology that's in large part based on the goal of improving transparency, it was odd that the Ethereum Foundation itself was extremely opaque. It didn't disclose its financial statements, and nothing was known about its internal structure. There wasn't even a simple official organization chart to be found. While many in the community criticized this about the foundation, few were willing to criticize Vitalik himself, even though he had the final say.

Still, together with ConsenSys, the EF remained the biggest supporter of the Ethereum ecosystem through its grants and events. In March 2018, winners of the EF's first wave of grants were announced. The scope had been broadened out from a focus on scaling to include teams building a better user experience and improving security.

The exception to the downward slope of ICO funding in 2018 was one spike in June. Behind that spike was the biggest ICO ever: $4.2 billion raised by Cayman Islands–based Block.one for its blockchain project called EOS. BitShares cofounder Daniel Larimer was the company's CTO. The crowdsale, which lasted for the entire year leading up to June 1, was meant to fund a platform for decentralized applications to compete with Ethereum. EOS could be used as an example to show there was still interest in funding blockchain companies with ICOs, but the way the sale was structured and its association with one of its advisors led to more skepticism about crypto instead. Of course, the amount raised again prompted accusations that crypto startups had become too greedy and were in the space just to get rich quick. The amount raised would make EOS the second-biggest IPO in the United States in 2018 after Spotify, which raised $9.2 billion.

Unlike other large ICOs, Block.one was able to withdraw funds raised before the sale ended, and the EOS token was available to trade on exchanges almost immediately after the offering started. This raised some red flags. Block.one could potentially repeatedly withdraw ether raised and put it back in the sale to inflate volume and attract more buyers, and the ability to trade EOS tokens in the secondary market when holdings were still relatively centralized could have led to market manipulation, said ConsenSys-backed data analytics firm Alethio. The company withdrew funds ninety-three times during the token sale, according to the report. Others criticized the project because ten addresses owned 50 percent of the tokens. Beyond centralization around token holders, the project itself is designed to be controlled by just twenty-one block producers, which allows EOS to have a much higher throughput than Ethereum (potentially millions of transactions per second, it claims), but increases the risk of collusion among nodes. Block.one denies that it was involved in price manipulation of its token and says it's unaware of manipulation by any other parties.

And then there was the question of who was behind the project. Comedian John Oliver called this out in a *Last Week Tonight* segment on Bitcoin, where he mercilessly mocked a video where the cowboy-hat donning early Block.one advisor Brock Pierce said "everything that exists is no longer going to exist in the way that it does today, everything in this world is about to get better." Oliver called him a "sleepy creepy cowboy from the future," and suggested people google "Brock Pierce scandal." If viewers did, they'd see lawsuits that surfaced in 2000 from three employees of Pierce's first company, web video business Digital Entertainment Network, saying that he and two of his associates pressured them for sex when they were minors. Pierce, who has denied the accusations, paid more than $21,000 to settle one employee suit, according to a Reuters article, while the other cases were dropped.

EOS was far from the only new blockchain wanting to be the "Ethereum killer." Many smart contract platforms were popping up, claiming to have more advanced technology that allowed for hundreds and sometimes even thousands of transactions per second, compared with Ethereum's fifteen. Charles Hoskinson was building Cardano, with its ADA token. Unlike the unwieldy web of developers and volunteers building for and on Ethereum, Charles wanted to run a very structured ship. There are three entities creating what he calls a "third-generation blockchain": nonprofit, Switzerland-based Cardano Foundation, which helps oversee the development of the Cardano blockchain; Japan-based engineering firm IOHK, which has been contracted to build Cardano; and Japan-based Emurgo, a venture investment firm and startup incubator to support the Cardano and general blockchain ecosystem. Its crowdsale excluded US citizens to diminish regulatory risk and ADA tokens were sold mostly to Japanese investors. Instead of the decentralized and disorganized approach to research in Ethereum, Cardano moved slowly and carefully with peer-reviewed, open source code.

Some also believed Polkadot, built by Gavin Wood's Parity Technologies, would compete with Ethereum, though Gavin emphatically denies this is the case as Polkadot isn't a smart contract platform, but a protocol to connect all the different blockchains and make them interoperable. Still, as Vitalik gets all the credit for Ethereum even though Gavin feels he was the technical mind behind its initial implementation, it probably wouldn't be the worst thing to happen to him if Polkadot ended up beating Ethereum after all. There was also Dfinity, Stellar, Tron, NEO, Steem, Loom, Waves, Tezos, and others, vying to become the dominating decentralized applications platform, or at least the preferred platform for a specific use case. Ethereum developers and fans would scoff at most of them, pointing out how they compromise on security, decentralization, or both to increase throughput. But the question was whether users would even care. These new platforms had the advantage of starting out with faster blockchains, instead of having to upgrade the network while it was running and rely on a risky migration onto a second chain, like Ethereum—that is, if they ship, as many still haven't.

Aurel, the Romanian Ethereum miner, thought this was a huge disadvantage to the second-biggest cryptocurrency and is now betting on its competitors. He was more or less forced into the decision. His landlord raised electricity costs and with the ether price declining, it wasn't worth it to mine anymore, so he shut down the entire operation. That made him look at the space with more attention and he decided to sell all his ether, too, and use the gains to invest in proof-of-stake chains. He had contributed to proof-of-work, but it was now clear to him that proof of stake was the way forward. He'd earn a yield on his stake, instead of having to set up a whole mining operation.

Aurel wasn't the only one losing his patience. Union Square Ventures cofounder and early crypto investor Fred Wilson argued at a conference in October 2018 that Ethereum was "blowing" its lead, and that to stay ahead it should be run with the organized structure and professional management of a company.

"If all of us who own Ethereum could go to Vitalik and say, 'Look, this thing you got going in Switzerland isn't working. Fire those fuckers who don't know what the hell they're doing, put somebody great on there who can help you build this into a monster,'" he said, "there's no mechanism to do that, and it's painful just sitting there, holding the asset, watching them whittle the value away, and you're like 'God dammit, I know what to do here, just look at it, every great company has done this, just do that.' And they don't do it!"

"Ethereum killers" is one of the few topics that can prompt Vitalik to drop his mostly peaceful demeanor. He said at a conference that projects like EOS are "centralized piles of trash." Responding to a tweet by Tron founder Justin Sun, where he listed the reasons why his blockchain was better than Ethereum, Vitalik joked that Sun had copied Ethereum's white paper.

[Reason number] 8. Better white paper writing capability (Ctrl+C + Ctrl+V much higher efficiency than keyboard typing new content).

Ethereum would get an advantage to all the upstarts. In June the director of the SEC's Division of Corporation Finance, William

Hinman, said he considers ether not to be a security. Digital tokens aren't in themselves securities, but the way they're sold can be, and most often are, securities offerings, he said in a conference. That had been said by SEC officials many times before, but what was new about Hinman's statements was that he said the networks that digital tokens are built on can become decentralized enough over time so that the digital asset stops being a security, even if it was when it was sold. In the case of bitcoin, he said, the network on which it functions "is operational and appears to have been decentralized for some time, perhaps from inception." Putting aside the crowdsale, he said in the "present state of ether, the Ethereum network and its decentralized structure, current offers and sales of ether are not securities transactions."

Hinman had clarified that in his opinion, bitcoin and ether aren't securities and trading those cryptocurrencies wouldn't break any laws. No other cryptocurrencies were included in the statement. It wasn't clear whether SEC officials think Ethereum's crowdsale wasn't an unregistered securities offering, just that the platform and ecosystem was decentralized enough that it didn't rely on a third party at that moment.

Steven Nerayoff, who helped come up with the term "utility token" and get the opinion letter from Pryor Cashman, was on a retreat in Israel with employees and investors of his crypto fund Alchemist when Hinman made those statements. They were on a bus near the Masada ruins when Steven's nephew, who works with him in the fund, saw the news.

"Steve! Ether's not a security!" he said, grabbing him by the arm and shoving his phone up to his face.

"Thank God!" he said. It was very appropriate that they were in the Holy Land.

But the best news of the year for crypto was that the owner of the New York Stock Exchange, trading giant Intercontinental Exchange (ICE), said it would launch a cryptocurrency trading platform called Bakkt. There would be a physically delivered Bitcoin futures contract settled daily to make merchant adoption easier. To prove the point, the announcement of the exchange in early August was coupled with the news that Starbucks would accept Bitcoin payments through the Bakkt system. Other big names like Microsoft, the Boston Consulting Group, and Fortress Investment were also sprinkled in the release. That cheered up the crypto community a bit, but then the November launch date came and went with still no Bakkt, as rumors fluttered that not even a giant like ICE had been able to secure a green light from regulators.

Starting in July, the SEC amped up its anti-ICO proceedings and filed twelve cases, cracking down on issuers, trading venues, and promoters of the crypto crowdfunding mechanism through the end of the year. Most of the SEC's actions were announced in November, when ether dropped below $150 and continued sliding. Crypto hedge funds shuttered on dismal returns as bitcoin plunged almost 80 percent from its high, ether sank almost 90 percent, and the great majority of the smaller cryptos lost more than 90 percent of their value. ICO investors were left with worthless coins as startups abandoned their projects and went off with whatever money they had left; mainstream financial media moved on to other flashy news, like cannabis companies' IPOs; and the BTC ticker was quietly retired from the scrolling price band in Bloomberg TV and CNBC.

Not even ConsenSys could brave the brutal bear market and so had to become more constrained. By the end of 2018 it shifted its model into the so-called ConsenSys 2.0, which placed a greater focus on profitability and accountability for the more than fifty Ethereum ventures being built inside the company. One of the first decisions made under this new direction was to lay off 13 percent of its 1,200 staff.

Richard, the kitesurf addict who did some front-end design for Ethereum in the early days, had been able to sell part of his ether near the top but he was still feeling the pain of the downturn. He had felt so disgusted with the ICO model after his trip to Curacao for the Filecoin ICO that he started to distrust most teams raising many tens of millions of dollars, and the crypto space in general started to feel like a sticky swamp. When he looked at the money he was making, there was no denying it was great, but there was still this nagging, uneasy feeling deep in his stomach. One day he realized what it was. Guilt. He was rich but didn't feel he deserved it. He didn't think anyone in crypto deserved the money that had been poured into the sector.

Still, he believed there was something of value under all the trash. He continued to build a cryptocurrency wallet but decided against a token sale for fundraising. In August 2017, he and his team used a traditional crowdfunding website and got about $1.3 million to continue building Balance. Richard also got informal commitments from investors who said they'd continue supporting the project when that money ran out. That time came in 2018, but they all pulled the plug. After the market rout, they didn't have any money, either, or appetite to go into crypto. Richard had no choice but to reinvest his gains into his project to help keep it afloat. He wasn't as rich anymore, but at least the guilt was gone.

Then on the last month of the year, ether dropped below $100 for the first time since May 2017.

Ethereum developers try to pretend the price doesn't matter and avoid talking about it, but a lower price makes the network more vulnerable to attacks, and for many, even if they loathed to admit it, it was also a psychological blow. Unfortunately for Mariano Conti of MakerDAO, who had taken out a loan backed by ether when it was around $800 with the expectation that it would climb higher, the cryptocurrency had slumped by the time he got his ether back. He would have been better off cashing it out and buying a car with that. Still, it amazed him that he was able to take out a loan against his own money, using nothing but his digital wallet and digital coins, going only through computer code running on Ethereum's decentralized network. He tried to keep his chin up through the slump in chat rooms and Skype calls with other developers. But in the endless two weeks in mid-December, when ether went into double-digit prices and fell to as low as $82, he lay awake in the hot and sticky Argentine summer nights trying to clear his head, but dark thoughts kept making their way back in. Should he start looking for another job? Was this it for Ethereum?

30

The Party

Mariano Conti only had to think back to a few weeks earlier in Prague to push away the dark thoughts and doubts about the future of Ethereum. Like many of his fellow Ethereans, he had descended on the Czech Republic for the fifth Ethereum developer summit, Devcon4. He got off the subway station and appeared directly in front of the conference space the Ethereum gang would occupy from October 30 to November 2, 2018. It was an expansive four- to five-story gray concrete-and-glass building in a quiet neighborhood about thirty minutes from Prague's old town. A ribbon of screens wrapping around one side of the building, flashing rainbow colors and the words "welcome to devcon iv," clashed with the bland 1970s design.

He ran into people he had met at other Ethereum conferences and hackathons as soon as he approached the entrance and got in the long, winding line with them. There was no trace of the bear market inside. Tickets had sold out and now about three thousand programmers, designers, and other "builders" (as the Devcon website described its attendees) filled the 140,000-square-foot conference space. The theme of the conference was "building," but being crypto it had been modified into something more memeable and the word "buidl," emerged as a play on "hodl," the mantra of the bull market. The market had crashed, but there were twice as many people at Devcon 2018 as there were at the Cancun conference near the height of the bubble a year before.

Vitalik was actively trying to diminish his role in the Ethereum community. He didn't want to be seen as a larger-than-life, charismatic leader. Instead he wanted to gradually blend into the background and become one of many researchers focusing on proof-of-stake and scaling solutions, so that the network didn't need him for its survival. In early October he said on Twitter, "I think ethereum can absolutely survive me spontaneously combusting tomorrow at this point." Later that month, when Ethereans were getting ready for yet another upgrade, called Istanbul, Vitalik pointed out that the code changes for the hard fork "happened with *zero* involvement from The Great Dictator™."

Still, Vitalik's update on the state of Ethereum was one of the most anticipated talks of the gathering. It had been scheduled for October 31, 2018, which happened to be the tenth anniversary of Satoshi Nakamoto's Bitcoin white paper. Vitalik noted the timing first thing: "Ten and binary counting!" He went on to describe all the great things that Serenity, also known as Ethereum 2.0, would bring. "Casper! Scaling! EWASM!" he exclaimed. The acronym EWASM referred to Ethereum WebAssembly, a set of standards to execute computer programs used in the broader development space and meant to replace the Ethereum Virtual Machine.

Serenity would allow Ethereum to become "the world computer" as it was meant to be, "not a smart phone from 1999 that can process 15 transactions per second and maybe potentially play snake," Vitalik said. Serenity will be "even more decentralized than today," and have "hopefully about 1,000 times higher scalability." He didn't set a date for the launch of Serenity, but reassured the assembled that it was "really no longer so far away." Projected behind him was a slide that said, "Mandatory cute animal picture," and a picture of a beaver that seemed to be smiling and about to hug the camera.

At the end of Devcon, Vitalik and other Ethereum Foundation members, including one wearing a onesie with pumpkins printed all over it, got onstage to sing, "B-U-I, B-U-I, B-U-I-D-L, radical markets are coming to you, don't ICO when there's work to do." Lyrics were projected on a screen and the rest of the conference room sang and clapped along. Videos of the performance appeared online immediately, prompting Bitcoiners to criticize Ethereum for being a bit of a cult and Vitalik its leader. Awkwardly festive moments like this were not unusual for Ethereans, who were often inclined to wear weird costumes and dance on stage. They loved their emojis, memes, and pictures of rainbows, unicorns, and llamas just as much as crypto-speculators loved their Lambos.

But it wasn't just optimism and cute animals in Prague. In the two days previous to Devcon, over two hundred Ethereans gathered in an old theater. They were the Fellowship of Ethereum Magicians, a self-organized entity that had formed earlier that year with the goal of coming together in person, before large Ethereum conferences, to discuss the platform's and community's problems and take concrete action toward fixing them. At each "unconference" they would split into tracks, or "rings," to talk about different topics, from scaling to education and security. It was a necessary step as the foundation was deliberately diminishing its role so the broader community could take the lead. Aya Miyaguchi, the new ED, called this philosophy "beauty in subtraction" at a talk in Prague.

One of the best-attended rings, with around fifty people there and not enough chairs to sit on, was the business model track. They were mostly twentysomething-year-old, shaggy, pale, skinny developers and engineers, maybe a couple of years out of college—and they were a little scared. Creating a business was hard enough, and they were doing it in a new field and using open source, which has been notoriously hard to monetize; most had no business experience. Many there had done ICOs and lost most of their money in the bear market, while others were looking to raise funding for projects and found there was no investor interest anymore. The main question was, How could they find a more sustainable model to support open source development? They brainstormed, drawing inspiration from what others had done before in the traditional "Web 2" world, and soon different ideas started to emerge: Subscriptions, e-commerce, ads, grants. It felt like they were all coming together after a storm, trying to find warm patches of land to dry off and keep going.

By the end of 2018 and early 2019, the first Ethereum killer app, ICOs, had sizzled out. From an exponential climb month to month in 2017 to a record $2.1 billion in January 2018, amounts raised in token sales since then had steadily tapered off and were down to a couple of hundred millions in 2019. The novel fundraising mechanism hadn't died, but it had to be reined in. US participants were often excluded, sales were made privately and sometimes only to accredited investors, and issuers were demanding more information from token buyers. Investors had become more discerning, and the word "ICO" had become synonymous with scammy projects where startups stuck a token in the middle of a (sometimes fake) business to deceive gullible investors.

New fundraising models started to emerge, with varying degrees of success and many just marginally better than the token sales that proliferated in 2017. Initial Exchange Offerings, or IEOs, where cryptocurrency exchanges manage the sale on behalf of startups for a fee and list the tokens on their trading platforms, are one example. Security Token Offerings, or STOs, where startups seek approval from regulators to sell digital tokens to accredited investors, also emerged. The SEC even started to approve traditional IPOs where retail investors were able to buy compliant ERC20 tokens. Some of these were viable, albeit measured, alternatives. In general, the days when hundreds of millions would flow into digital wallets from anonymous users all over the world in minutes were over.

For many developers who were building Ethereum itself, the Ethereum Foundation continued to be an important source of funding, which still left many teams feeling they were in a precarious situation. Preston Van Loon, one of the developers working on one of the most advanced Ethereum 2.0 implementation at Prysmatic Labs, tweeted out at the end of 2018 that his team's biggest distraction was that they had to have other full-time jobs—Preston was a programmer at Google. Vitalik unexpectedly dropped into the conversation and tweeted, "Just sent 1000 eth. Yolo," with a link to the transaction.

Vitalik's Twitter name is 'Vitalik Non-giver of Ether," a response to the many scammers posing as him on the platform trying to trick people into handing over crypto. Many Twitter users saw the irony. "Vitalik Non-giver of Ether > Just sent 1000 eth. I DONT KNOW WHAT TO BELIEVE ANYMORE," was one of the most liked responses.

One of the developers at Lighthouse, which was building another Ethereum 2.0 implementation, said they could also "turn 1k ETH into more developers!" and Vitalik responded, "Guess I have to," and sent ETH their way. Then, a developer from blockchain design and consultancy firm ChainSafe said, "I will quite literally drop out if we got $100K in ETH." After some back-and-forth so Vitalik could make sure it wasn't an "evil hacker impersonating Chainsafe," he sent over the funds and said, "I expect results!"

While the community celebrated Vitalik's deus ex machina move, these exchanges further showed exactly what venture capitalist Fred Wilson was cautioning against—that fundamental infrastructure projects for Ethereum were short on funds and that no amount of whimsical benevolence from Vitalik, using his own money, would make up for the lack of steady funding and structure required to take Ethereum to the next level. Journalist Laura Shin asked Vitalik to address the venture capitalist's criticism directly in a live recording of her *Unchained* podcast in March 2019.

"There's definitely been people from time to time who have just said, 'yeah, we need to go in with guns blazing and fire those bastards, get 40 people in and stick them in the middle of Silicon Valley, and get them to pay $10,000 a month in rent, get them to work for 16 hours every day for six months, rah, rah, and we got Ethereum 3.0, man!'" he said, earning the laughter and applause from the audience. "And, like . . . no."

Vitalik was happy with the way Ethereum was structured, without one single, central entity controlling development, but rather many different companies and foundations voluntarily organizing to build what's needed. Some will fail and some will succeed, he reasoned, and what seems like chaos to outside observers will result in a stronger path to Ethereum 2.0.

In the meantime, many developers were not waiting around for Serenity. They were using workarounds and scaling tools that were already live to keep building. Ameen Soleimani was at the helm of one of the companies doing this successfully. SpankChain, his brainchild, had a working platform, actual users, and revenue one year after it had ICO'ed in 2017. It's a platform for adult entertainers to get crypto in exchange for performing on live video, ensuring the transaction can go through without interference, as banks and regulators often do in the porn industry. With SpankChain, porn was pushing forward cryptocurrency adoption just like it did with electronic payments through the internet. By the end of 2018, SpankChain had almost six thousand active users and had paid about $70,000 in cryptocurrency to more than thirty webcam models since the site launched in April. They were doing this using state channels, a Layer 2 technology that allows users to send instant payments with crypto.

Ethereans also started to build new solutions for governance, as a traditional management team, whose existence wouldn't be questioned in a regular startup, became a potential single point of failure in decentralized systems. In that context, the term DAO started to reappear. One of the first DAOs to handle a project's governance was MakerDAO's system, but then other organizations started to emerge as a way to find a more permanent way to fund projects in the community, as the EF's funds would eventually run out. Ameen of SpankChain was also behind MolochDAO, a decentralized, autonomous organization meant to collect funds for Ethereum projects. Its members can vote on which projects to fund, much like the original DAO. Vitalik, the foundation, Joe Lubin, and ConsenSys all donated money. In a sign that the community had fully healed from its most traumatic event ever and wasn't afraid to explore how smart contracts could help run more transparent and efficient organizations, a handful of other DAOs started popping up.

Another big trend was emerging in Ethereum, and Alvaro Yermak, the Argentine bank teller who went through the *corralito* almost twenty years ago was benefiting from it, just like he did with Bitcoin. In September 2018, five years after Alvaro bought his first BTC, he was married and vacationing with his wife and her child in the Brazilian beach town of Natal. They had saved for months for that trip and made the reservations back in March. Emma, who calls Alvaro "dad," had been counting the days since then. One day, they were checking their emails in the hotel lobby before going to the beach. Emma was tugging at their T-shirts for them to hurry up.

They were about to head out when Alvaro thought about looking at his Bitcoin wallet balance. The market had been horrible that year but still, he continued to buy fractions of coins whenever he had a few pesos saved up. Just like during the 2001 crisis, Alvaro's job at the bank gave him a firsthand look at the economy. President Mauricio Macri had come to power after a decade of Kirchner rule to rescue the country from the claws of populism and corruption, but Argentina just couldn't avoid falling into the same traps: mounting dollar debt and a widening budget deficit. By 2018, the peso was in free fall again and inflation spiraled to 50 percent. If bills cycling through the economy can be compared to blood pumping through the body, Alvaro had his fingers on the pulse. He had been promoted to supervise the ATMs in Tucuman and could tell how fast money was changing hands in a country that still uses cash for much of its transactions and where bill denominations haven't kept up with inflation. People were quickly leaving the machines dry. Salaries weren't keeping up with inflation and people were having a hard time making ends meet. Taking out loans, especially long-term ones like mortgages, was out of the question for most as interest rates skyrocketed.

So when Alvaro checked his Ripio digital wallet (where he bought and stored his bitcoin) from the hotel lobby in Brazil, he was surprised to see a new "loans" button. Valeria and Emma had grabbed their beach towels and were waiting by the lobby's revolving door.

"Hold on a second, I think I just spotted an opportunity here," he said.

Alvaro requested 4,500 pesos, or a little more than $100 at the time, just to test how it worked. The app had verified his account with a copy of his ID and a pay stub a few months ago and didn't ask for anything else this time. Two days later he had an extra 4,500 pesos in his digital wallet, which he would have to pay back, plus 6 percent interest, at the end of the month. He couldn't believe it. He was able to get a loan when he was away on vacation, with sand between his toes, without having to sit at the bank and sign on the dotted lines while making small talk with a bored account manager. It just took a couple of clicks and two days. Most important, he would pay way below the market rate.

A few days after he got back home, he applied for a second loan for 75,000 pesos, and again had the money in his account within two days. He immediately used it to continue making his usual investment: he bought more bitcoin. The cryptocurrency slumped almost 6 percent in September, but Alvaro wasn't worried. He's in it for the long haul. Also, the peso weakened 8 percent in the same period.

What Alvaro didn't know was that on the other side of his loan wasn't Ripio lending him the money. There was an investor, who could be anywhere in the world but let's say South Korea because many of Ripio's enthusiasts are concentrated there. The application exchanged Alvaro's ether for the Ripio Credit Network's token, called RCN, and from RCN to pesos and then back again when the loan was paid. The lender got his loan plus interest back in ether. The loan itself was a smart contract that automatically executed the exchange. The Ethereum-based digital token and network enabled a worker in a far-flung province of Argentina to borrow from an anonymous investor, who was probably on the other side of the world.

Neither knew who the other was. There were far fewer intermediaries involved in the process than with a regular bank loan, so Alvaro was able to get a better rate, and the global network allowed him access to a larger pool of potential lenders. The investor on the other side made a sizable return.

Alvaro has a bank account, but someone without one, which is half of the Argentine population and about 60 percent of Latin America, can also get access to credit. All they need is an internet connection and a computer or cell phone. They can use cash to charge their digital wallets in the same payments collecting services at corner bodegas and subway stations that they use to pay bills and charge cell phones. In 2018 about 20 percent of Ripio's 300,000 wallet users didn't have a credit card.

A new Ethereum-based phenomenon was emerging and like ICOs previously, it was one of the main drivers of innovation in the blockchain space. Crypto startups like MakerDAO and Ripio were creating a whole new financial system from scratch. They were ditching the old ways of banking, where financial firms control users' information, hold their money, and sit in the middle of transactions taking a cut. Instead, all the services traditionally offered by banks and brokers, from lending to trading and betting, are being built on the Ethereum blockchain.

While there are varying degrees of centralization, these platforms tend to be peer-to-peer apps that increase users' control of their funds and their information, no third party is required to transact, and, outside of expensive sustained attacks such as more than 50 percent of miners colluding or spamming the network, third parties can't censor or stop transactions, either.

Because these apps run on the public Ethereum blockchain, it means the flow of funds is transparent and anyone can take the open source code and inspect it. They can even fork a project and modify it. The movement came to be known as "decentralized finance," or DeFi, and also "open finance." It was banking without banks.

While ICOs had disrupted fundraising, open finance was arguably going even further. It's not just about fundraising; it's about the entire financial system. These projects were taking better advantage of the programmable nature of Ethereum, exploring how to recreate the more complex aspects of finance, like loans and derivatives, in a decentralized way. The "Web 3" vision, where Ethereum would be the world computer running a new blockchain-based version of the internet, was far from realized, but the largest smart contracts platform was making strides in the important sector of finance.

Collateral became a popular way for platforms to issue loans without having to screen each users' credit score. For example, traders would deposit 150 ether into a smart contract to get 100 Dai, which they often used to buy more cryptocurrency. In some ways it's less convenient than getting credit without putting up any assets, but it also eliminated the need to provide any personal information or deal with any humans at all. The whole process is done automatically, in a few minutes, from anywhere. By early 2020, the amount of money being used as collateral to back loans and other transactions in decentralized finance crossed $1 billion, from just $10 million a year earlier. There was real value being transacted, and though it was mainly used to speculate, its advocates argued it was only early days and eventually a broader audience would also be shunning their banks and taking out loans in DeFi platforms.

MakerDAO was the backbone of this emerging, financial ecosystem as the majority of the assets being used as collateral to back up loans was deposited in the platform. Users locking up ether on MakerDAO got Dai in return, the stablecoin that's linked to the price of the dollar. The platform started to become something like the ecosystem's central bank, except instead of being controlled by a small group of old economists, users everywhere could issue Dai against their ether and vote on the interest rate that regulates the price of Dai so it remains at $1. And MakerDAO was just one part of this ecosystem. There were applications for lending, payments, exchanges, insurance, identity, issuing derivatives, and more.

Bancor, the decentralized liquidity pool cofounded by Galia Benartzi, was another one of these. Like Uniswap, Kyber Network, 0x, and other decentralized exchanges, the protocol she had helped create was giving people the ability to transact without a middleman. For much of 2017 and 2018, Bancor would be mostly thought of as the company that raised $153 million in three hours during the ICO mania, and was lumped together with opportunists who proliferated at the time. Now, finally, two years later, it was part of this growing blockchain-based financial ecosystem, and its reputation had started to recover. By mid-2019, forty thousand people had exchanged $2 billion on the platform.

It wasn't just this grassroots financial movement using Ethereum. Big companies were building on the decentralized network more than ever. Some two years after JPMorgan's CEO Jamie Dimon labeled Bitcoin a "fraud," the US bank launched its own cryptocurrency created on Quorum, an enterprise-focused version of Ethereum. Microsoft and Amazon use Ethereum for their blockchain-as-a-service platforms, which aims to help users implement distributed ledger technology. Accounting firm EY built tools to allow companies to privately create, trade, and destroy tokens on top of Ethereum, in a project called Nightfall.

By the time New York blockchain week came around in mid-2019, there were no Lambos or Aston Martins, no parties at strip clubs making headlines. But stats on Ethereum were healthier than ever. The network had higher transaction volume than Bitcoin and four times the number of developers, according to a report by Electric Capital. Gas spent was at the highest since December 2017, and the number of accounts opened continued to climb. The incentive for quick ICO money was gone, but developers continued building on the network, this time with the more sustainable aim of delivering value to users. As DeFi and DAOs flourished on Ethereum, bitcoin was on its way to cross $10,000 again. While ether lagged its rally, it also recovered from the 2018 lows, staying safely away from double-digit territory.

The value proposition of uncensorable money for crypto remained, but an added macro trend would become relevant. There was rising awareness that long-ago scrappy upstarts Facebook and Google had now become megacorporations serving as the main gateways to the internet, and that regardless of their company logos, they were very much able to "do evil." For too long, users had neglected to question what they were giving away to use these platforms "for free." The Cambridge Analytica scandal, which revealed that the consulting firm had used thousands of people's Facebook data without their consent to influence political events including Brexit and US elections, put the issue in the forefront of public discourse. People are handing over all the minute details of their lives, including second-to-second GPS location, private chats, and surreptitious recordings of conversations, and these companies are profiting from that data. Blockchain technology offers an alternative to that dark future, where people would take back control of not just their money, but their personal information, too.

At the end of New York blockchain week, in a sun-drenched, industrial-sized coworking space in Brooklyn, Ethereans gathered for a hackathon. They filed in from Friday evening, crowded into whatever desks and tables they could find to set up their laptops, and started typing away through Sunday. There were about four hundred of them making Ethereum dapps. Maybe the new CryptoKitties would be built that weekend. Maybe even from the very CryptoKitties team; Dapper Labs was there promoting its new game, Cheeze Wizards. They hadn't left Ethereum, scaling problems and all. Jeff Scott Ward, who had quit ConsenSys, was there, figuring out what to do next. Ameen Soleimani of Spank-Chain and MolochDAO and Mariano Conti of MakerDAO were there, too.

Not at the hackathon but still in Ethereum, Richard Burton was building the Balance wallet, emphasizing better user experience—the effort failed to gain enough traction, though, and he had to shut

down the company by the end of the year. On the other coast, Taylor
Monahan's wallet, now called MyCrypto, continued to be one of
the most-used in Ethereum, and Taylor was seeking to integrate her
application with the new decentralized platforms that kept popping
up. Vlad Zamfir continued researching Casper CBC and blockchain
governance. Texture's sanctuary was the high-tech music studio in
his Oakland mansion, where he spent much of his time, though he
continued to watch Ethereum closely and advocated for a more open
Ethereum Foundation. More tangentially related to Ethereum now,
Ming continued to recover from her time at the helm of Ethereum,
watching how the platform developed from a safe distance at a sea-
side location. Mihai and Roxana were back in Romania, close to family and building Akasha, a blockchain-based social network, while
Jeff Wilcke was also enjoying time with his family and building
video games in the Netherlands. Amir was still supporting different
blockchain projects from the shadows.

In 2019 Steven Nerayoff continued to fund and support blockchain companies investing in some of the space's top or most buzzed-
about projects, including tZERO, ZCash, Algorand, and others. He
also worked on bringing regulation to the industry. Still, it was a tough
time as he was involved in a legal dispute with one of the startups he
advised.

Gavin Wood's Web 3 Foundation had conducted a second sale
of DOT tokens at a valuation of $1.2 billion and was getting ready
to launch the Polkadot network around the new year. Joe Lubin was
similarly raising money for ConsenSys, which was also rumored to
be valued at around $1 billion, and was operating as a full-fledged
Ethereum-startup factory. Charles Hoskinson was painstakingly
building Cardano so that every line of its code was bulletproof. He
was also enjoying his crypto riches with a brand-new Lambo and
a huge ranch with horses and goats frolicking about near Boulder,
Colorado. Anthony Di Iorio stepped down as CEO of Decentral,
the maker of the Jaxx cryptocurrency wallet, and while he remained

chairman, he shifted his focus into the health and wellness space with his own consultancy. He had also cashed out $28 million of his cryptos to buy a 16,000-square-feet penthouse on the fifty-something floor of the St. Regis in Toronto. And hackers everywhere continued to build other Ethereum killers.

Back at the hackathon in Brooklyn, internet friends were becoming real-life friends. They were all building projects that work with each other's projects. They had stuck around through the depths of the market crash. And now they were getting to see firsthand what would emerge from the ashes. They were typing away at their keyboards, *building*. Yes, the potential still felt infinite. It's wasn't work; it was a celebration. *We're still here, and we're stronger.* No one was in a hurry to leave that party, not the one in Brooklyn, nor the Ethereum party that was still going on in semi-abandoned warehouses, overcrowded apartments-turned-offices, and makeshift hacking hubs around the world.

Vitalik arrived at the New York hackathon with two friends who quickly scattered, leaving him to walk alone to the coffee stand and make himself a cup of tea. Yes, he still controlled the foundation, which he had mostly closed off to the world, maybe as a way to protect it from the chaos of the early days. Or maybe as a way to protect the dream of an infinite machine from the grubby hands of an avaricious world. And yes, he was still widely revered as the creator of Ethereum, even as he tried to wean the community off his influence. Where it mattered the most, in the technical decisions about the protocol, Vitalik was just one voice among a group of other core developers and researchers. He looked like just another young geek, just another idealistic crypto-anarchist wearing a funny T-shirt that might very well feature unicorns and rainbows. Most people around him were busy hacking, and everyone else was engrossed in excited conversation. He looked around and joined one of these small groups. He was just one more Etherean. Almost.

■ ■ ■

After that first Ethereum hackathon, when developers gathered to build dapps right before the peak of the bubble, similar events were held in cities all over the globe. Two years later, in November 2019, the gang was back where it all started, in Waterloo, Canada. About two hundred young developers filled the auditorium for the opening ceremony on Friday night, some balancing laptops on their knees while others peeled off layers of clothes as they shook the frigid temperatures away. It was dark outside and it would start snowing soon.

I sat with Vitalik onstage to talk about what the past two years were like for Ethereum. Back in 2017, he was very vocal in expressing concern about how market valuations didn't justify actual value being created by cryptocurrencies. I asked him if, with ETH at under $200 and BTC at under $10,000, that was still the case.

"Two years ago people's expectations were definitely getting far ahead of the reality," he said. "Now on the one hand the hype is lower, and on the other hand the reality is better. And I think that's good on both fronts. We've made a lot of progress."

Specifically, Ethereum developers have made progress on scalability, proof of stake, and decentralized finance and other applications, he said.

Still, Ethereum was seldom seen in major news headlines anymore and crazed investors had moved on, which might have led an outsider to think the wild ride was over for the second-biggest crypto. To Vitalik the opposite was true. Ethereum was stronger than ever, and creating concrete value. "Looking forward to when it starts doing that on a much larger scale," he said.

And would he go as far to say that ETH is undervalued?

Developers listening raptly to what Vitalik had to say would implicitly give their own answers over the weekend as they pushed total applications created at hackathons to one thousand. But Vitalik demurred. ". . . No comment," he said. Ethereans laughed and soon after started emptying out the room. They were ready to continue building.

Acknowledgments

I'm immensely grateful for the support, trust, encouragement, and help of so many amazing human beings, without whom this book simply would not exist.

I'd like to thank Hollis Heimbouch, my editor at HarperCollins, for her brilliant insights and thoughtful guidance on how to best shape this story, for giving me the freedom to decide on its direction, for her confidence in me and patience throughout. I'm also grateful to the entire HarperCollins team, who took a chance on this first-time author: the copy editors, designers, lawyers, and everyone involved in the production of this book.

I'm grateful to Dan Mandel, my agent, who helped me turn what initially was a rough idea into an actual book proposal and advocated for me in front of the world's greatest publishers. His advice was invaluable in wading through the world of book publishing, which was foreign to me. His persistent encouragement helped me get through times of insecurity, which inevitably crept through along the process.

Of immeasurable importance, too, are all my sources, who took many hours off their busy schedules to tell me their stories, who patiently explained complicated technical terms, who generously shared research material and connected me to their networks, and who in many cases let down walls and opened up their hearts to me. I do not take that trust you deposited in me lightly, and I worked tirelessly, for two years, to accurately represent our conversations. They're too many to name here, and some would also like to remain anonymous.

Acknowledgments

I'd like to especially highlight the help of Alan Krassowski and Alex Van de Sande, who thoroughly reviewed the manuscript—in its entirety in the case of Alan, and a section in the case of Alex—and scrutinized it for any technical inaccuracies. Of course, any mistakes that made their way to the final copy are my own responsibility.

When I first started this process, officially in June 2018, I was still a Bloomberg News reporter. My managers at the time supported and encouraged me throughout, even when the path I took resulted in my decision to leave the newsroom, of which I had been a happy member for eight years. I'd like to especially thank Madeleine Lim, who mentioned I should write a story about ICOs after seeing my interest on crypto—the story catapulted my side job as a crypto reporter—and has rooted for me along the way, and Michael Regan, who put up with me taking time from my role as Markets Live blogger to write about crypto, and leaving the small team on my book leave and then later as I followed a different direction.

Other Bloomberg colleagues I'd like to mention even if they weren't as involved in the book writing process are Rodrigo Orihuela, who first pointed me to Bitcoin, back in 2013. I have him to thank for my first-ever story about crypto. I also want to thank David Papadopoulos and Laura Zelenko, who advocated to hire me at Bloomberg in the first place when I had one foot out the door after the internship.

I want to also thank Nick Tomaino, with whom I shared my ambition to write a book about crypto when it was just an idea. In late 2017, Nick planted the idea in my head to write a book about how Ethereum was created.

I've left for the end those who have been with me from the very start with unconditional support; my family. Infinite gratitude goes to my husband, Chris, who reassured me (and also endured me) when I was stressed, insecure, anxious, worried, and all the not-so-wonderful-but-necessary feelings I know I'm not the first author to feel in this process. And who also shared my pride, happiness, and satisfaction in having completed a lifelong dream in the best way I knew how. Before anyone else, he was sounding board, proofreader, and editor. Huge thanks go to my mother, who has pushed me to become a writer since the first time she read the short stories I scribbled in my childhood journals. Thanks for being my biggest fan, always.

Notes

1: Mooning

5   poured into this crowdfunding mechanism that year: "Funds Raised in 2018," ICO Data, 2018, https://www.icodata.io/stats/2018.

5   Canada, Mexico, and Brazil in that time, combined: Ey, *Big vs. Agile? Global IPO Trends: Q4 2018*, 2018, https://www.ey.com/Publication /vwLUAssets/ey-global-ipo-trends-q4-2018/$FILE/ey-global-ipo -trends-q4-2018.pdf.

2: Cypherpunks' Fever Dream

11   an anonymous digital currency: David Chaum, "An Anonymous Digital Currency: Blind Signatures for Untraceable Payments," in David Chaum, Ronald L. Rivest, and Alan T. Sherman, eds., *Advances in Cryptology: Proceedings of CRYPTO 82* (New York : Plenum Press, 1983), http://www.hit.bme.hu/~buttyan/courses/BMEVIHIM219/2009 /Chaum.BlindSigForPayment.1982.PDF.

12   Timothy May wrote in the manifesto: Timothy May, "The Crypto Anarchist Manifesto," November 22, 1992, https://activism.net/cypher punk/crypto-anarchy.html.

17   "ongoing chain of hash-based proof-of-work": Satoshi Nakamoto, "Bitcoin P2P E-cash Paper," Cryptography Mailing List, October 31, 2008, https://satoshi.nakamotoinstitute.org/emails/cryptography/1 /#selection-75.18-83.27.18.

18   Satoshi Nakamoto wrote in the paper: Satoshi Nakamoto, "Bitcoin: A Peer-to-Peer Electronic Cash System," 2008, https://bitcoin.org/bitcoin .pdf.

22   "Bitcoin offers a way to fix this": Vitalik Buterin, reply to "Bitcoin Weekly Looking for Writers," BitcoinTalk, March 25, 2011, https://bit cointalk.org/index.php?topic=4916.msg72174#msg72174.

3: The Magazine

25   "suddenly crash at any time": Vitalik Buterin, "Causes Behind the Bitcoin Price Rally," *Bitcoin Weekly*, May 15, 2011, https://web.archive

.org/web/20130916232908/http://bitcoinweekly.com:80/articles/causes
-behind-the-Bitcoin-price-rally.

27   "available payment options": "The First Issue of Bitcoin Magazine
Goes to Print," Matthew N. Wright, PRWeb, May 2, 2012, http://www
.prweb.com/releases/2012/5/prweb9463303.htm.

28   Mihai kept the magazine going: "Bittalk Media Ltd Announcement,
September 9, 2012," *Bitcoin Magazine*, September 9, 2012, https://web
.archive.org/web/20120913060903/http://bitcoinmagazine.net
/announcement/.

4: The Rabbit Hole

32   at the beginning of the year: Carrie Kirby, "Bitcoin 2013 to Draw
1,000, and the Winklevii, to San Jose This Weekend," CoinDesk, May 17,
2013, https://www.coindesk.com/bitcoin-2013-to-draw-1000-and-the
-winklevii-to-san-jose-this-weekend/.

35   risks and common sense: Enric Duran, "I Have 'Robbed' 492000
Euros Whom Most Rob Us in Order to Denounce Them and Build Some
Alternatives Society," *Enric Duran* (blog), 2008, https://enricduran.cat
/en/i-have-robbed-492000-euros-whom-most-rob-us-order-denounce
-them-and-build-some-alternatives-society-0/.

5: The Swiss Knife

37   wrote for a *Bitcoin Magazine*: Vitalik Buterin, "Bitcoin at Porcfest,
Part 0: Exploring Boston and New Hampshire," *Bitcoin Magazine*, June 15,
2013, https://bitcoinmagazine.com/articles/Bitcoin-at-porcfest-part
-0-exploring-boston-and-new-hampshire-1371335040/.

38   strike against them: Vitalik Buterin, "Bitcoiners from Around the
World Meet in Amsterdam," *Bitcoin Magazine*, September 29, 2013,
https://bitcoinmagazine.com/articles/bitcoiners-from-around-the-world
-meet-in-amsterdam-1380482873/.

41   exchange (1 BTC for 100 MSC): J. R. Willett, "It's here: The Second
Bitcoin Whitepaper," BitcoinTalk, January 6, 2012, https://bitcointalk.org
/index.php?topic=56901.0.

42   "Anybody can do that": Digital Magus, "Bitcoin 2013 - Day 2 - Bitcoin
in the Future, part 4 of 5," YouTube, uploaded May 22, 2013, https://www
.youtube.com/watch?v=4bMf4xZg_4U&feature=youtu.be&t=4m19s.

43   wrote in the paper: Nick Szabo, "Formalizing and Securing
Relationships on Public Networks," *First Monday* 2, no. 9, (September
1997), https://ojphi.org/ojs/index.php/fm/article/view/548/469.

43   wanted to change that: Nick Szabo, "Smart Contracts: Building
Blocks for Digital Markets," 1996, http://www.fon.hum.uva.nl/rob

/Courses/InformationInSpeech/CDROM/Literature/LOTwinter
school2006/szabo.best.vwh.net/smart_contracts_2.html.

45 "more generalized way": Vitalik Buterin, "Ultimate Scripting: A
    Platform for Generalized Financial Contracts on Mastercoin," 2014,
    https://web.archive.org/web/20150527194453/http://vbuterin.com
    /ultimatescripting.html.

47 "adopted his ideas": Colored Coins Google Groups, https://groups
    .google.com/forum/#!forum/bitcoinx.

6: The White Paper

54 and debate championships: Centre for Education in Mathematics
    and Computing, "International Olympiad in Informatics," University of
    Waterloo, 2010, https://cemc.math.uwaterloo.ca/contests/computing
    /canada_ioi.html.

54 that didn't really stick: "Testimonials from Alumni," Abelard School,
    https://www.abelardschool.org/students-testimonials.

56 40 bytes from 80 bytes: "Bitcoin Core Version 0.9.0 Released,"
    Bitcoin.org, March 19, 2014, https://Bitcoin.org/en/release/v0.9.0#how
    -to-upgrade.

56 "volunteer network resource": Jeff Garzik, reply to "[ANN][XCP]
    Counterparty Protocol, Client and Coin (built on Bitcoin)—Official,"
    BitcoinTalk, March 21, 2014, https://bitcointalk.org/index.php?topic
    =395761.msg5815887#msg5815887.

7: The First Responders

65 become a new UTXO: Flora Sun, "UTXO vs Account/Balance
    Model," Medium, April 14, 2018, https://medium.com/@sunflora98
    /utxo-vs-account-balance-model-5e6470f4e0cf.

70 "Worrying and Love Crypto": Charles Hoskinson and Brian Göss,
    "Bitcoin or How I Learned to Stop Worrying and Love Crypto," Udemy,
    October 2013, https://www.udemy.com/bitcoin-or-how-i-learned-to
    -stop-worrying-and-love-crypto/.

71 combining their efforts: Charles Hoskinson, "Announcing Project
    Invictus: a P2P Exchange Collaboration," BitcoinTalk, June 8, 2013, https://
    bitcointalk.org/index.php?topic=229315.msg2412906#msg2412906.

72 "without Fiat Deposits": Daniel Larimer, "0.5 BTC Bounty—Creating
    a Fiat/Bitcoin Exchange without Fiat Deposits," BitcoinTalk, June 2, 2013,
    https://bitcointalk.org/index.php?topic=223747.0.

73 many more, they argued: Stan Larimer, "Bitcoin and the Three Laws
    of Robotics," Let's Talk Bitcoin! Network, September 14, 2013, https://
    letstalkbitcoin.com/bitcoin-and-the-three-laws-of-robotics.

Notes

73   Bitcoin Conference in October: Daniel Larimer, "Introducing
     Keyhotee—Next Generation Identity, DNS, Messaging, and Wallet,"
     BitcoinTalk, October 24, 2013, https://bitcointalk.org/index.php
     ?topic=317462.0.
73   "firing of their CEO": sumantso, reply to "BitShares and
     Mastercoin—a Comparison," BitcoinTalk, January 2, 2014, https://
     bitcointalk.org/index.php?topic=325425.60.
74   implementation in London: Nermin Hajdarbegovic, "Ethereum
     Launches 'Cryptocurrency 2.0' Network," CoinDesk, January 23, 2013,
     https://www.coindesk.com/ethererum-launches-cryptocurrency-2-0-net
     work.

8: The Miami House

78   email and asked to meet: Guy Grandjean and James Ball, "Bitcoin:
     The Fastest Growing Currency in the World—Video," *Guardian*, March 22,
     2013, https://www.theguardian.com/technology/video/2013/mar/22
     /bitcoin-currency-video.
79   coders who could help: Vitalik Buterin (@VitalikButerin), "The
     earliest emails from @gavofyork reaching out to me in Dec 2013. Thanks
     a lot for Gav's crucial contributions to ethereum!," Twitter, August 10,
     2017, https://twitter.com/VitalikButerin/status/895518902817480708.
84   bigger potential was there: Vitalik Buterin, "Mastercoin: A Second-
     Generation Protocol on the Bitcoin Blockchain," *Bitcoin Magazine*,
     November 4, 2013, https://bitcoinmagazine.com/articles/mastercoin-a
     -second-generation-protocol-on-the-bitcoin-blockchain-1383603310/.

9: The Announcement

88   minimalistic Berlin apartment: "North American Bitcoin Conference
     Coming to Miami," Marketwired, January 8, 2014, https://globenews
     wire.com/news-release/2014/01/08/1061356/0/en/North-American
     -Bitcoin-Conference-Coming-to-Miami.html.
89   answers one by one: BitShares, "Dan Larimer and Vitalik Buterin at
     the North American Bitcoin Conference in Miami," YouTube, uploaded
     April 17, 2014, https://www.youtube.com/watch?v=mP82Xm
     UNgNM.

10: The Town of Zug

93   corporate tax rates: KPMG, *Clarity on Swiss Taxes*, 2018, https://
     assets.kpmg.com/content/dam/kpmg/ch/pdf/clarity-on-swiss-taxes
     -2018-en.pdf.

324

11: The Spaceship

104 connected to the 2009 post: Satoshi Nakamoto, March 7, 2014, reply to
Satoshi Nakamoto, "Bitcoin Open Source Implementation of P2P Currency,"
P2P Foundation, February 11, 2009, http://p2pfoundation.ning.com/forum
/topics/bitcoin-open-source?commentId=2003008%3AComment%3A52186.

12: The White-Shoe Lawyers

110 to define what ether is: US Securities and Exchange Commission,
"SEC Issues Proposal on Crowdfunding," news release no. 2013-227,
October 23, 2013, https://www.sec.gov/news/press-release/2013-227.

113 there would always be a backup: Jeff Wilcke, "Homestead Release,"
Ethereum Foundation Blog, February 29, 2016, https://blog.ethereum
.org/2016/02/29/homestead-release/.

113 Paper is the reference: Andreas M. Antonopoulos and Gavin Wood,
Mastering Ethereum: Building Smart Contracts and Dapps (Sebastopol, CA:
O'Reilly Media, 2018), https://www.oreilly.com/library/view
/mastering-ethereum/9781491971932/ch01.html.

14: The (Non)Investment

126 women who showed up: John Scianna, "Texas Bitcoin Conference,"
Bitcoin Magazine, April 2, 2014, https://bitcoinmagazine.com/articles
/texas-bitcoin-conference-1396465256/.

128 applications on top of it: Kanton Zug, Commercial Register, https://
zg.chregister.ch/cr-portal/auszug/auszug.xhtml?uid=CHE-292.124.800#.

130 in an online chat: Pete Dushenski, "A Guide to Buying 5000 Ether/
Bitcoin, 2.5x More Than Ethereum's Genesis Sale Offers," *Contravex*
(blog), July 23, 2014, http://www.contravex.com/2014/07/23/a-guide
-to-buying-5000-ether-bitcoin-2-5x-more-than-ethereums-genesis-sale/.

15: The Ether Sale

133 prices in September 2014: Vitalik Buterin, "Launching the Ether
Sale," *Ethereum Foundation Blog*, July 22, 2014, https://blog.ethereum
.org/2014/07/22/launching-the-ether-sale/.

136 "let's do this": EtherCasts, "Ethereum Pre-Sale," YouTube, uploaded
July 23, 2014, https://www.youtube.com/watch?feature=player_embedded
&v=2PAHMxQCDAQ#t=216.

138 "other," Mihai wrote: Mihai Alisie, "Mihai's Ethereum Project Update. The First Year," *Ethereum Foundation Blog*, March 14, 2015, https://
blog.ethereum.org/2015/03/14/ethereum-the-first-year/.

140 a lot of people: Preston Byrne, "Whether Ether Is a Security," *Preston Byrne* (blog), April 23, 2018, https://prestonbyrne.com/2018/04/23 /on-ethereum-security/.

140 May 2019 report found: "The Economic Impact of Ether Whales on the Market," Chainalysis, May 15, 2019, https://blog.chainalysis.com /reports/the-economic-impact-of-ether-whales.

140 "so damn smooth": Hasu, "Ethereum Presale Dynamics Revisited," Medium, April 27, 2018, https://medium.com/@hasufly/ethereum-pre sale-dynamics-revisited-c1b70ac38448.

16: Takeoff

146 "Paul," he said: Paul is a pseudonym for the investor's real name.

148 bugs or setbacks: Vitalik Buterin, "Olympic: Frontier Pre-Release," *Ethereum Foundation Blog*, May 9, 2015, https://blog.ethereum .org/2015/05/09/olympic-frontier-pre-release/.

155 4:26 p.m. in Berlin: Etherscan, Block #1, https://etherscan.io /block/1.

155 someone else wrote: Ethereum/go-Ethereum chat archives, Gitter, 2015, https://gitter.im/ethereum/go-ethereum/archives/2015/07/30.

17: The Shrinking Runway

163 "anyhow," Vitalik wrote: "We just went from $530 to sub $500 in under a minute," Reddit thread, 2014, https://www.reddit.com/r/Bitcoin /comments/2diqyy/we_just_went_from_530_to_sub_500_in_under_a /cjpxgln/.

163 "a little under two": Vitalik Buterin, "The Evolution of Ethereum," *Ethereum Foundation Blog*, September 28, 2015, https://blog.ethereum .org/2015/09/28/the-evolution-of-ethereum/.

167 Web 3 dream a reality: Gavin Wood, "The Last Blog Post," *Ethereum Foundation Blog*, January 11, 2016, https://blog.ethereum.org/2016 /01/11/last-blog-post/.

18: The First Dapps

170 Ethereum smart contracts: Jack Peterson, Joseph Krug, Micah Zoltu, Austin K. Williams, and Stephanie Alexander, "Augur: A Decentralized Oracle and Prediction Market Platform (v2.0)," November 1, 2019, https://www.augur.net/whitepaper.pdf.

171 he wrote on GitHub: Vitalik Buterin, "Standardized_Contract_APIs," GitHub, June 23, 2015, https://github.com/ethereum/wiki/wiki/Standard ized_Contract_APIs/499c882f3ec123537fc2fccd57eaa29e6032fe4a.

171 with their thoughts: Alex Van de Sande, "Let's talk about the coin standard," Reddit, 2015, https://www.reddit.com/r/ethereum /comments/3n8fkn/lets_talk_about_the_coin_standard/.

172 issue being discussed: Fabian Vogelsteller, "ERC: Token standard #20," GitHub, November 19, 2015, https://github.com/ethereum/EIPs /issues/20.

173 ended up implementing: Rune Christensen, "Introducing eDollar, the ultimate stablecoin built on Ethereum," Reddit, 2015, https://www .reddit.com/r/ethereum/comments/30f98i/introducing_edollar_the _ultimate_stablecoin_built/.

175 companies to build on: Jeff Wilcke, "Homestead Release," *Ethereum Foundation Blog*, February 29, 2016, https://blog.ethereum.org/2016 /02/29/homestead-release/.

176 world had Ethereum: Gavin Andresen, "Bit-thereum," *GavinTech* (blog), June 9, 2014, http://gavintech.blogspot.com/2014/06/bit -thereum.html.

19: The Magic Lock

177 Slock.it's blog posts: Slock.it, "Decentralizing the Emerging Sharing Economy," Medium, *Slock.it Blog*, December 2, 2015, https://blog.slock .it/slock-it-decentralizing-the-emerging-sharing-economy-cf19ce09b957 ?c=20150901_vision%22%20%5Cl%20%220_blog.

180 automating governance rules: Christoph Jentzsch, "Decentralized Autonomous Organization to Automate Governance, Final Draft—Under Review," 2016, https://web.archive.org/web/20180913233456/https:// download.slock.it/public/DAO/WhitePaper.pdf.

20: The DAO Wars

186 a blog post about it: Peter Vessenes, "More Ethereum Attacks: Race-to-Empty Is the Real Deal," *Vessenes* (blog), June 9, 2016, https:// vessenes.com/more-ethereum-attacks-race-to-empty-is-the-real-deal/.

187 "the contract recursively": eththrowa, "Bug discovered in MKR token contract also affects the DAO," The DAO website, June 12, 2016, https:// web.archive.org/web/20160702202124/https://forum.daohub.org/t/bug -discovered-in-mkr-token-contract-also-affects-thedao-would-allow-users -to-steal-rewards-from-thedao-by-calling-recursively/4947.

187 "'recursive call' bug discovery": Stephan Tual, "No DAO Funds at Risk Following the Ethereum Smart Contract 'Recursive Call' Bug Discovery," Medium, *Slock.it Blog*, June 12, 2016, https://blog.slock.it /no-dao-funds-at-risk-following-the-ethereum-smart-contract-recursive -call-bug-discovery-29f482d348b.

188 mechanism was faulty: Dino Mark, Vlad Zamfir, and Emin Gun
  Sirer, "A Call for a Temporary Moratorium on The DAO," Hacking,
  Distributed, May 27, 2016, http://hackingdistributed.com/2016/05/27
  /dao-call-for-moratorium/.

188 "Am I wrong?": Phil Daian, "Analysis of the DAO Exploit," Hacking,
  Distributed, June 18, 2016, http://hackingdistributed.com/2016/06/18
  /analysis-of-the-dao-exploit/.

188 trigger the vulnerability: Phil Daian, "Chasing the DAO Attacker's
  Wake," Phil Does Security, June 19, 2016, https://pdaian.com/blog
  /chasing-the-dao-attackers-wake/.

189 Some trading venues complied: pigeons, "Conversation between
  Vitalik and Exchanges," Steemit, 2016.

197 "truly, 'The Attacker'": Anonymous, "An Open Letter," Pastebin,
  June 18, 2016, https://pastebin.com/CcGUBgDG.

200 someone replied: Alex Van de Sande (@avsa), "DAO IS BEING
  SECURELY DRAINED. DO NOT PANIC," Twitter, June 21, 2016,
  https://twitter.com/avsa/status/745313647514226688?lang=en.

21: The Fork

203 called "DAO Wars": Peter Szilagyi, "DAO Wars: Your Voice on the
  Soft-Fork Dilemma," *Ethereum Foundation Blog*, June 24, 2016, https://
  blog.ethereum.org/2016/06/24/dao-wars-youre-voice-soft-fork-dilemma/.

204 jam up the network: Tjaden Hess, River Keefer, and Emin Gun Sirer,
  "Ethereum's DAO Wars Soft Fork Is a Potential DoS Vector," Hacking,
  Distributed, June 28, 2016, http://hackingdistributed.com/2016/06/28
  /ethereum-soft-fork-dos-vector/.

204 running the show: Peter Szilagyi, "The Network Strikes Back
  (1.4.9)," GitHub, June 29, 2016, https://github.com/ethereum/go
  -ethereum/releases/tag/v1.4.9.

205 the software upgrade: Andreas M. Antonopoulos, "Ethereum Fork
  History," Ethereum Book, GitHub, 2016, https://github.com/ethereum
  book/ethereumbook/blob/3a21b603899e27427ca64fc5d3fd57af96a3
  cbd8/forks-history.asciidoc.

206 worked without a glitch: Alex Van de Sande (@avsa), "Watching the
  successful hard fork. Congratulations to the team for another smooth
  transition!," Twitter, July 20, 2016, https://twitter.com/avsa/status
  /755764078098915328.

207 didn't last long: Initiative for CryptoCurrencies and Contracts
  (@initc3org), "Heady days in Ithaca: Vitalik Buterin + IC3 Co-Directors
  celebrate Ethereum Hard Fork with champagne and forks," Twitter,
  July 26, 2016, https://twitter.com/initc3org/status/75800069888161
  3824/photo/1.

208 "and special interests": "Keep the Original Censorship Resistant
Ethereum Going," Ethereum Classic website, 2016, https://web.archive
.org/web/20160802024753/https://ethereumclassic.github.io/.

211 "lost a single dime": Ptelepathetique Movies, "The DAO Explained
(with Griff Green) Burning Man 2016," YouTube, uploaded October 7,
2016, https://www.youtube.com/watch?v=mmVkpfivr8Q.

22: The Shanghai Attacks

215 praise from the community: Vitalik Buterin, "Geth 1.4.12: From
Shanghai with Love, hotfix for recent DoS issues. Please update!" Reddit,
2016, https://www.reddit.com/r/ethereum/comments/53fbi0/geth
_1412_from_shanghai_with_love_hotfix_for/.

218 year to about 250: "New Dapps per Month," State of the Dapps,
https://www.stateofthedapps.com/stats/platform/ethereum#new.

23: The Burning Wick

225 misogynistic messages instead: giatrosgiatros, "Stop Bashing MEW,"
Reddit, 2016, https://www.reddit.com/r/ethereum/comments/5cfap3
/stop_bashing_mew/d9w12vd/.

24: Accidentally Ether Rich

228 would go higher: Nathaniel Popper, "Bitcoin Price Soars, Fueled by
Speculation and Global Currency Turmoil," *New York Times*, January 3,
2017, https://www.nytimes.com/2017/01/03/business/dealbook/bit
coin-price-soars-fueled-by-speculation-and-global-currency-turmoil.html.

232 constant in 2017: US Securities and Exchange Commission,
"Self-Regulatory Organizations; Bats BZX Exchange, Inc.; Order
Disapproving a Proposed Rule Change, as Modified by Amendments
No. 1 and 2, to BZX Rule 14.11(e)(4), Commodity-Based Trust Shares,
to List and Trade Shares Issued by the Winklevoss Bitcoin Trust," news
release no. 34-80206, March 10, 2017, https://www.sec.gov/rules/sro
/batsbzx/2017/34-80206.pdf.

232 the crypto Super Bowl: Stan Higgins, "Consensus 2017 Recap: The
Biggest Main Stage Moments," CoinDesk, May 27, 2017, updated May 29,
2017, https://www.coindesk.com/consensus-2017-recap-biggest-main
-stage-moments.

232 "never quite like this": Jeff John Roberts, "3 Reasons Why Bitcoin
Broke $2,000," *Fortune*, May 21, 2017, http://fortune.com/2017/05/21
/bitcoin-2000/.

234 "I love this stuff": Sarah Krouse, "Bitcoin's Unlikely Evangelist:
Fidelity CEO Abigail Johnson," *Wall Street Journal*, May 23, 2017,

https://www.wsj.com/articles/fidelity-ceo-bringing-blockchain-to-the
-masses-harder-than-it-seemed-1495548000.
234 tokens on Ethereum: "Blockchain Venture Capital," CoinDesk, May 16,
2014, updated November 14, 2018, https://www.coindesk.com/bit
coin-venture-capital.

25: The New IPO

241 mood to celebrate: Bancor, "Bancor Network Token (BNT)
Contribution & Token Allocation Terms," Medium, June 5, 2017, https://
medium.com/@bancor/bancor-network-token-bnt-contribution-token
-creation-terms-48cc85a63812.
243 "blockchain," Bitfinex tweeted: Bitfinex (@bitfinex), "We are
suspending all ETH withdrawal until the network backlog subsides and
we are able to reliably post transactions to blockchain," Twitter, June 21,
2017, https://twitter.com/bitfinex/status/877539782678786051.

26: The Friendly Ghost

246 "religion: crypto": Vitalik Buterin, "About Me," personal website,
https://about.me/vitalik_buterin.
248 most economic power: Vitalik Buterin, "Slasher: A Punitive Proof-of-
Stake Algorithm," *Ethereum Foundation Blog*, January 15, 2014, https://blog
.ethereum.org/2014/01/15/slasher-a-punitive-proof-of-stake-algorithm/.

27: The Boom

253 coins were surging: Nathaniel Popper, "Move Over, Bitcoin. Ether
Is the Digital Currency of the Moment," *New York Times*, June 19, 2017,
https://www.nytimes.com/2017/06/19/business/dealbook/ethereum
-bitcoin-digital-currency.html.
256 it "warrants watching": Evelyn Cheng, "Top Wall Street Strategist
Sees Bitcoin 'Cannibalizing' Gold, Worth as Much as $55,000," CNBC,
July 7, 2017, https://www.cnbc.com/2017/07/07/strategist-tom-lee
-weighs-sees-bitcoin-going-as-high-as-55000.html.
257 "corrections and all else": John McAfee (@officialmcafee), "Bitcoin
now at $16,600.00. Those of you in the old school who believe
this is a bubble simply have not understood the new mathematics
of the Blockchain, or you did not cared enough to try. Bubbles are
mathematically impossible in this new paradigm. So are corrections and
all else," Twitter, December 7, 2017, https://twitter.com/officialmcafee
/status/938938539282190337?lang=en.
257 lingo with crypto: Fitz Tepper, "What the Hell Is Happening to

Cryptocurrency Valuations?," TechCrunch, June 7, 2017, https://tech crunch.com/2017/06/07/what-the-hell-is-happening-to-cryptocurrency -valuations/.

259 said in a July 25 statement: US Securities and Exchange Commission, "Report of Investigation Pursuant to Section 21(a) of the Securities Exchange Act of 1934: The DAO," news release no. 81207, July 25, 2017, https://www.sec.gov/litigation/investreport/34-81207.pdf.

263 of the Filecoin ICO: Stan Higgins, "$257 Million: Filecoin Breaks All-Time Record for ICO Funding," CoinDesk, September 7, 2017, updated September 8, 2017, https://www.coindesk.com/257-million -filecoin-breaks-time-record-ico-funding.

28: Futures and Cats

268 first half of 2018: Hugh Son, Dakin Campbell, and Sonali Basak, "Goldman Is Setting Up a Cryptocurrency Trading Desk," Bloomberg News, December 21, 2017, https://www.bloomberg.com/news/articles /2017-12-21/goldman-is-said-to-be-building-a-cryptocurrency-trading -desk.

268 algorithmic trading: "Cryptocurrency Investment Fund Industry Graphs and Charts," Crypto Fund Research, https://cryptofundresearch .com/cryptocurrency-funds-overview-infographic/.

278 million, at the peak: Vitalik Buterin's Ethereum address, Etherscan, https://etherscan.io/address/0xab5801a7d398351b8be11c439e05c5b 3259aec9b#analytics.

29: The Crash

283 selling digital assets: "SEC Cyber Enforcement Actions," US Securities and Exchange Commission, https://www.sec.gov/spotlight /cybersecurity-enforcement-actions.

288 to manipulate crypto markets: "Tether Response to Flawed Paper by Griffin and Shams," Tether, November 7, 2019, https://tether.to/tether -response-to-flawed-paper-by-griffin-and-shams/.

289 as much as 95 percent: "Market Surveillance Report—August 2018," Blockchain Transparency Institute, https://www.bti.live/report-august 2018/.

289 were Christmas cards: Matt Robinson, "SEC Issues Subpoenas in Hunt for Fraudulent ICOs," Bloomberg News, February 28, 2018, updated March 1, 2018, https://www.bloomberg.com/news/articles/2018-03-01 /sec-is-said-to-issue-subpoenas-in-hunt-for-fraudulent-icos.

290 groundbreaking technology: Camila Russo, "Bitcoin Speculators, Not Drug Dealers, Dominate Crypto Use Now," Bloomberg News, August 7,

2018, https://www.bloomberg.com/news/articles/2018-08-07/bit coin-speculators-not-drug-dealers-dominate-crypto-use-now.

291 forcing it back to earth: "ICO Treasury Balances," Diar, https://diar .co/ethereum-ico-treasury-balances/.

293 cases were dropped: Joseph Menn, "Bitcoin Foundation Hit by Resignations over New Director," Reuters, May 16, 2014, https://www .reuters.com/article/us-bitcoin-foundation-resignations/bitcoin -foundation-hit-by-resignations-over-new-director-idUSBREA 4F02B20140516.

30: The Party

303 and clapped along: CoinDesk, "Devcon 4—Ethereum's Big Sing-a-long," YouTube, uploaded October 31, 2018, https://www.youtube.com /watch?v=xC8DrG5KSLU.

305 liked responses: Vitalik Buterin (@VitalikButerin), "Just sent 1000 eth. Yolo," Twitter, December 18, 2018, https://twitter.com/Vitalik Buterin/status/1075181710730506240.

305 "And, like . . . no": Fred Wilson, "Video of the Week: Vitalik Buterin—The Unchained Podcast Interview," *AVC* (blog), March 30, 2019, https://avc.com/2019/03/video-of-the-week-vitalik-buterin-the -unchained-podcast-interview/.

309 a credit card: Cash Essentials, *World Cash Report 2018*, https://cash essentials.org/app/uploads/2018/07/2018-world-cash-report.pdf.

309 banking without banks: Delphi Digital, *Thematic Insights: Decentralized Finance*, March 2019, https://www.delphidigital.io/defi.

ABOUT THE AUTHOR

CAMILA RUSSO is founder and editor in chief of the cryptocurrency content platform The Defiant. She was a Bloomberg News reporter for eight years, covering emerging markets, European stocks, and digital assets from Buenos Aires, Madrid, and New York City. She also worked at *El Mercurio*, the largest newspaper in Chile, her home country. Russo is one of the most influential cryptocurrency reporters, speaking at the leading industry events and appearing in major media outlets. She has a master of science degree from Northwestern University's Medill School of Journalism and a bachelor's degree from Pontificia Universidad Catolica de Chile. She lives in New York City.